D1809619

UK Economic and Social Change

1700-2019

Supplementary Volume 3

*Being an investigation of the evidence that reveals the **best known facts** regarding the quantifiable economic and social history of the peoples of the United Kingdom of Great Britain and Northern Ireland (but particularly the English peoples) since the 18th century; including their population, economy, the role of the state, earnings, income inequality, living costs, household expenditure, housing, the retreat of real poverty, the air quality of their environment and their life expectancy.*

Collated, graphically presented with text written by:

J. R. Cooper

A data collation, analysis and presentation conducted from 2017 to 2023; but also founded upon five decades of the study of history, economics and the sociology of life and its political manifestations. Sources are derived from the most respected academic, authoritative and best researched origins. All underpinned by the thorough use of valid mathematical principles and the scientific methodology.

Title font Georgia
Text font Cambria
Chart font Arial

Self published with IngramSpark
Printed by Lightning Source UK Ltd.

Paperback (2023)   ISBN: 978-1-7395094-6-0
Hardback (2023)   ISBN: 978-1-7395094-0-8
Supplementary Volume 1 (2023)   ISBN: 978-1-7395094-1-5
Supplementary Volume 2 (2023)   ISBN: 978-1-7395094-2-2
Supplementary Volume 3 (2023)   ISBN: 978-1-7395094-3-9
Supplementary Volume 4 (2024)   ISBN: 978-1-7395094-4-6
Exploring Climate History (2024)   ISBN: 978-1-7395094-5-3

Dedication

Dedicated to my mother, father, sister and grandmothers.

Thank you for your unconditional love, care, support, guidance and tolerance (of which you needed a great deal).

To my maternal grandmother, who knew great hardship throughout her life, losing her father when she was aged three, losing her third baby in infancy, my grandfather in and out of work throughout the 1930's; with many debilitating consequences to her health and well-being.

To my paternal grandmother, losing her mother when she was six, forced to foster her first son (my father) for the first six years of his life due to extreme hardship in the 1930's; losing her second baby in infancy.

But also dedicated to my maternal great-grandmother, a lady I never met, but who was clearly a very resourceful and strong lady.

She was widowed in 1909, aged 32, with 3 young children (including her youngest, my maternal grandmother) and pregnant with her fourth child.

With only the Poor Law to turn to, instead she picked stones from local farmer's fields for coppers (old farthings, halfpennies and pennies) and took in washing.

She has described herself in the 1911 census as "Charwoman".

She had been forced to give her fourth child into the permanent care of her parents at her birth, yet still mistakenly listed her in her 1911 census return, before crossing her out from that return.

In 1926 her eldest daughter and son-in-law both died of tuberculosis within months of each other, leaving her to bring up her first new-born grandchild. Then in 1938 her eldest son also died of tuberculosis.

These ladies and the millions of other people of the time and all the millennia before, knew what **real poverty** was and struggled through.

Acknowledgements

I feel honoured to be able to thank several good friends for their reviews of aspects of the initial research, the presentations I have built of my findings, their notes and references and now this book.

In particular I thank Bill Young, a very good friend for many years now, for his careful and forensic checking of my blunders and his guidance regarding the understand-ability of the data, as I have tried to present it. Also MS for his checking of my presentations and then the pre-publication edition of this book, chapter by chapter, using his printer's and type-setter's eye to try to avoid blunders on the page, as well as the understanding of the narrative and spotting my many "apostrophic" errors.

I have also carefully checked the graphics and my explanations of these with my Mother in particular, as she has very strong views on politics and social organisation which I must confess are not at all in accord with my own in many respects. This has helped enormously to keep me scrupulously levelled in all facets of my interpretation of my findings.

Also I am very grateful further to Bill Young, my Mother, Rachel Turner and Alaine Mardle for their reading of the first printed draft and their notes and corrections of my errors and the oversights they have found therein and their suggestions for improvements throughout.

I have tried my very best to be even-handed and driven entirely by the "facts", the **best known facts** I could find from the evidence. All in the light of my natural and overpowering scepticism of all loud mantras of faith and ideologies (religious or secular).

If I have failed to be scrupulously honest, even-handed and factually correct then that is my error and no one else's.

Table of Contents

Air Quality, Road Transport, Energy and Life Expectancy

"Energy is Eternal Delight"

William Blake:

The Marriage of Heaven and Hell,

'The voice of the Devil',

1792-1795

A commentary on the current (2017/2019) media and campaigning discussion

As the UK and the world's population, life expectancy and wealth have increased over the last 200 years or so, and quite dramatically over the last few decades throughout the world, so the recent clamour by some campaigning and political causes has grown ever more shrill.

Whilst most of the campaigning to continuously improve people's lives throughout the world was and is justified, sadly, in common with the current instant judgement "sound bite" approach to discussion of important matters, many campaigns now *"make a drama out of a crisis"* and they clearly put <u>their</u> moral judgement, ladled with liberal doses of self-righteous indignation, ahead of balanced facts and consequent reasonable action.

One such is the widespread campaigning regarding UK air quality in the 21st century.

Without any doubt, and by any measure, the air quality in the UK is better now than it has been, at least since the industrial revolution (with it's consequent, ultimate, rise in living standards for the vast majority of people in the UK).

Before that time, *in the bucolic age imagined by today's dreamers*, of course the air quality was cleaner; but the vast majority of people died very young. So much for clean air!!!!

And although in certain respects, the recent <u>rate of improvement</u> in London has slowed during the current century, UK air quality still remains cleaner than ever, even in London; well at least since London has been larger than a small developing town.

Those with any knowledge of the actual measures and known historical facts know this to be the case.

The most extreme recent (post Second World War) example of dreadful and deadly air quality was the infamous coal burning smog's of the 1950's.

They rightly set the course for the year on year improvements, <u>every year since</u>.

These modern campaigns, by latching on to the recent COMEAP (2010) and Royal College of Surgeon's (2015) reports on the effects of particulates and Nitrogen Dioxide on human health, and their statistically calculated "*premature*" death rates (<u>with extremely large range of uncertainties</u>), combined with their recent successful legal actions against the government (thanks to EU imposed legal limits), have caused the "temperature" of the issue to be raised to "*crisis*" and thence "*drama*", and gradually public perception is moved to some vague new state, mostly one of Chicken Little panic!

The campaigning tone and supporting media obfuscation, such as "*the growing problem of air pollution*", is simply not supported **at any time or place** by the actual measurements from any location in the UK, including even London.

Everywhere in the UK air pollution is currently declining year on year, including every year this century.

If, according to the COMEAP/RCS statistical estimate, 40,000 people in the UK were dying "*prematurely*" due to air pollution in 2010, including 9,400 people in London, **it follows inevitably** that in the 50 years <u>before</u> 2010 (probably even 200 years), due to air pollution being worse year on year before 2010, the numbers dying "*prematurely*" due to air pollution were higher and higher. And yet life expectancy soared in those 50 (and 200) years, <u>every year</u>!

Since, after 2010, air quality has continued to improve every year, **it**

again follows inevitably that the number of people calculated to be supposedly dying "*prematurely*" each year **must have fallen**, year on year, every year since!

Note also as referred to previously, the huge uncertainty about this statistical construct. This uncertainty yields confidence range limits from as low as just 1/6th of the estimate or 6,700, to as high as double the estimate, or 80,000, for the UK, and therefore from 1,600 to 19,000 for the London estimate!

In contrast to all such campaigns conceived on the zealous moral high ground, the prosaic actual facts, be they economic, financial, mathematical, chemical or physical, by all measures, show that we are healthier, wealthier and long lived than ever in human history.

No matter the naysayers and hand-ringers clamour that the sky is falling, that we are all dying (even *prematurely*), we still remain healthier, wealthier and longer lived than we poor everyday folk have EVER been in the whole of human history.

And yet the wealthier and healthier we have become the more miserable, niggardly, gloomy and doom laden many have become; it seems not also wiser!

Perhaps those same doom merchants would do as well to live the lives of the majority of the world's population, or the lives of their parents or grand parents, to put modern life in the UK for most in real perspective.

This is no call for complacency or rampant, unbridled emissions of air pollutants. There remain many, many issues to tackle, including slack, lazy government and rich individual and corporate greed, plus every day ignorance and complacency.

Rather it is a call for reason, balance and fact based argument, before dubious hysterical, zealous and knee jerk judgement.

And above all a call for firm, continuing governmental support for the REAL sustained improvements that have been wrought, so far, in people's lives in the last 100 years.

Rather than the modern penchant to ban or subsidise everything in a panicked sop to a minority of vitriolic dreamers, government, entirely paid for by the taxpayer ("there is no such thing as public money – there is only taxpayers' money"), should honestly and forthrightly live up to the broad social contract; to keep the nation safe, prevent excess of greed and set and impose the legal limits to balance economy and environment for everyone's benefit, **but with a light touch**.

UK Pollution (Air Quality), Cars

1970-2019 or two generations

Continuous improvement

UK Growth of population and road traffic

&

Life Expectancy

1900-2019

UK population (millions) and Life Expectancy at Birth (Years)

Wrigley/ HMD Life Expectancy (Left axis) — UK Population (Consistent) (Right Axis)

7

UK population and registered road vehicles

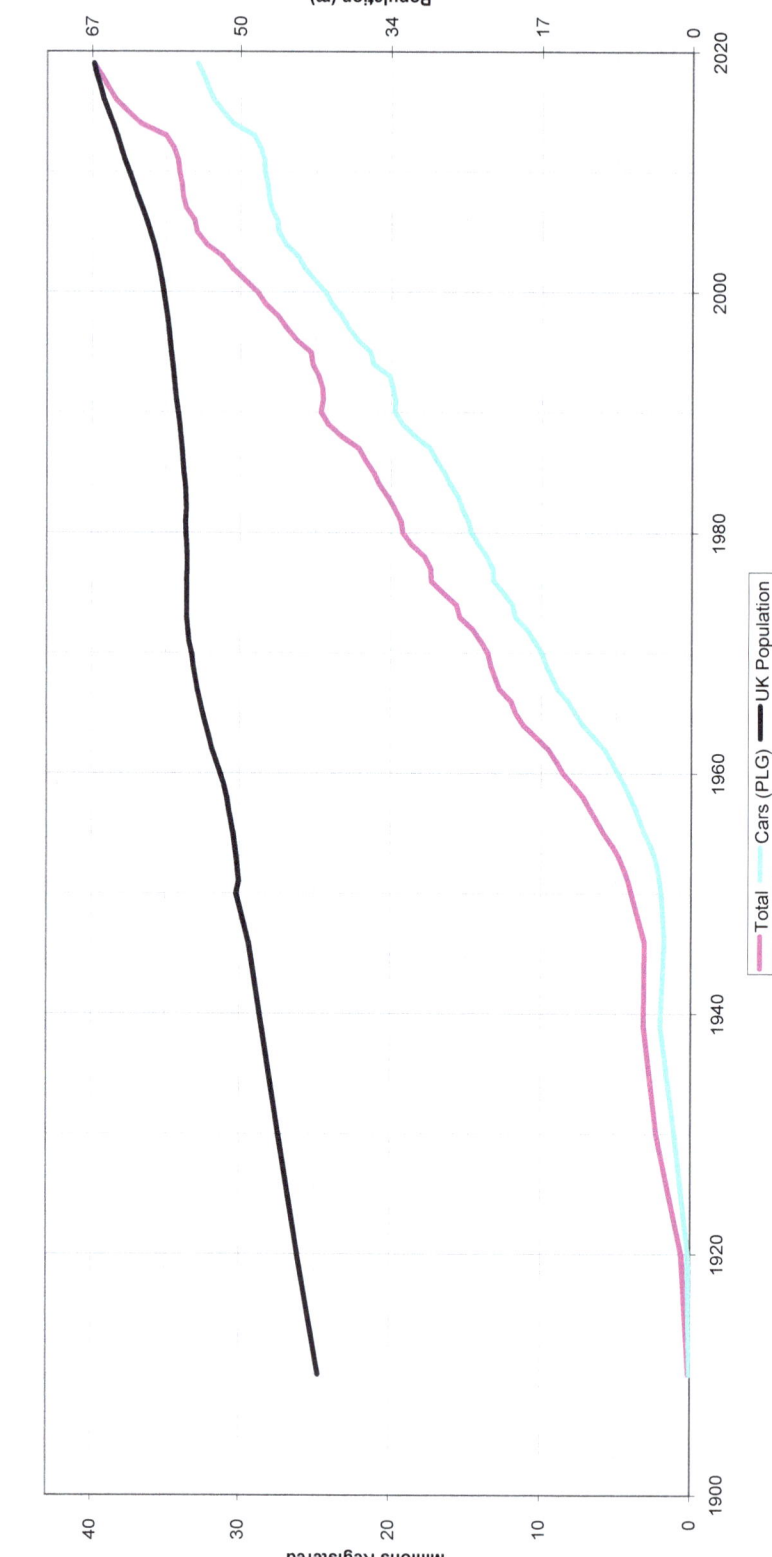

Population (m)

Millions Registered

Total — Cars (PLG) — UK Population

UK Growth of population and road traffic

&

Continuous improvement of air quality

1970-2019

UK population and registered road vehicles

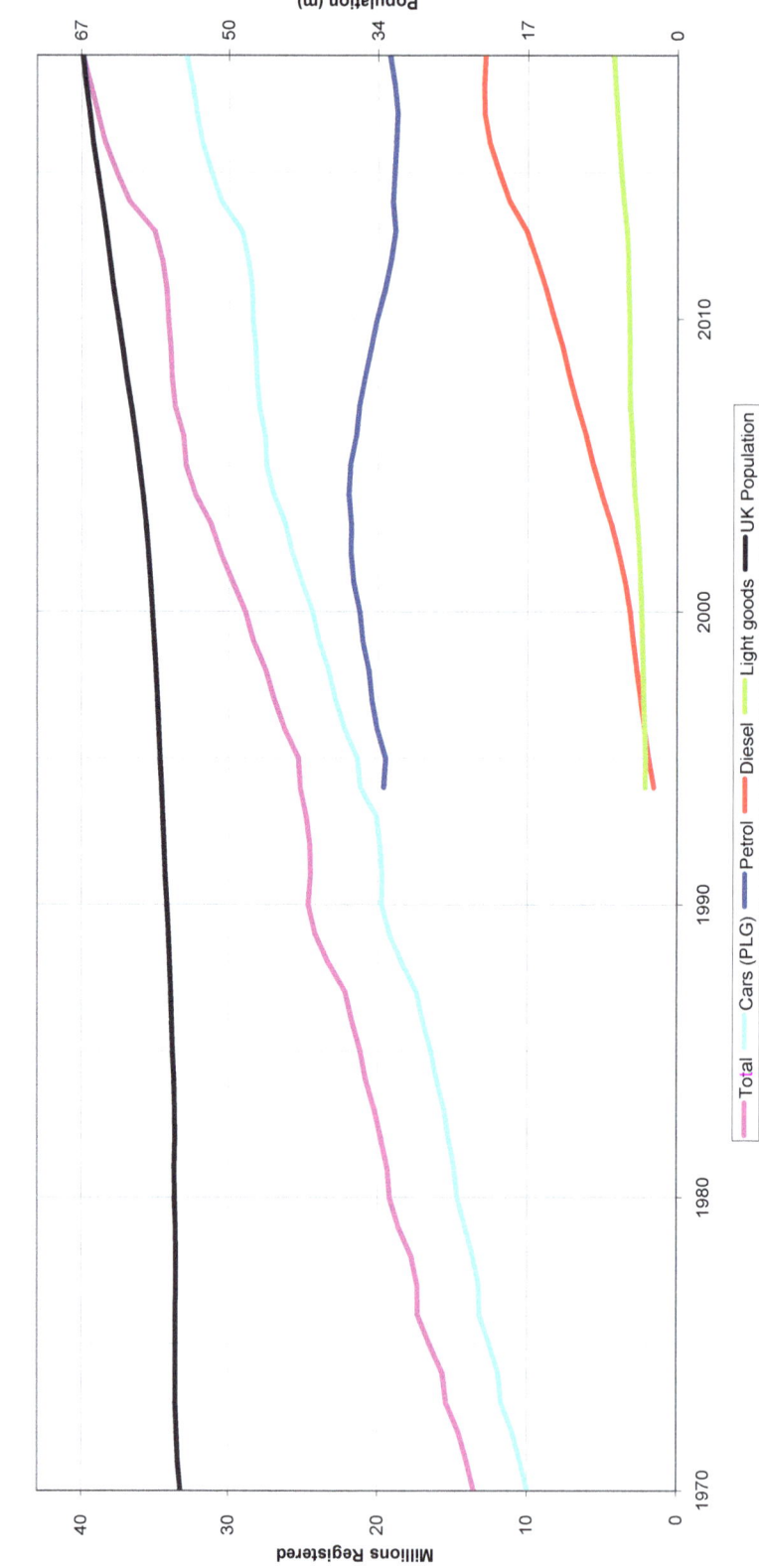

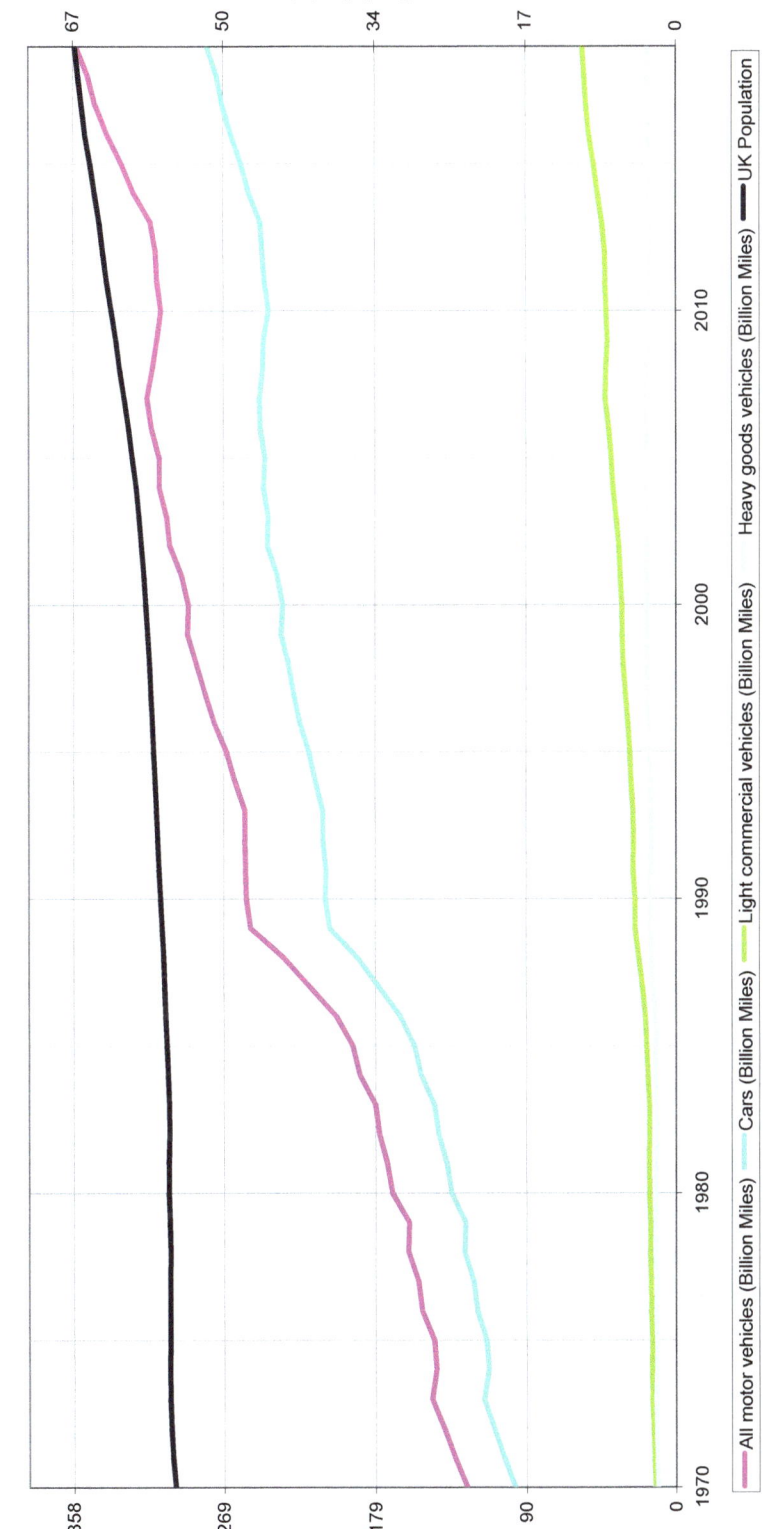

UK population and road miles travelled

11

UK population and fuel used by road vehicles (Diesel by type)

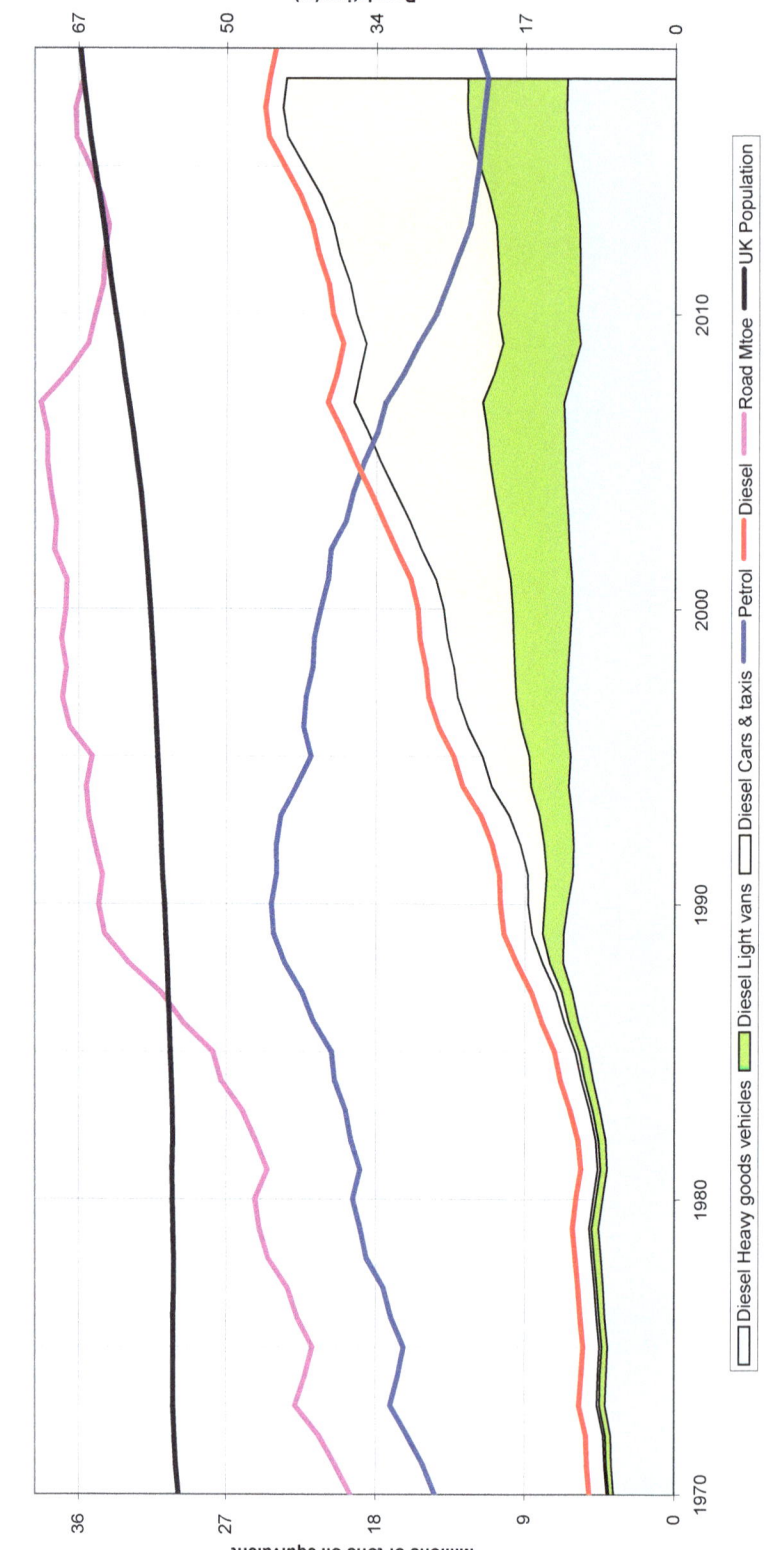

Legend: Diesel Heavy goods vehicles | Diesel Light vans | Diesel Cars & taxis | Petrol | Diesel | Road Mtoe | UK Population

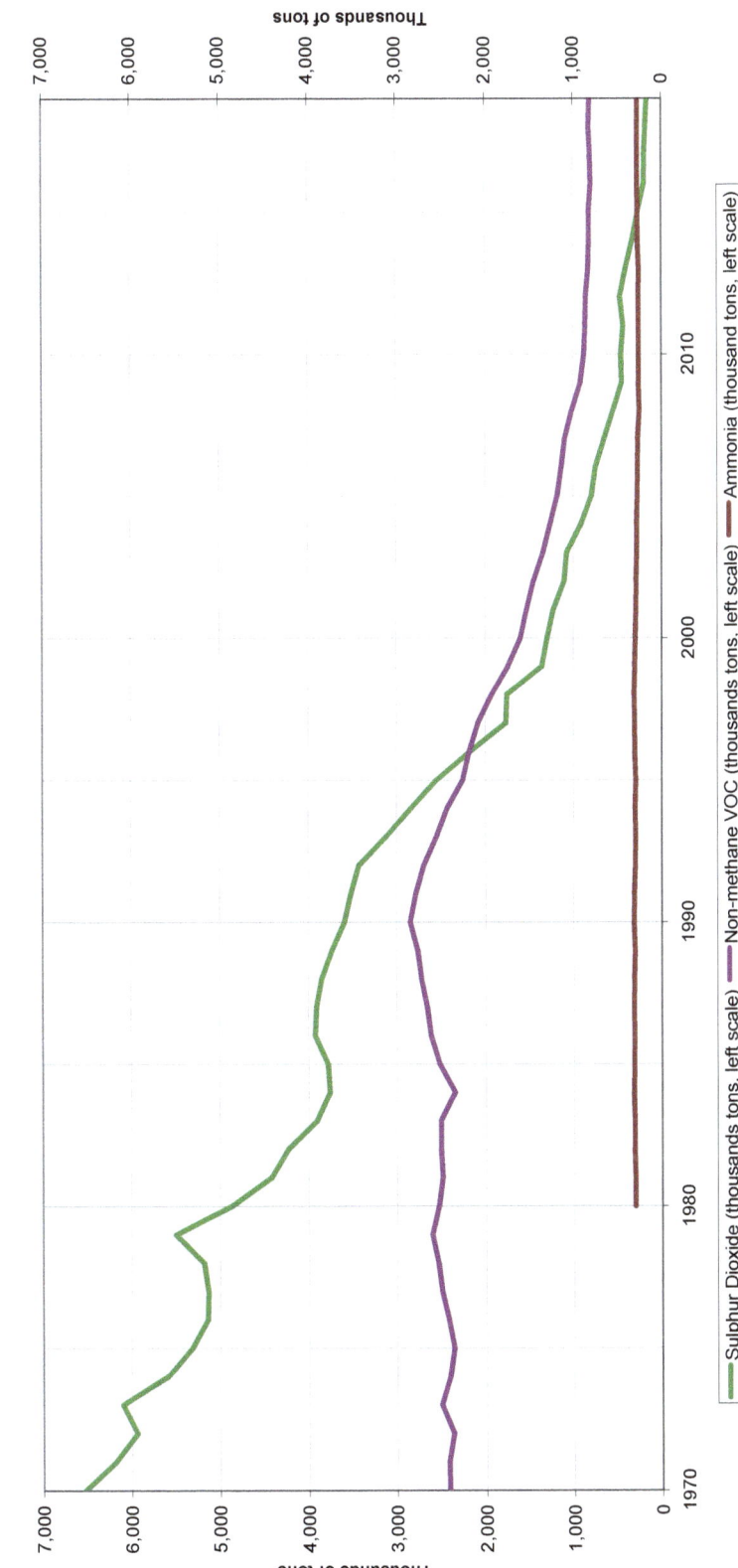

UK trend in weight of atmospheric pollutants (Defra)
Sulphur Dioxide, Non-methane volatile organic compounds and Ammonia

— Sulphur Dioxide (thousands tons, left scale) — Non-methane VOC (thousands tons, left scale) — Ammonia (thousand tons, left scale)

13

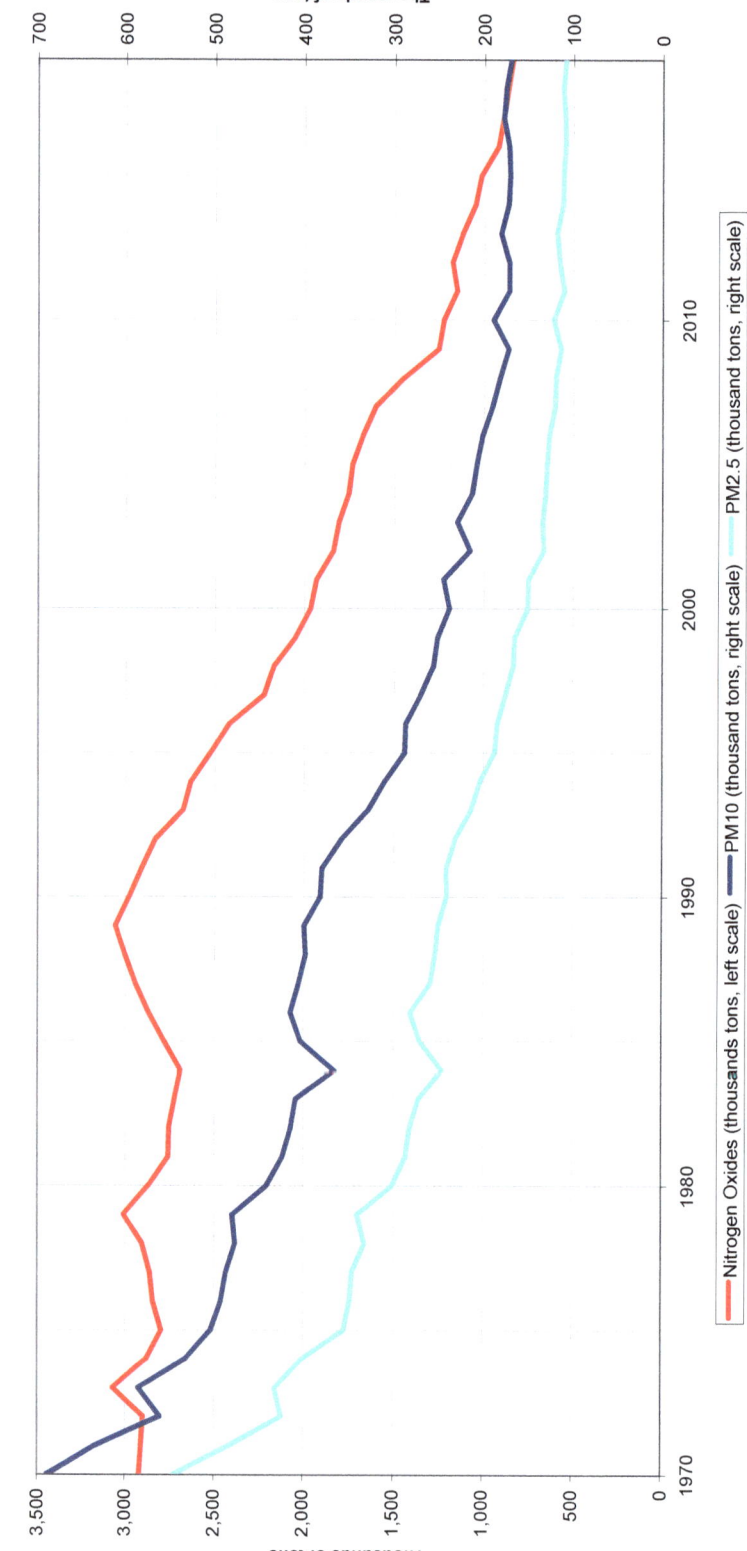

14

UK trend in weight of atmospheric pollutants (Defra/BEIS(NAEI))
(Road use contribution on (NOx as NO2 - 33%, 31% Diesel), (PM10 - 12%, 2.5% Fuel) and (PM2.5 - 12%, 4.0% Fuel))

Nitrogen Oxides (thousands tons, left scale) ——— PM10 (thousand tons, right scale) ——— PM2.5 (thousand tons, right scale)

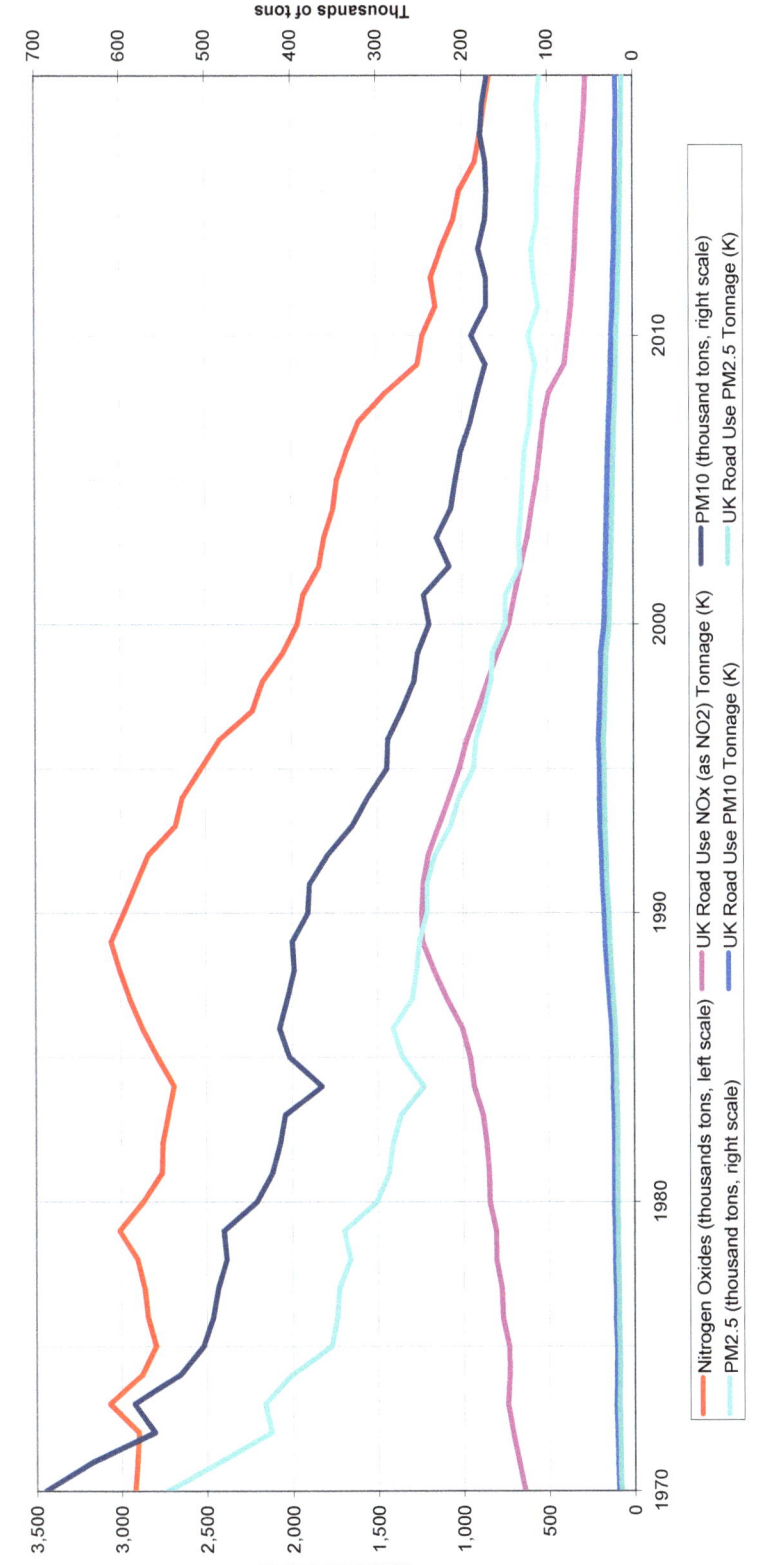

UK trend in weight of atmospheric pollutants (Defra/BEIS(NAEI))
(Road use contribution (NOx as NO2 - 33%, 31% Diesel), (PM10 - 12%, 2.5% Fuel) and (PM2.5 - 12%, 4.0% Fuel))

Legend:
- Nitrogen Oxides (thousands tons, left scale)
- PM2.5 (thousand tons, right scale)
- UK Road Use NOx (as NO2) Tonnage (K)
- UK Road Use PM10 Tonnage (K)
- PM10 (thousand tons, right scale)
- UK Road Use PM2.5 Tonnage (K)

15

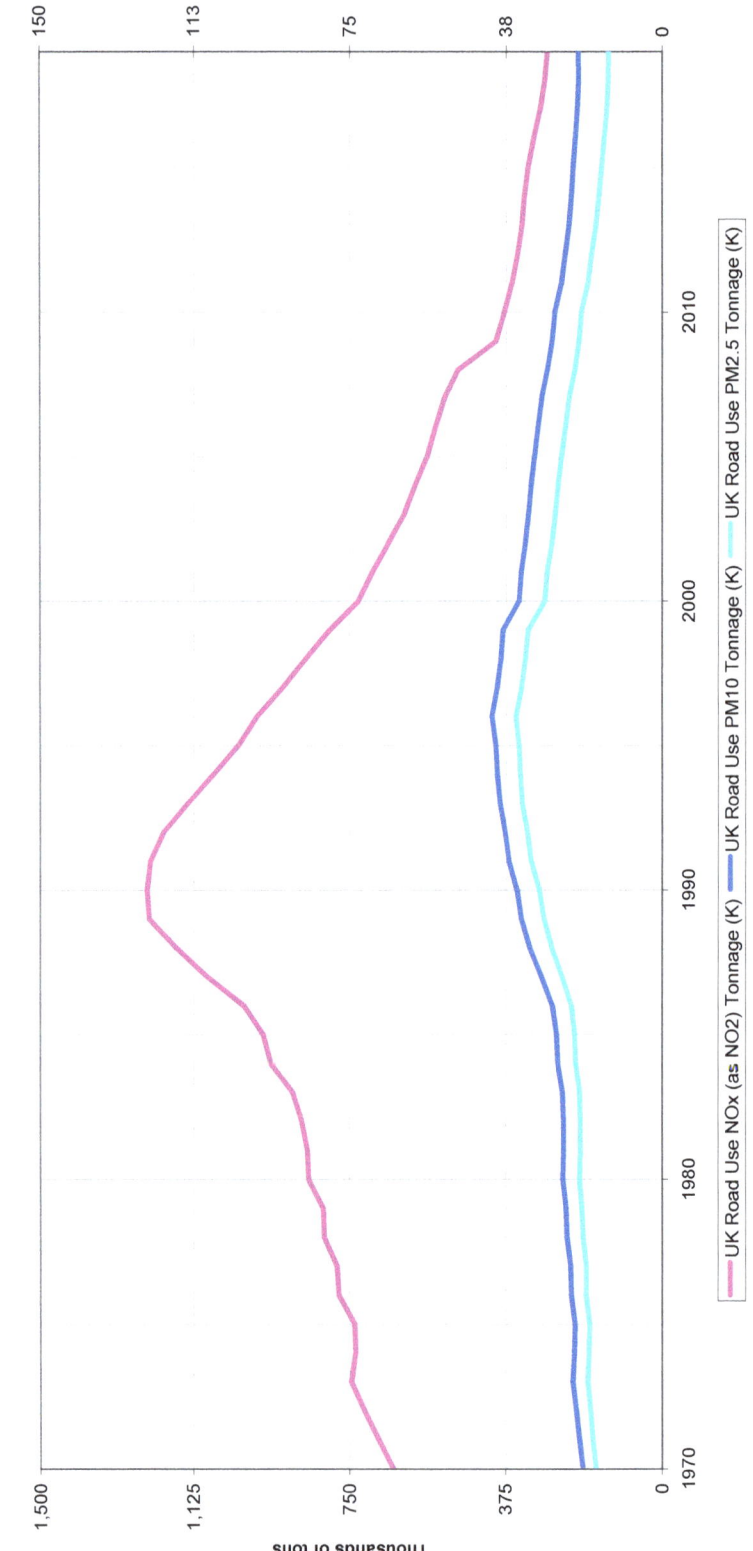

UK trend in weight of atmospheric pollutants (Defra/BEIS(NAEI))
(Road use contribution (NOx as NO2 - 33%, 31% Diesel), (PM10 - 12%, 2.5% Fuel) and (PM2.5 - 12%, 4.0% Fuel))

UK Road Use NOx (as NO2) Tonnage (K) — UK Road Use PM10 Tonnage (K) — UK Road Use PM2.5 Tonnage (K)

Non-pollutant emissions

CO2 metric tonnes per million miles driven

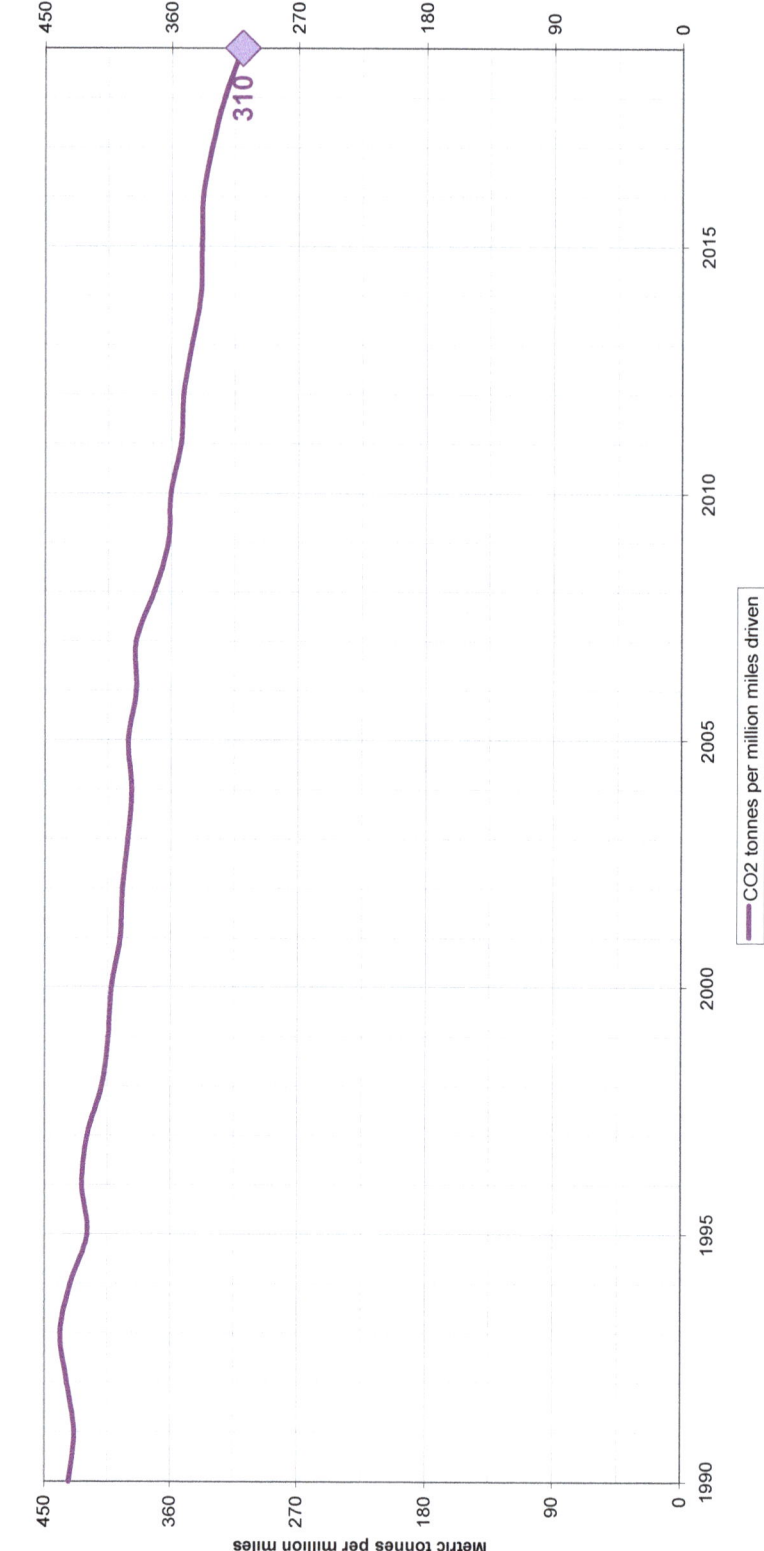

UK road transport CO2 emissions (metric tonnes per annum) per million miles - 28% reduction since 1990

Metric tonnes per million miles

310

— CO2 tonnes per million miles driven

UK Growth of population and road traffic

&

Continuous improvement of air quality

2000-2019

UK population and registered road vehicles

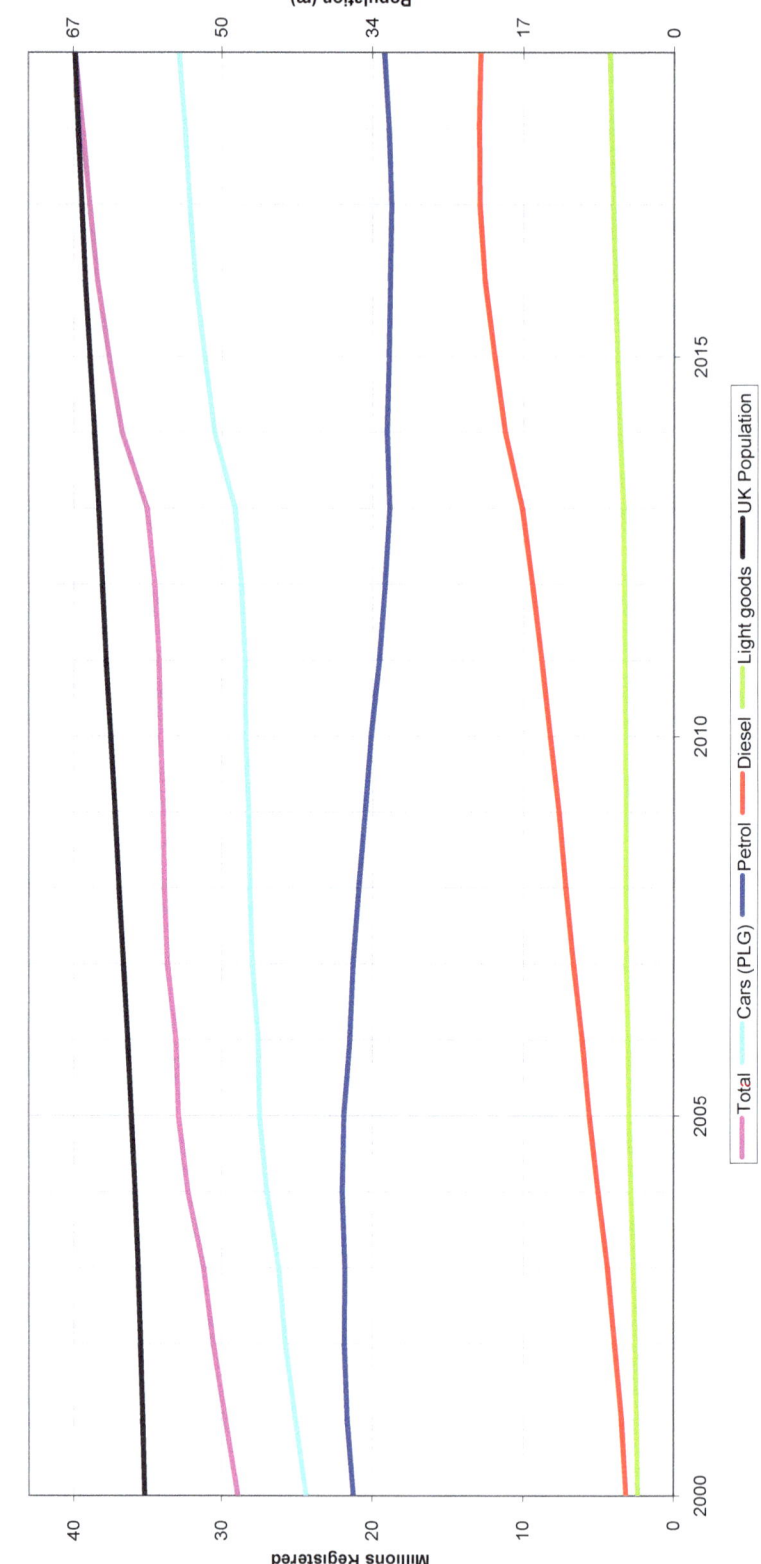

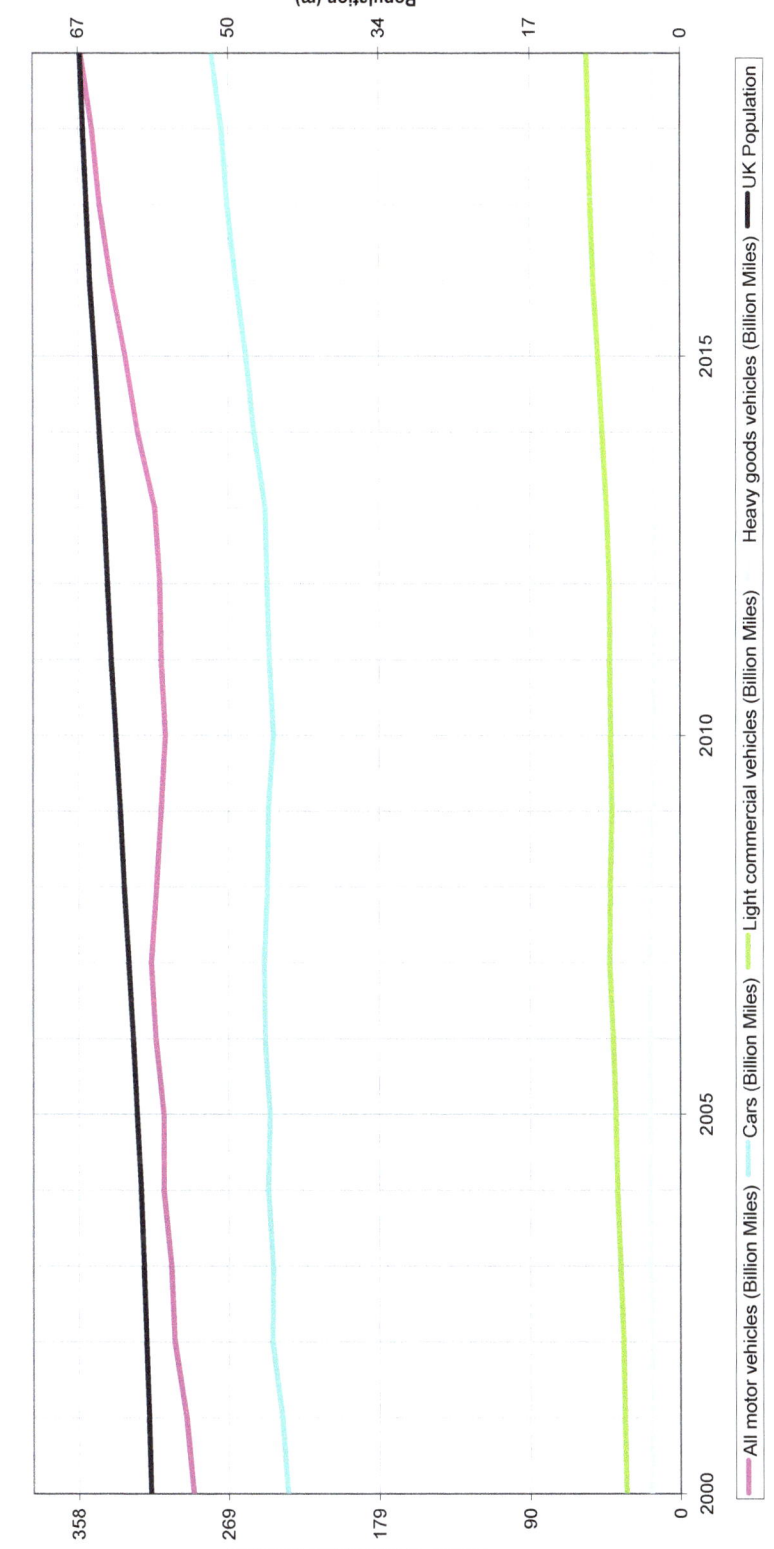

UK population and road miles travelled

21

UK population and fuel used by road vehicles (Diesel by type)

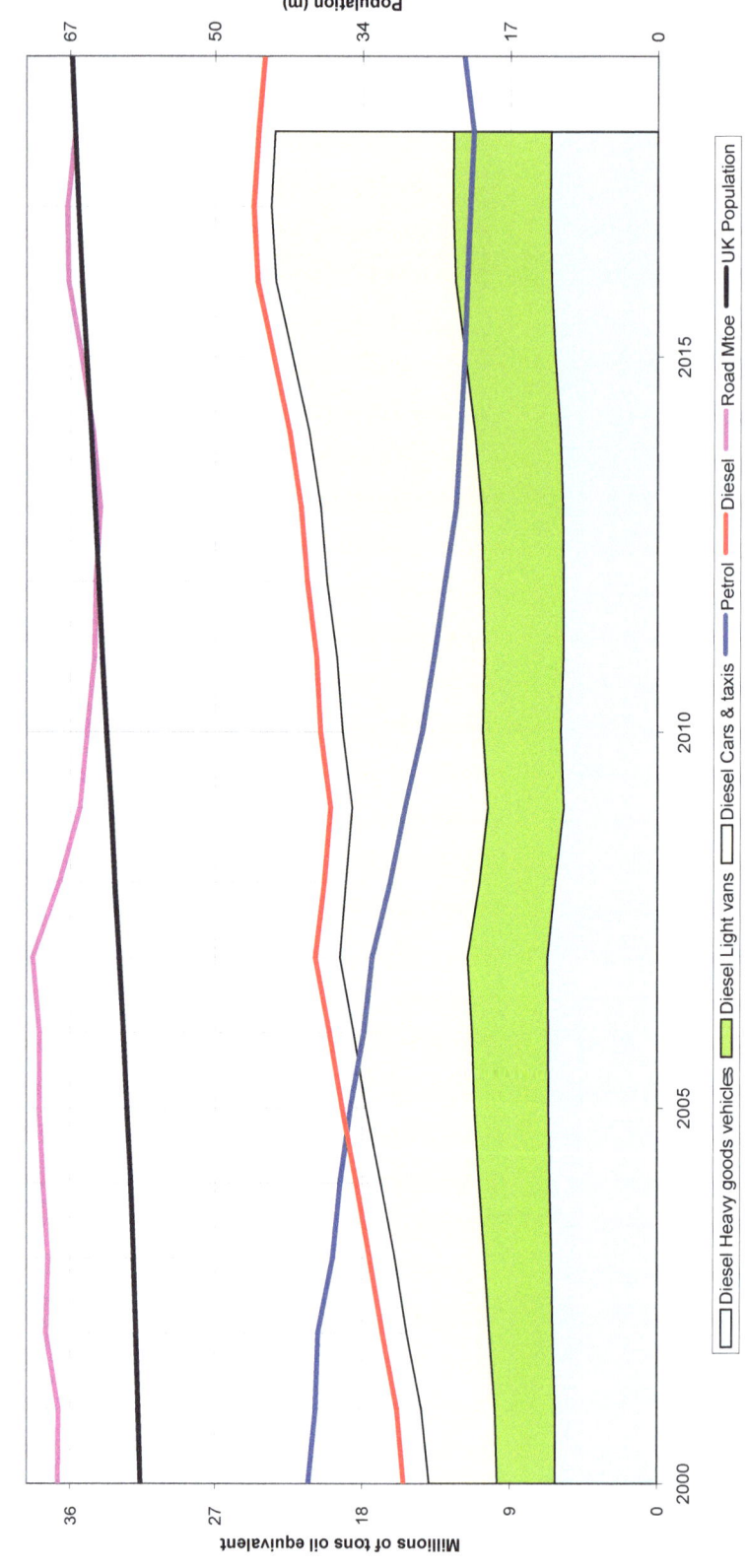

Diesel Heavy goods vehicles | Diesel Light vans | Diesel Cars & taxis | Petrol | Diesel | Road Mtoe | UK Population

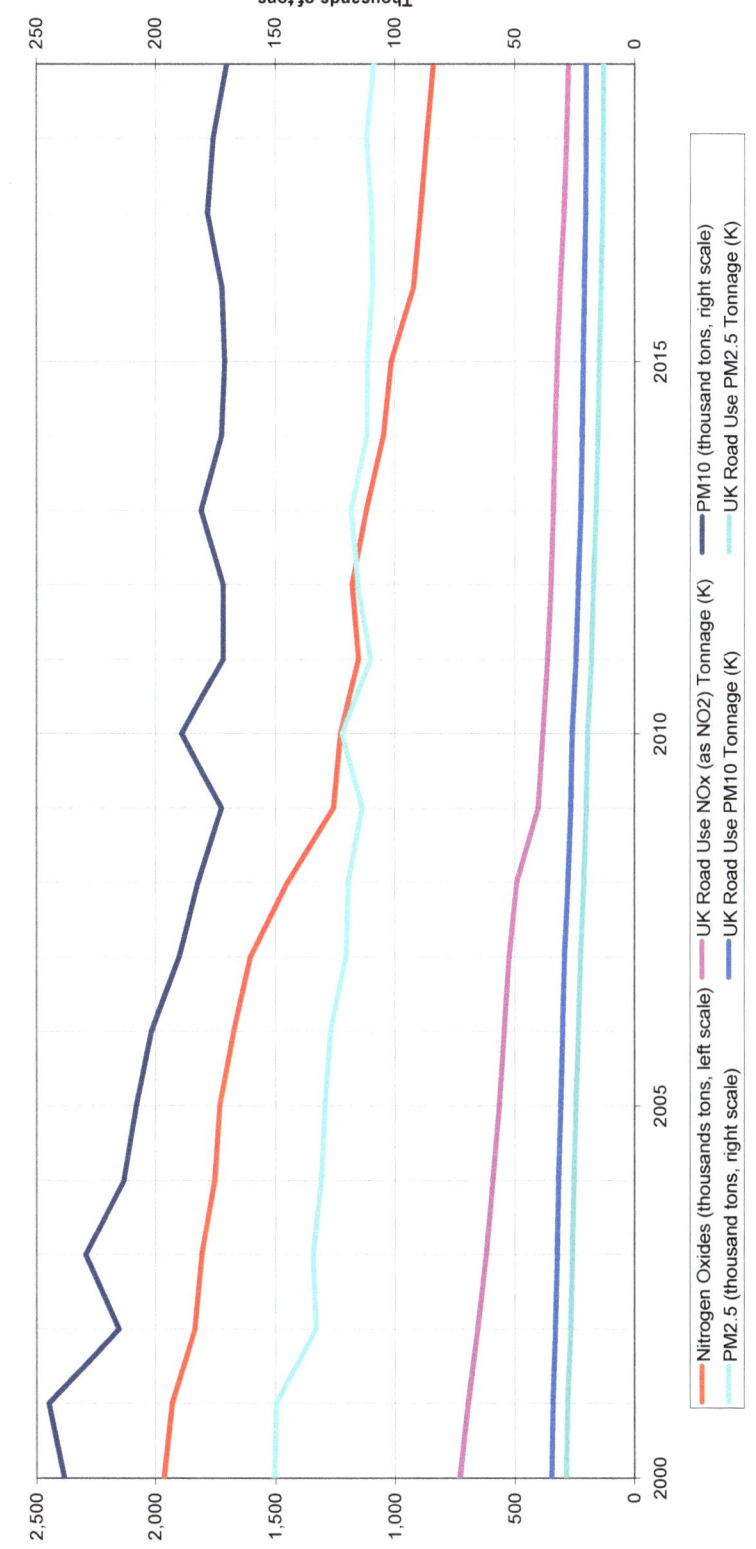

UK trend in weight of atmospheric pollutants (Defra/BEIS(NAEI))
(Road use contribution (NOx as NO2 - 33%, 31% Diesel), (PM10 - 12%, 2.5% Fuel) and (PM2.5 - 12%, 4.0% Fuel))

Thousands of tons

Nitrogen Oxides (thousands tons, left scale)
PM2.5 (thousand tons, right scale)
UK Road Use NOx (as NO2) Tonnage (K)
UK Road Use PM10 Tonnage (K)
PM10 (thousand tons, right scale)
UK Road Use PM2.5 Tonnage (K)

23

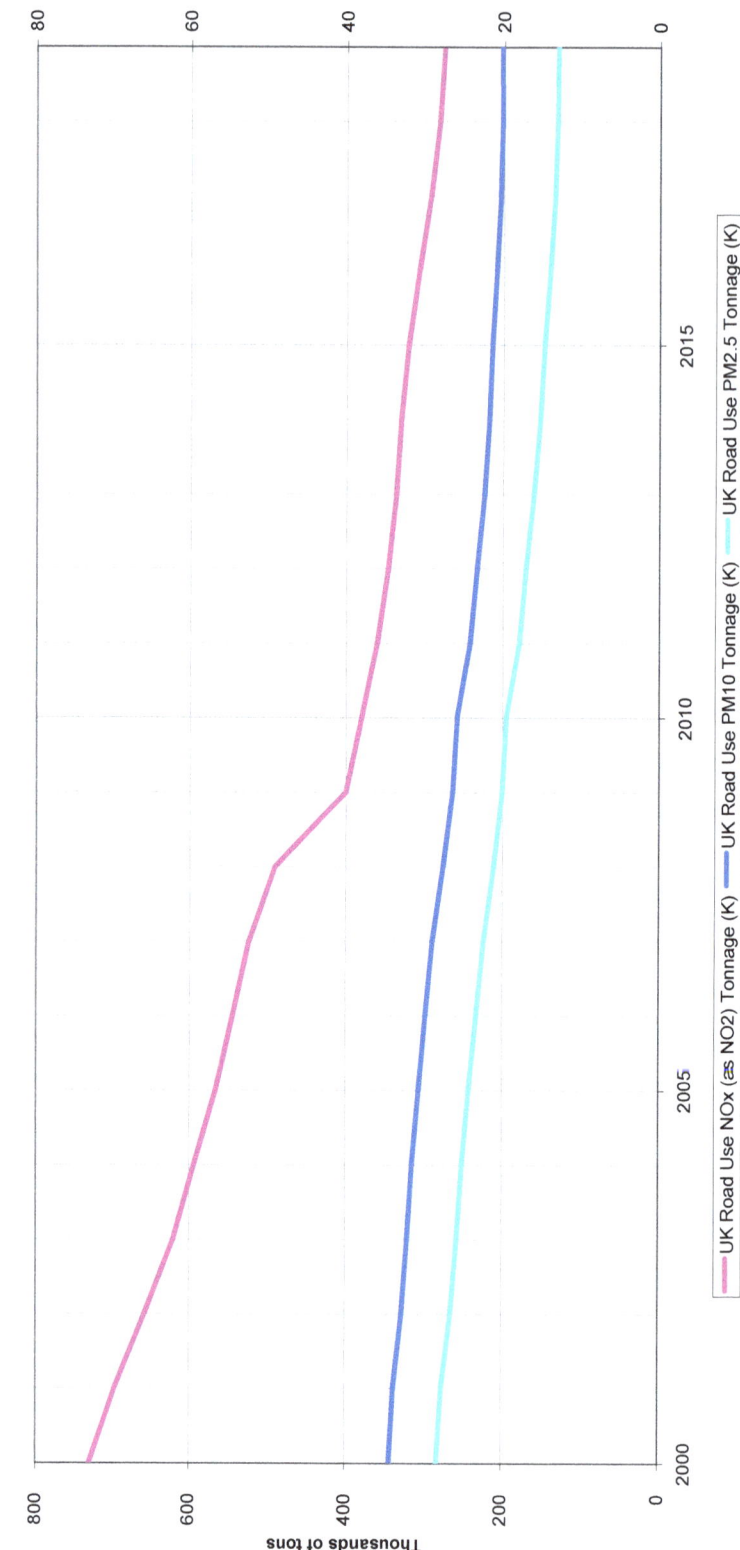

UK trend in weight of atmospheric pollutants (Defra/BEIS(NAEI))
(Road use contribution (NOx as NO2 - 33%, 31% Diesel), (PM10 - 12%, 2.5% Fuel) and (PM2.5 - 12%, 4.0% Fuel))

Thousands of tons

24

UK Road Use NOx (as NO2) Tonnage (K) UK Road Use PM10 Tonnage (K) UK Road Use PM2.5 Tonnage (K)

Life Expectancy of Londoners

&

Air pollutants in the UK and London: NO_x/NO_2, PM10 and PM2.5

2000-2019

Plus effect of 2020 Coronavirus "Lockdown"

London Life Expectancy (ONS Life Tables, 2001-2003 to 2017-2019 + PHE WICH Mortality, 2018 & 2019)

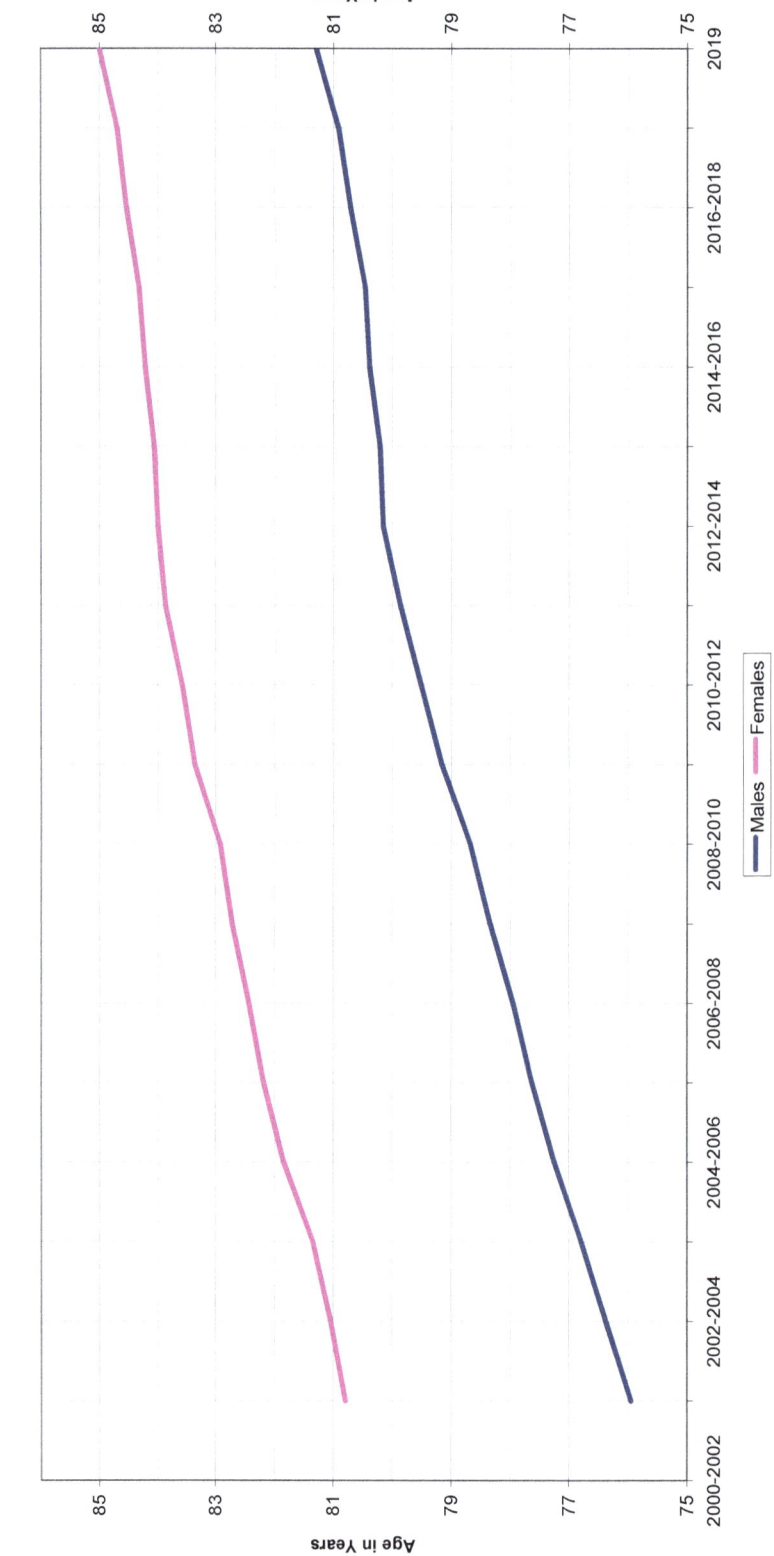

Legend: Males, Females

NO_x/NO_2

UK recent nitrous-oxide (NOx) & nitrogen dioxide (NO2) air pollutants

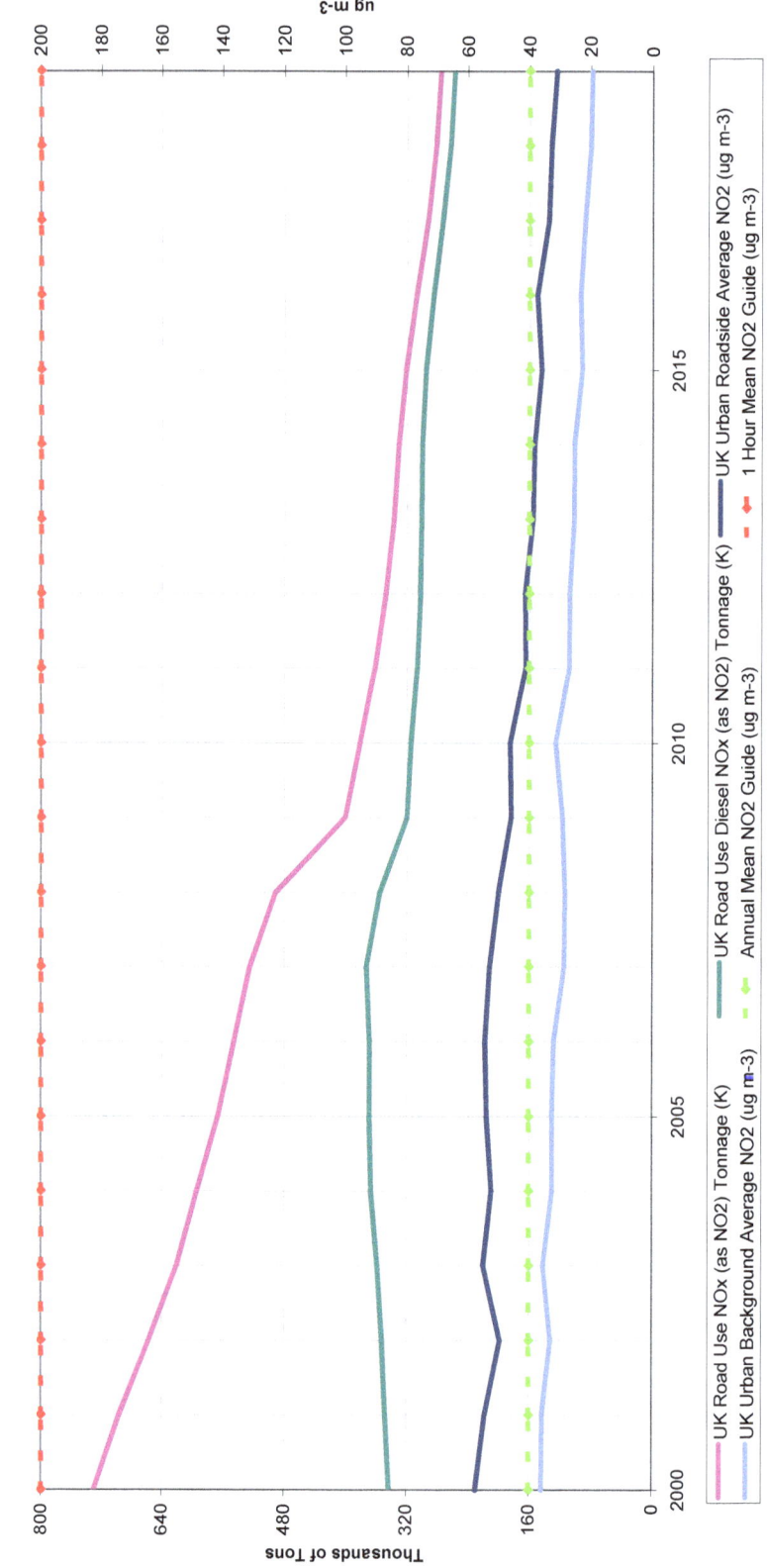

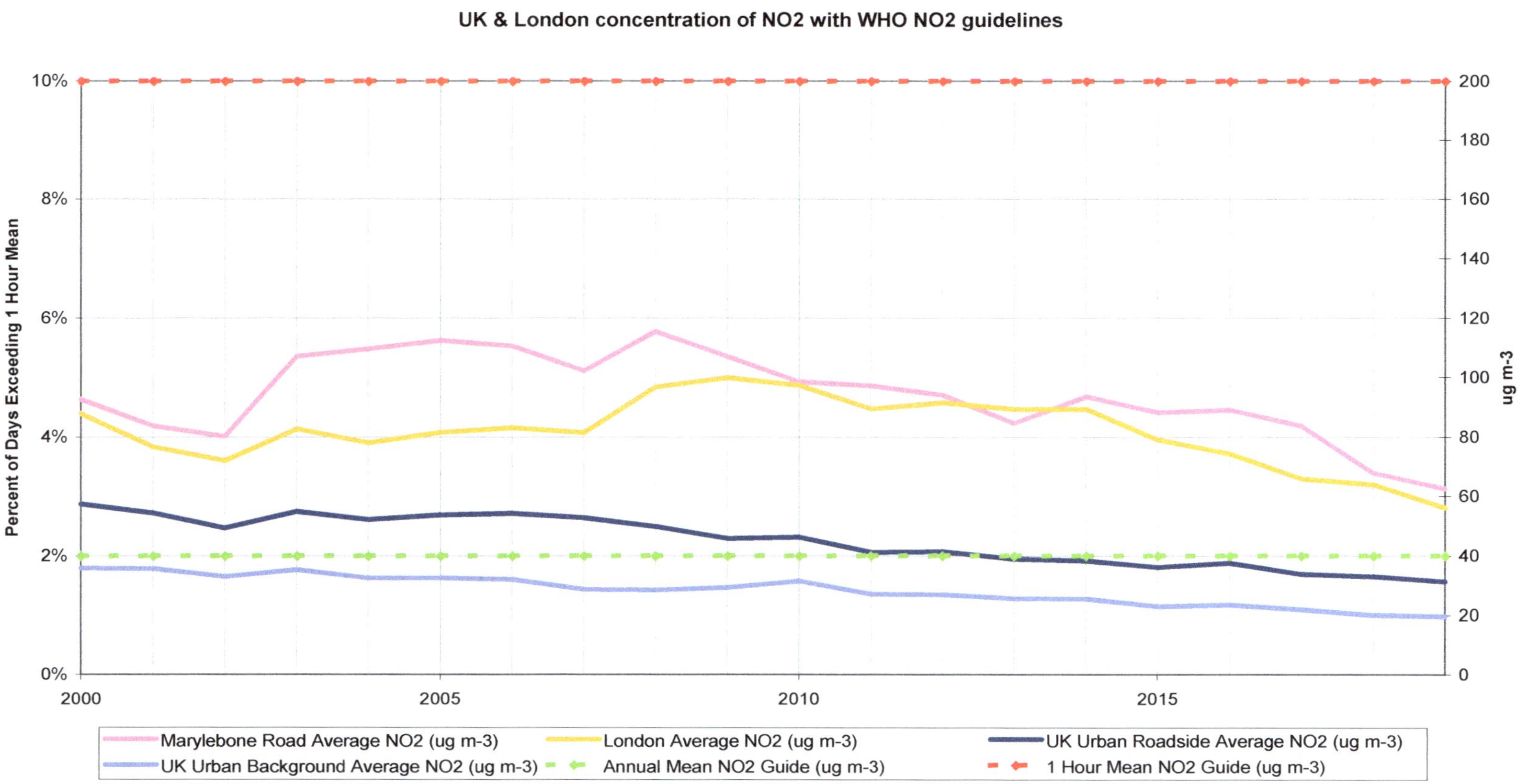
UK & London concentration of NO2 with WHO NO2 guidelines
Percent of Days Exceeding 1 Hour Mean
10%
8%
6%
4%
2%
0%
200
180
160
140
120
100
80
60
40
20
0
ug m-3
2000
2005
2010
2015
Marylebone Road Average NO2 (ug m-3)
London Average NO2 (ug m-3)
UK Urban Roadside Average NO2 (ug m-3)
UK Urban Background Average NO2 (ug m-3)
Annual Mean NO2 Guide (ug m-3)
1 Hour Mean NO2 Guide (ug m-3)

Marylebone Road, London % of hours per annum exceeding WHO NO2 guidelines

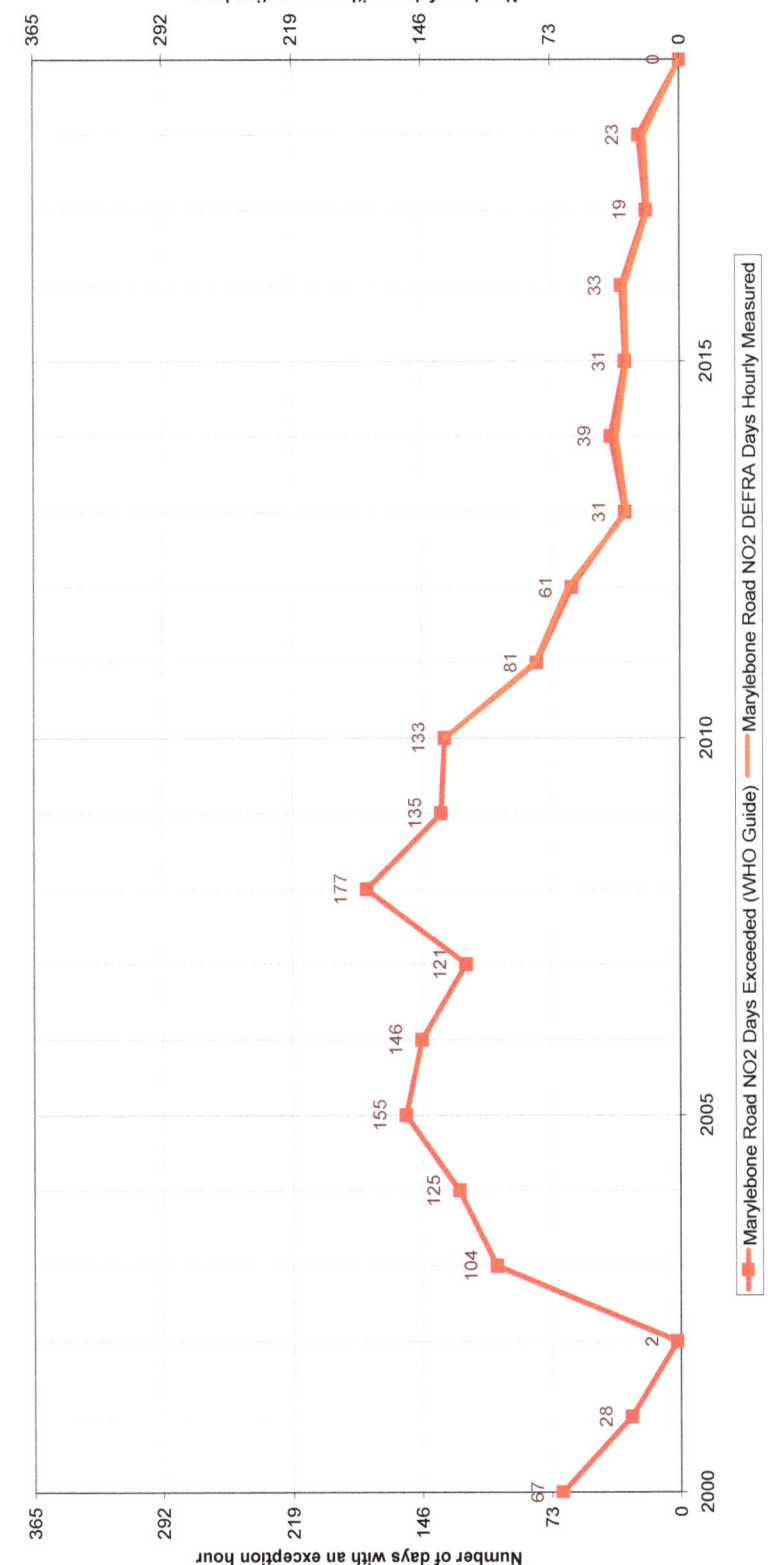

Number of days in which a measured exceptional hour of NO2 occurred (LAQ/Kings)

Number of days with an exception hour

Marylebone Road NO2 Days Exceeded (WHO Guide) — Marylebone Road NO2 DEFRA Days Hourly Measured

31

London NO2 Concentration (selected roads) plus Mayor's Office all roadside and background mean - Half-yearly

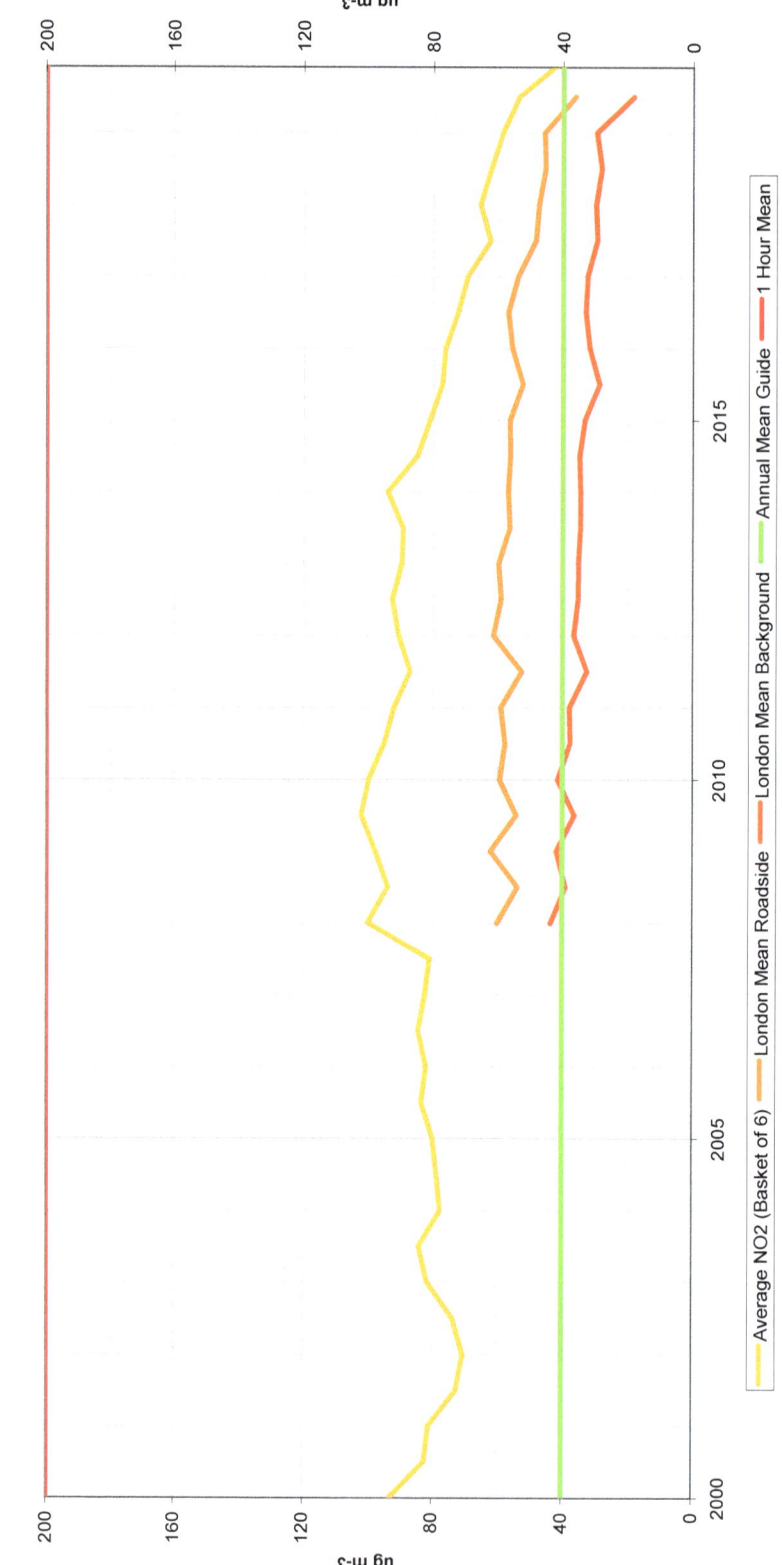

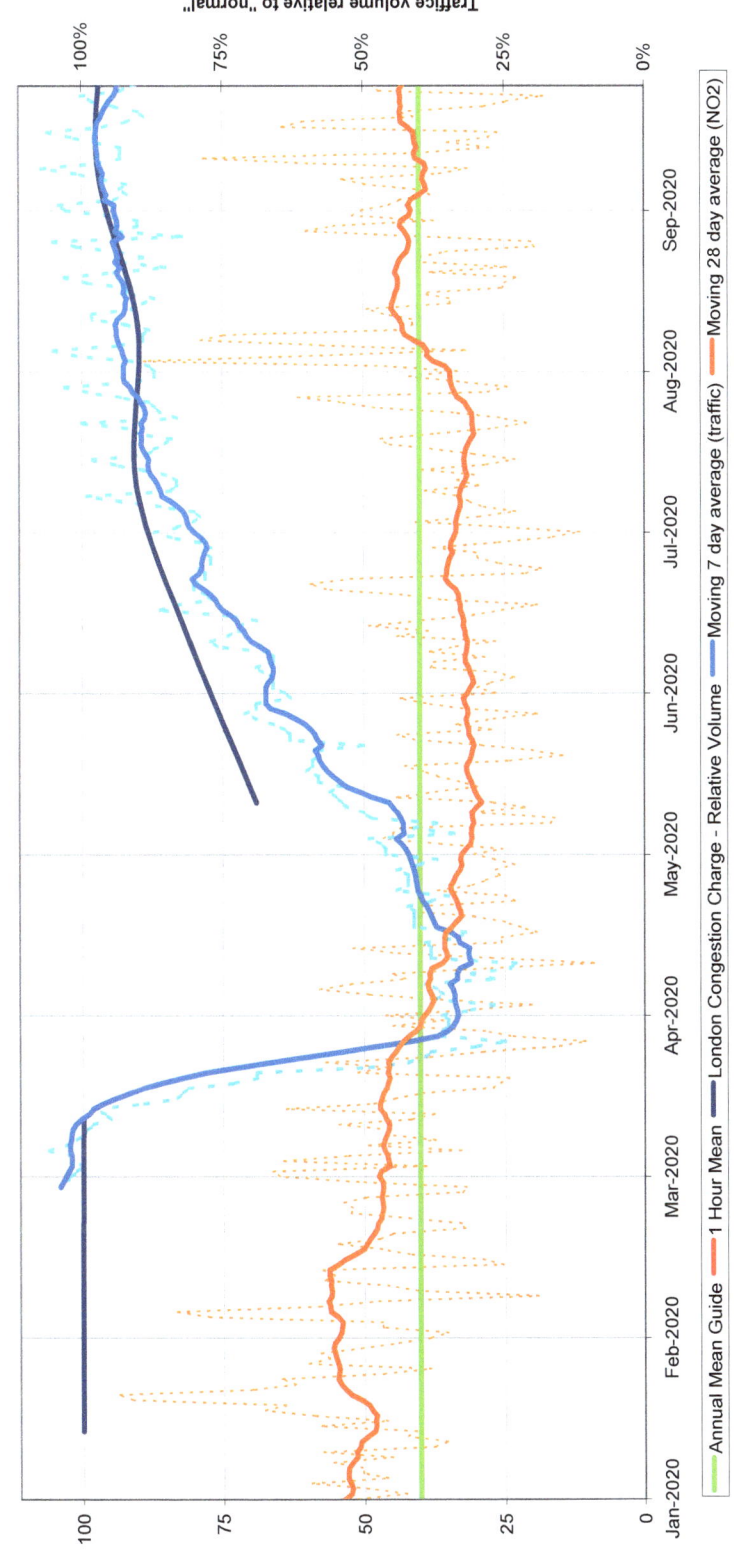

London (selected roads) Daily NO2 concentration January 2020 to August 2020
correlated to Coronavirus restrictions motor vehicle usage

Traffic volume relative to "normal"

ug m-3

— Annual Mean Guide — 1 Hour Mean — London Congestion Charge - Relative Volume — Moving 7 day average (traffic) --- Moving 28 day average (NO2)

33

PM$_{10}$ – Particulates under 10 microns

UK recent particulates (PM10) air pollutants

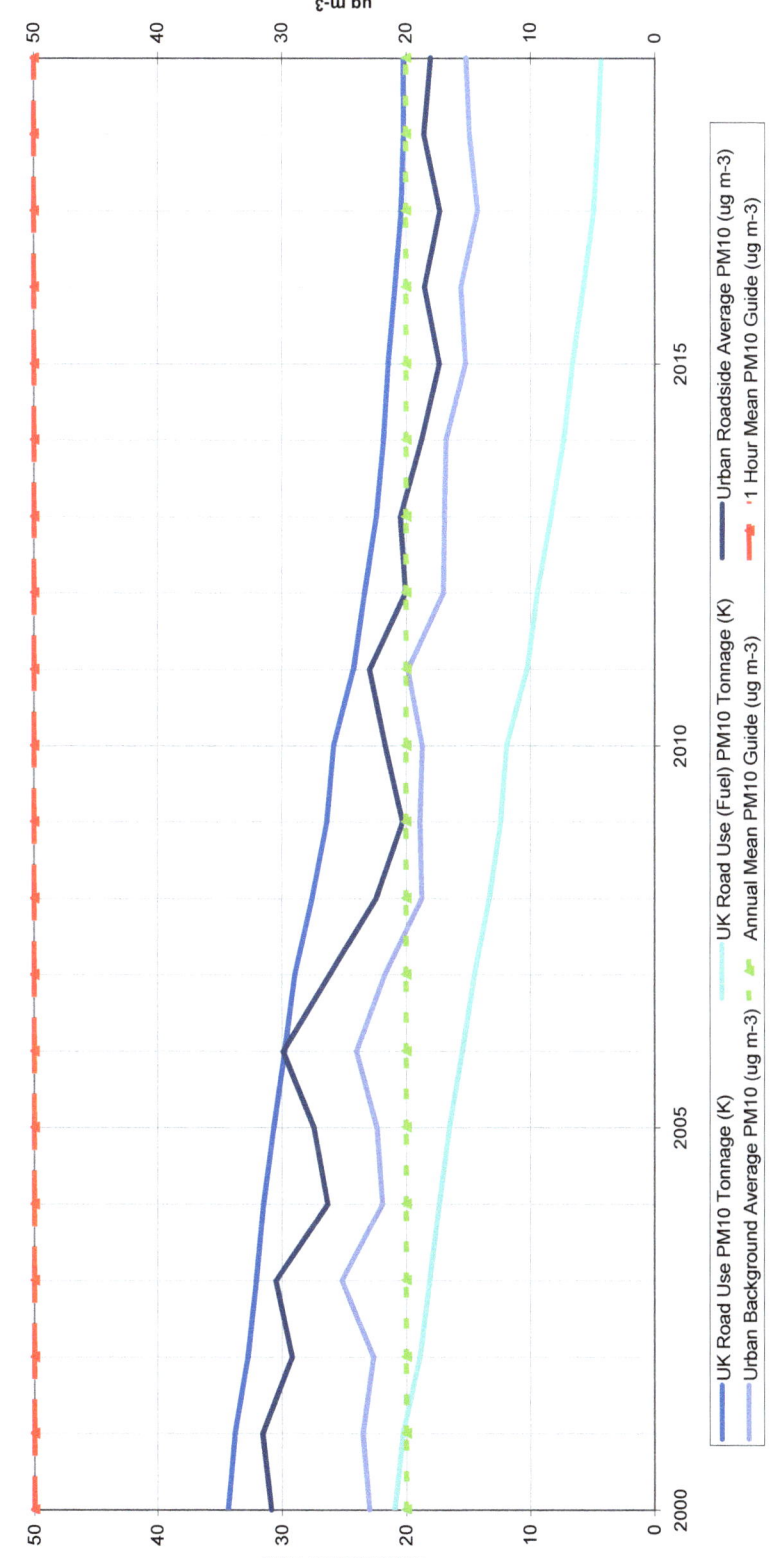

UK & London concentration of PM10 with DEFRA PM10 air pollutant trigger

Marylebone Road & London % of hours per annum exceeding DEFRA PM10 trigger

Number of days in which a measured exceptional hour of PM10 occurred (LAQ/Kings)

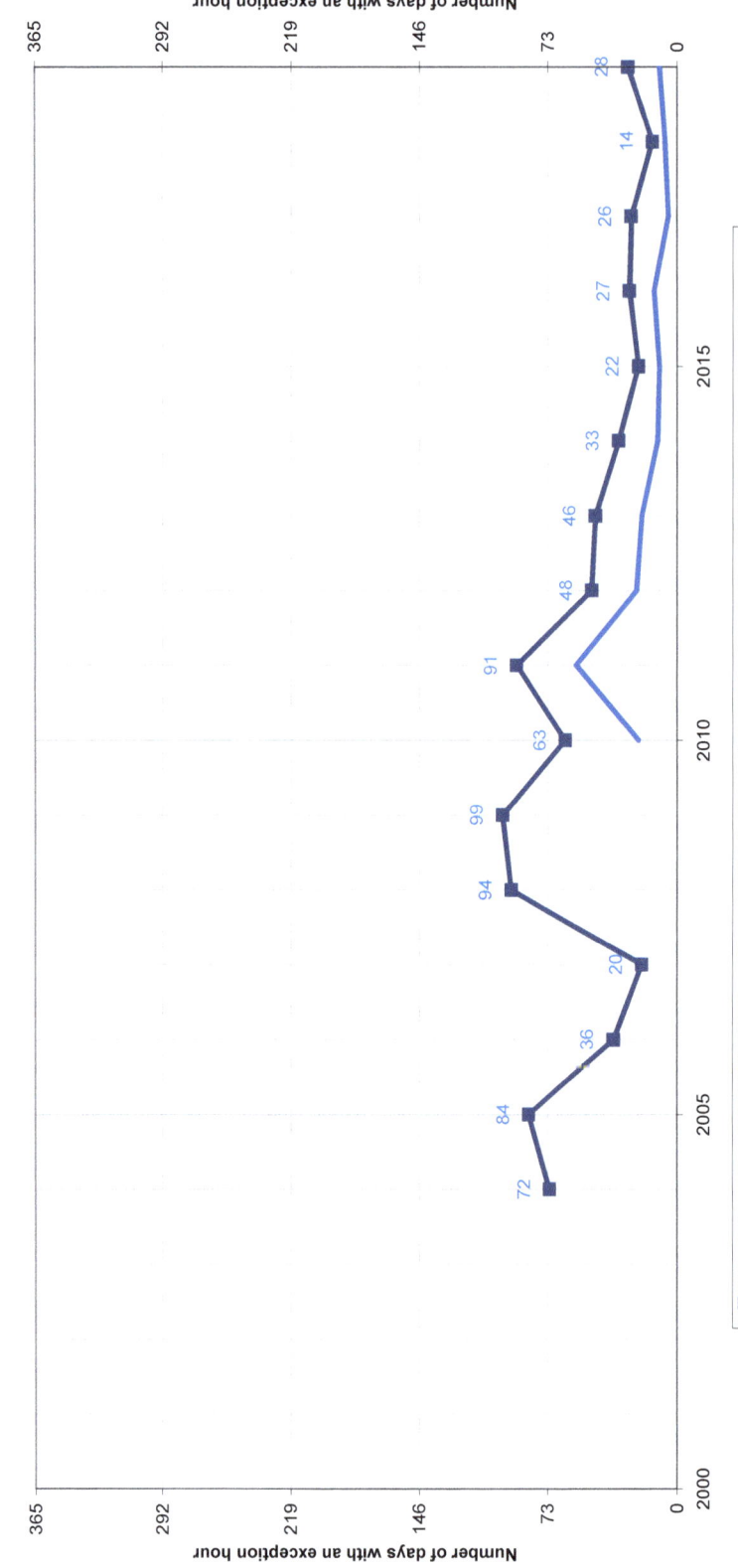

Marylebone Road FDMS PM10 Days Exceeded (defra Trigger) — Marylebone Road PM10 Defra Days Hourly Measured

London PM10 concentration (selected roads) plus Mayor's Office all roadside and background mean - Half-yearly

Legend: Average PM10 (Basket of Seven) | London Mean Roadside | London Mean Background | Annual Mean Guide | 1 Hour Mean

39

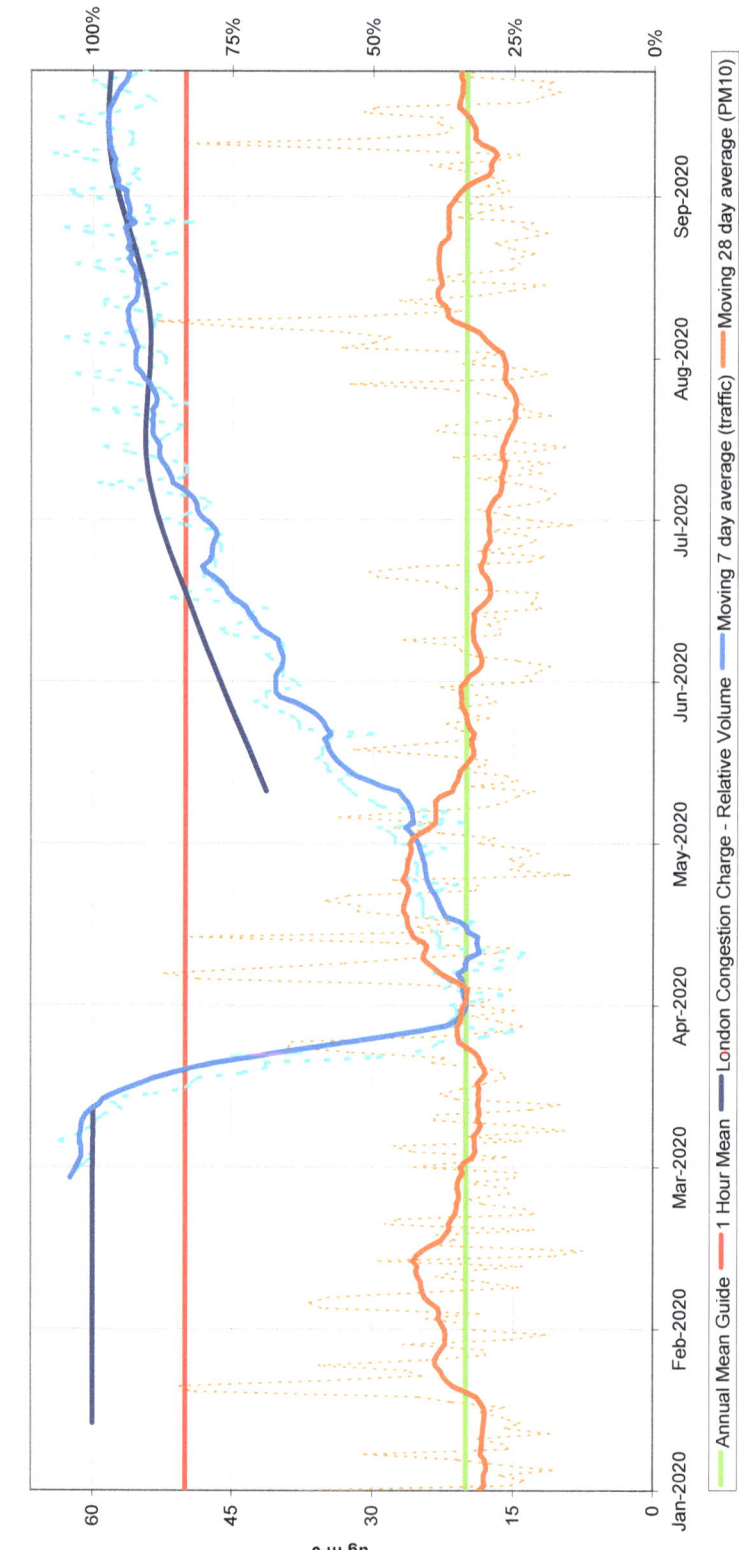

London (selected roads) Daily PM10 concentration January 2020 to August 2020
correlated to Coronavirus restrictions motor vehicle usage

Annual Mean Guide — 1 Hour Mean — London Congestion Charge - Relative Volume — Moving 7 day average (traffic) — Moving 28 day average (PM10)

PM$_{2.5}$ – Particulates under 2.5 microns

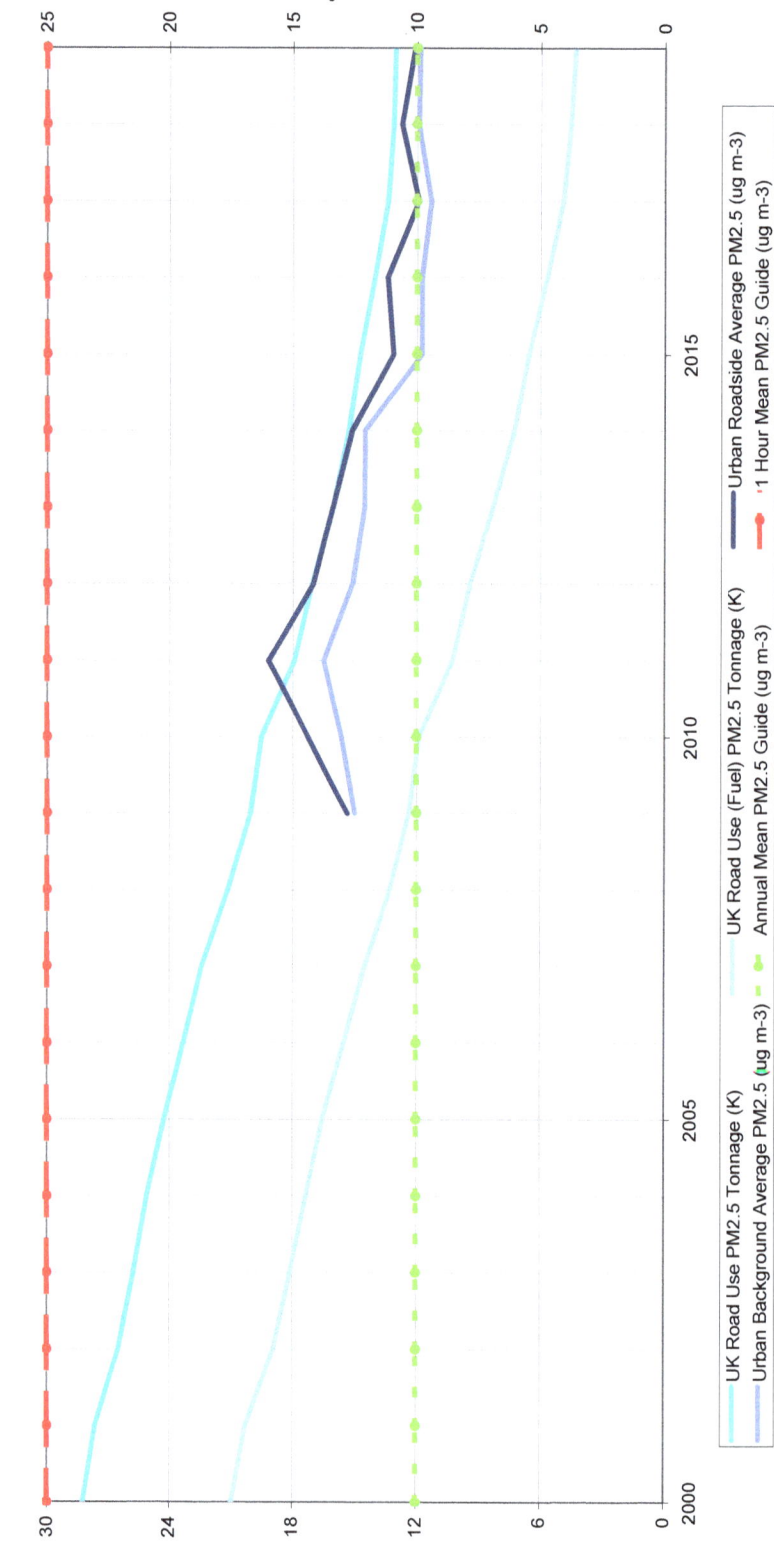

UK, London recent particulates (PM2.5) air pollutants

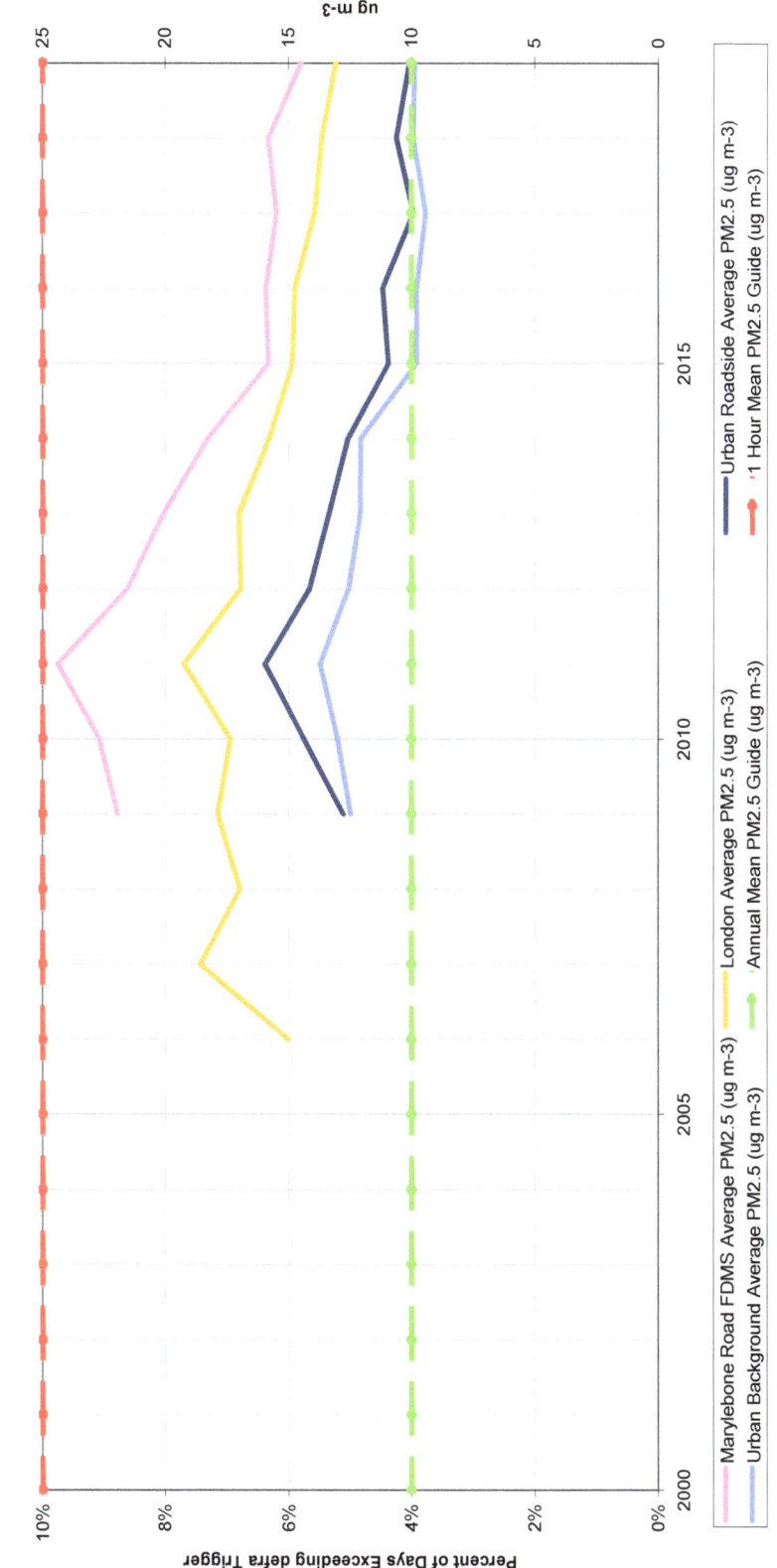

UK & London concentration of PM2.5 with DEFRA PM2.5 trigger

Marylebone Road FDMS Average PM2.5 (ug m-3) — London Average PM2.5 (ug m-3) — Urban Roadside Average PM2.5 (ug m-3)
Urban Background Average PM2.5 (ug m-3) — Annual Mean PM2.5 Guide (ug m-3) — 1 Hour Mean PM2.5 Guide (ug m-3)

43

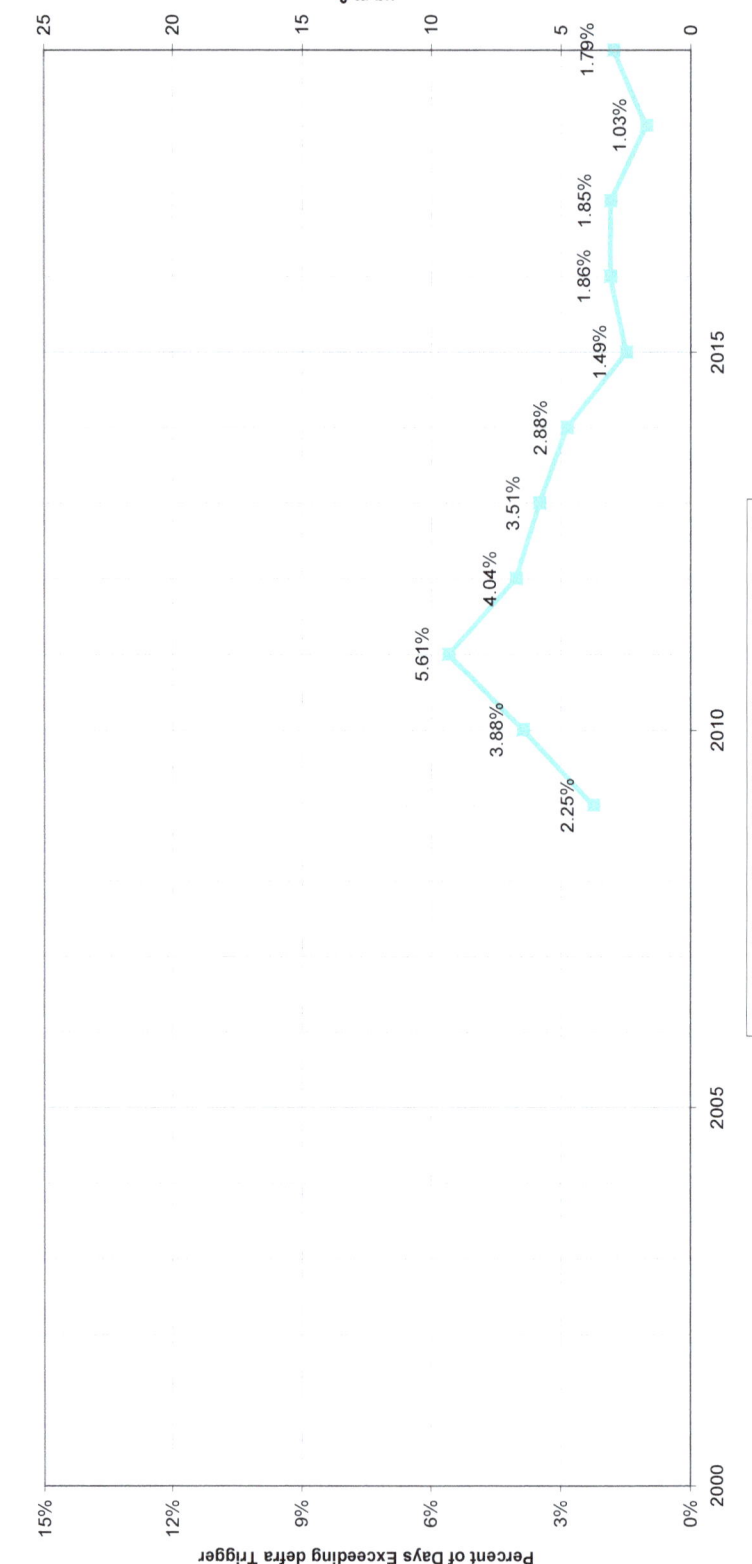

Marylebone Road & London % of hours per annum exceeding DEFRA PM2.5 trigger

Number of days in which a measured exceptional hour of PM2.5 occurred (LAQ/Kings)

Number of days with an exception hour

Marylebone Road FDMS PM2.5 Days Exceeded (defra Trigger) ——— Marylebone Road PM2.5 Days Exceeded (defra Trigger) ——— Marylebone Road PM2.5 DEFRA Days Hourly Measured

45

London PM2.5 concentration (selected roads) plus Mayor's Office all roadside and background mean - Half-yearly

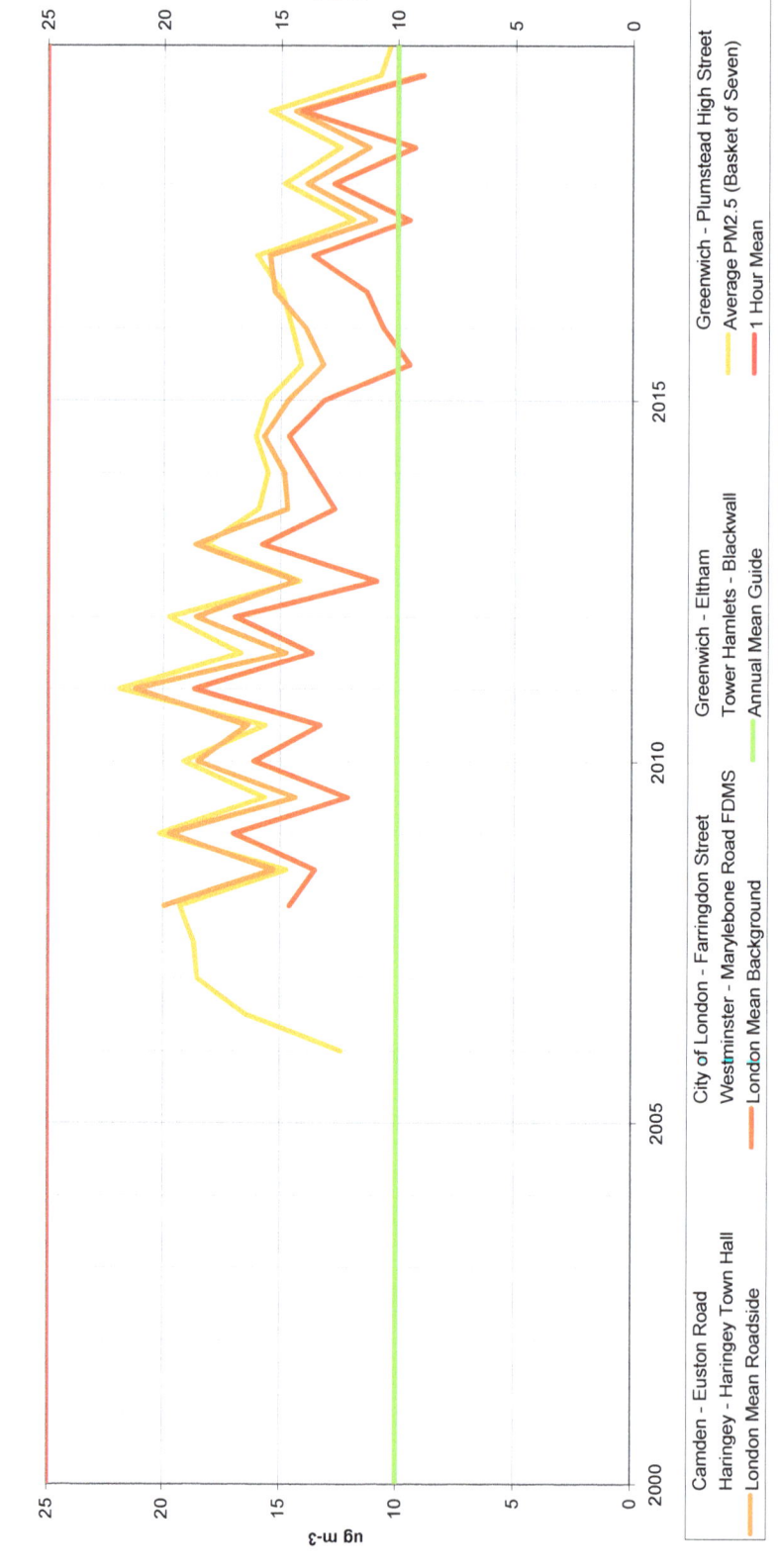

Camden - Euston Road
Haringey - Haringey Town Hall
London Mean Roadside

City of London - Farringdon Street
Westminster - Marylebone Road FDMS
London Mean Background

Greenwich - Eltham
Tower Hamlets - Blackwall
Annual Mean Guide

Greenwich - Plumstead High Street
Average PM2.5 (Basket of Seven)
1 Hour Mean

London (selected roads) Daily PM2.5 concentration January 2020 to August 2020
correlated to Coronavirus restrictions motor vehicle usage

Traffic volume relative to "normal"

ug m-3

— Annual Mean Guide — 1 Hour Mean — London Congestion Charge - Relative Volume — Moving 7 day average (traffic) — Moving 28 day average (PM2.5)

47

DEFRA, UK major roads and background Analysis for 2019 of NO_2

Plus

Capital City Foundation, Greater London Analysis and Modelling for 2010 of NO_2

DEFRA, UK analysis of geographical concentration of NO₂, 2019

Major roads and annual mean background

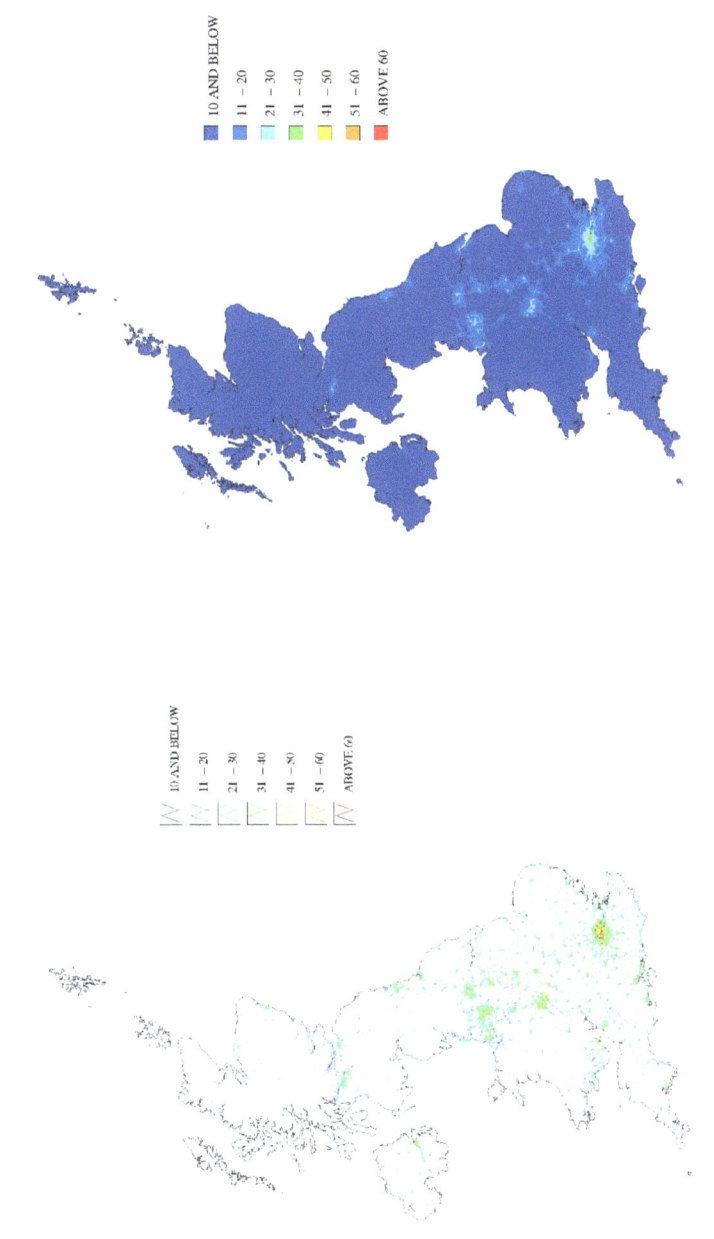

10 AND BELOW
11 — 20
21 — 30
31 — 40
41 — 50
51 — 60
ABOVE 60

London modelled concentration of NO$_2$, at 2010 relative high (*Capital City Foundation, Up in the Air 2015, Page 18*).

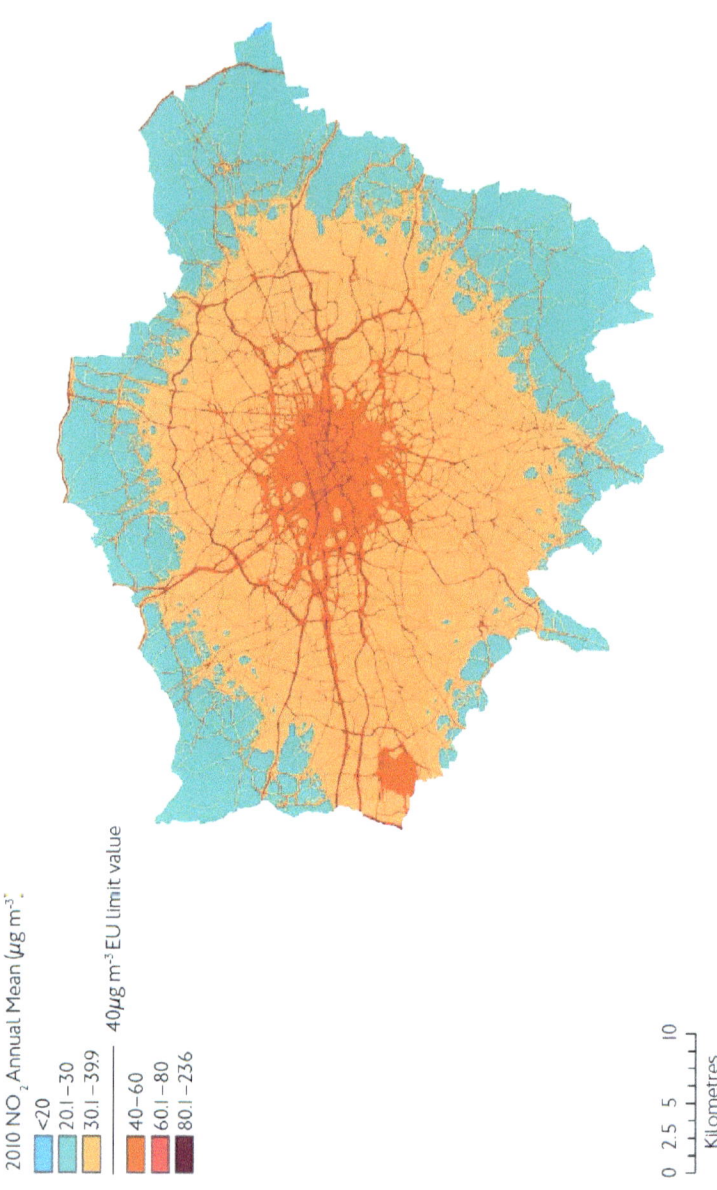

2010 NO$_2$ Annual Mean (μg m^{-3})

<20
20.1–30
30.1–39.9

40μg m^{-3} EU limit value

40–60
60.1–80
80.1–236

0 2.5 5   10

Kilometres

London modelled concentration of NO₂, 2025 projection - 2015 policies (*Capital City Foundation, Up in the Air 2015, Page 27*).

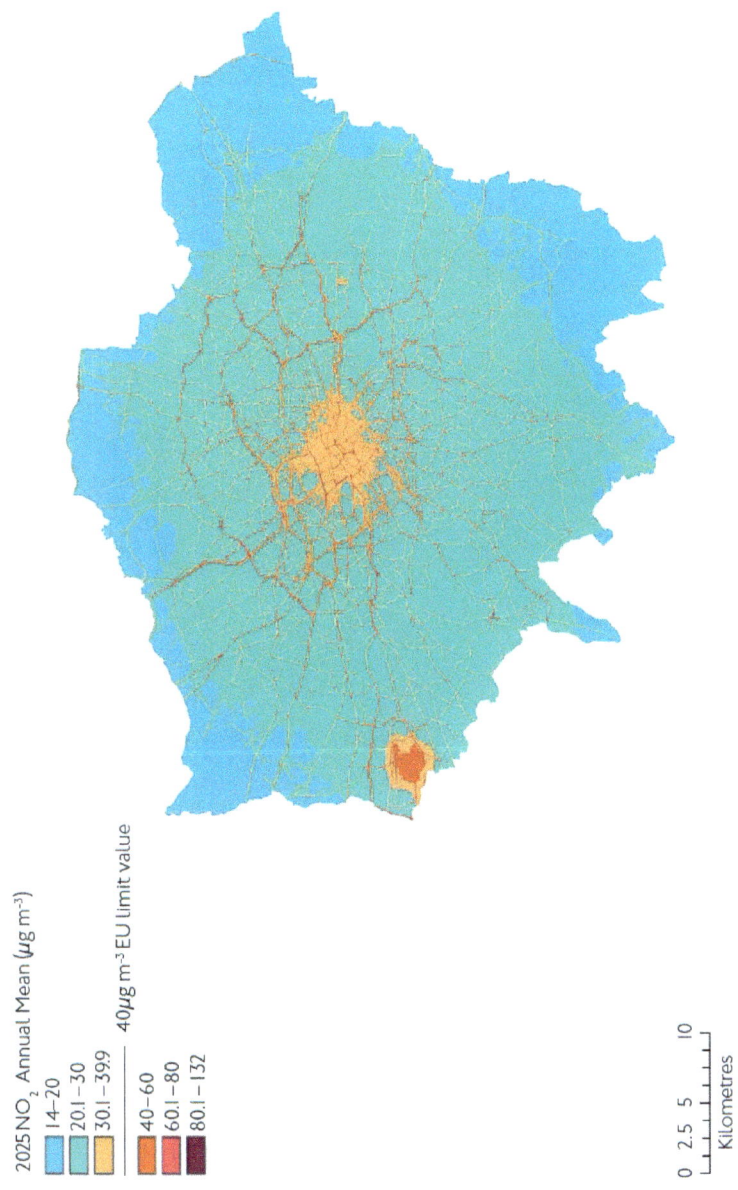

2025 NO₂ Annual Mean (μg m⁻³)

14–20
20.1–30
30.1–39.9
—— 40μg m⁻³ EU limit value
40–60
60.1–80
80.1–132

0 2.5 5   10
Kilometres

Part of a series - see also:

- UK Economic & Social Change – 1700-2019 – Three centuries of progress
  - UK Economy – 1700-1913 – An economy in transition
- UK Economy – 1900-2019 – Growth of the state & world war
- UK Economy – 1990-2019 – Quarter of a century of new changes
  - UK Economy – 1990-2019 – Stable income inequality
- UK Household Expenditure – 1700-2019 – Cost of Living
  - UK Housing – 1700-2019 – Growth of home ownership
- UK Pauperism, Poverty and Hardship – 1700-2019 – The Retreat of Real Poverty
  - UK Pollution (Air Quality), Cars – 1970-2019 – Continuous improvement
- UK Pollution (Air Quality), Energy – 1970-2019 – Continuous improvement
- UK Population & Life Expectancy – 1970-2019 – Continuous Improvement

UK Road Transport

Age of vehicles and fuel costs

1950-2020

GB age of private cars, including comparison with EU24 for 2017

1995-2020

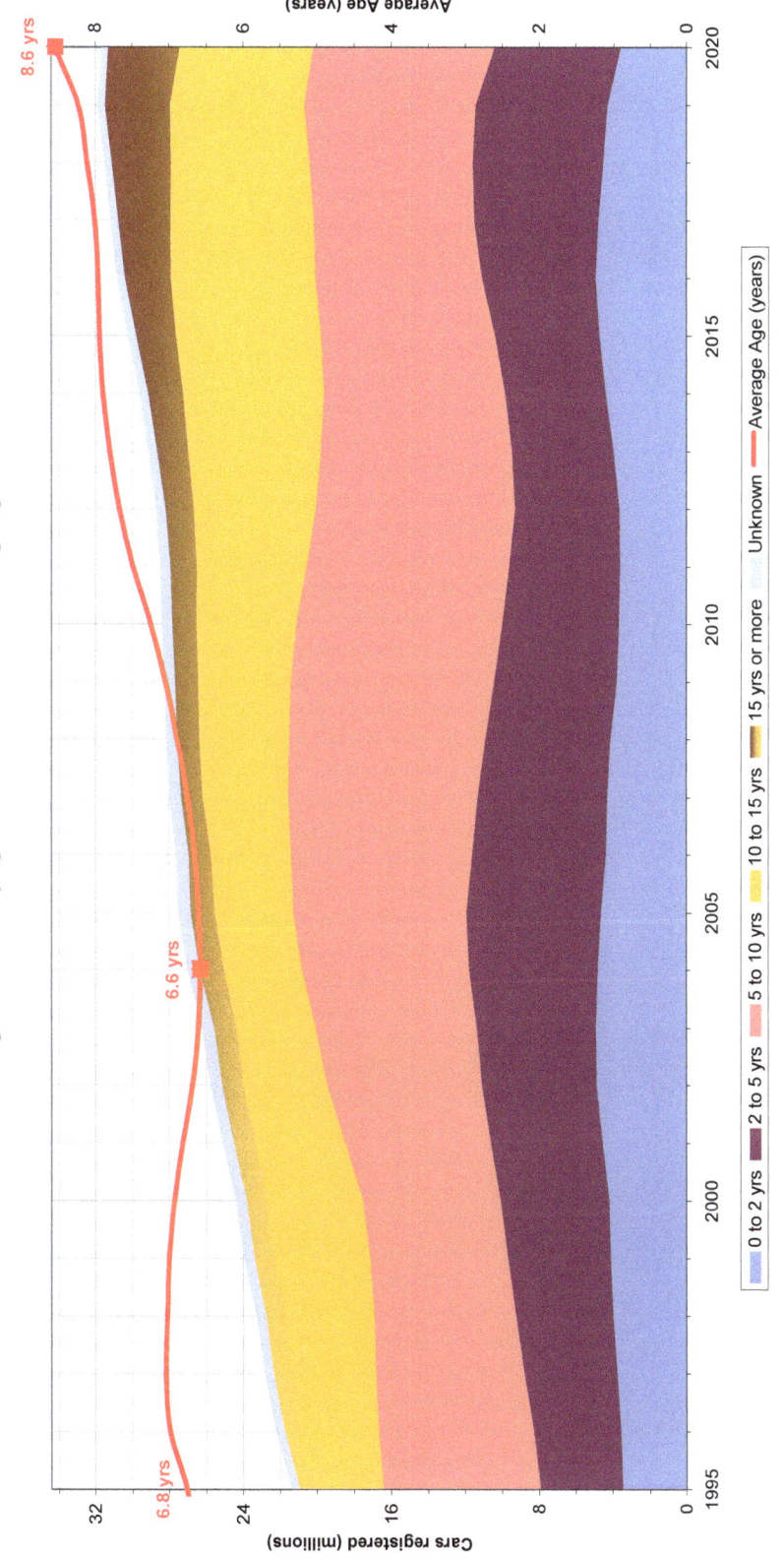

Number of registered cars by ages for Great Britain and average age of vehicles

Average Age (years)

Cars registered (millions)

0 to 2 yrs | 2 to 5 yrs | 5 to 10 yrs | 10 to 15 yrs | 15 yrs or more | Unknown | Average Age (years)

8.6 yrs

6.6 yrs

6.8 yrs

55

Percentage share of registered cars by age for Great Britain

Percentage share of cars by age

0 to 2 yrs 2 to 5 yrs 5 to 10 yrs 10 to 15 yrs 15 yrs or more Unknown

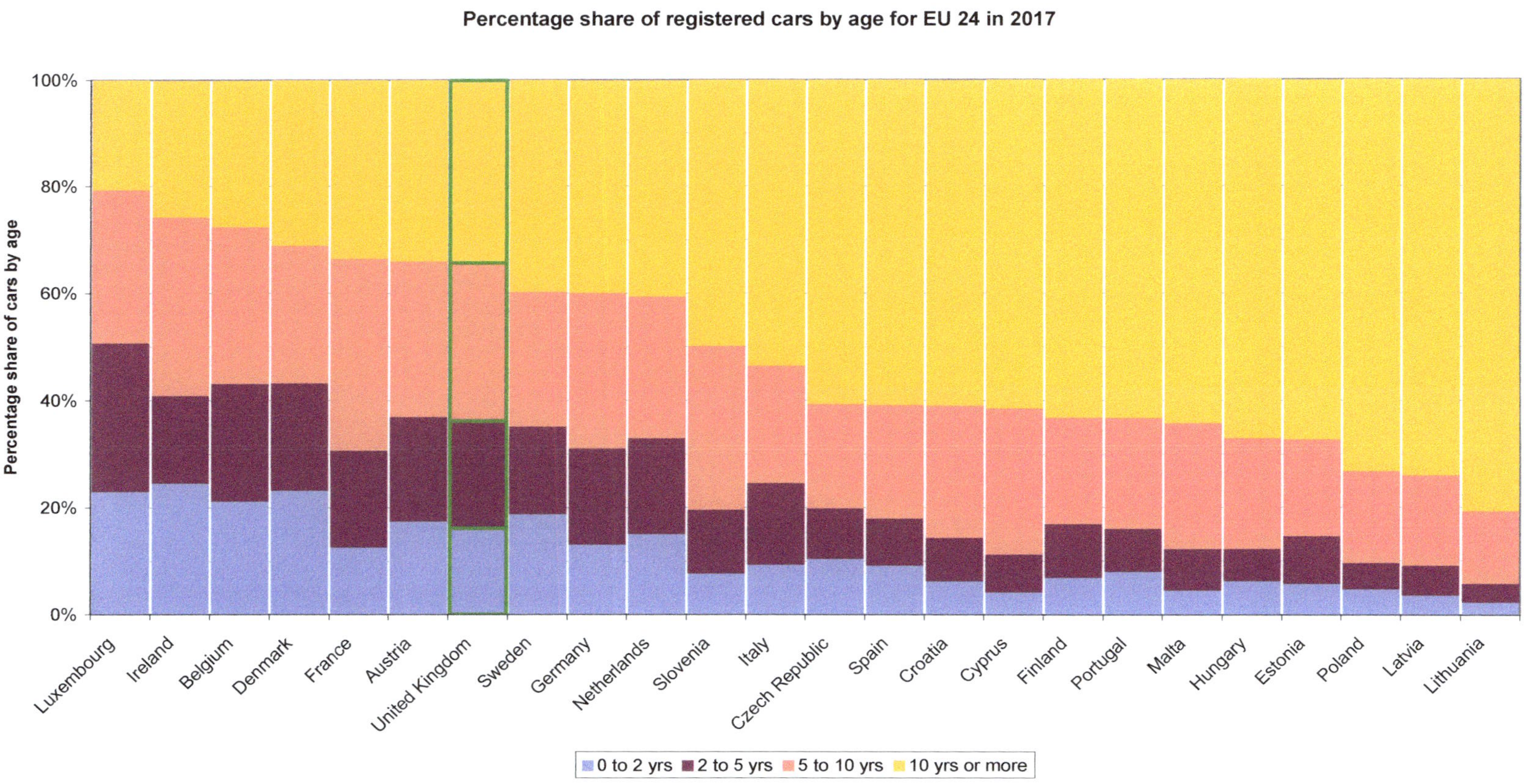

Percentage share of registered cars by age for EU 24 in 2017
Percentage share of cars by age
100%
80%
60%
40%
20%
0%
Luxembourg
Ireland
Belgium
Denmark
France
Austria
United Kingdom
Sweden
Germany
Netherlands
Slovenia
Italy
Czech Republic
Spain
Croatia
Cyprus
Finland
Portugal
Malta
Hungary
Estonia
Poland
Latvia
Lithuania
0 to 2 yrs
2 to 5 yrs
5 to 10 yrs
10 yrs or more

The real cost of fuel per litre

1954-2020

"Real" (CPI) Price of motor fuel (pence per litre) - from BEIS

Percent of motorist tax revenue spent on roads

"Real" pence per litre

Petrol: 2 star — Petrol: 4star/ LRP — Petrol: Super unleaded — Petrol: Premium unleaded — Diesel — % of Motorist Revenue spent on Roads

59

The taxation share of the cost of fuel

2003-2020

Percentage of motor fuel price which is taxation and pence per litre - from BEIS

Nominal pence per litre

Share of pump price which is taxation

Petrol: Percent Tax —— Diesel: Percent Tax ----- Petrol: Pump price (p/litre) ----- Diesel: Pump price (p/litre)

61

Share of government revenue from motorist (excluding VAT on fuel) and spending on the roads

2000-2019

UK Motorist Revenue and Transport Spending	2000-2019
All Transport Spending as a share of Motorists Revenue	**59.0%**
4.5 of which: local roads	10.3%
4.5 of which: national roads	13.0%
4.5 of which: local public transport	8.1%
4.5 of which: railway	24.4%
4.5 of which: other transport	3.2%
Non-road Transport subsidy	**35.7%**
Non-transport transfer to HM Treasury	**41.0%**
% of Government Revenue from motorists spent on Roads	**23.3%**

63

UK government revenue from the motorist, plus analysis of expenditure on roads, transport etc.

1999/2000 to 2020/2021

Revenue raised from the motorist - £'000	1999-00	2000-01	2001-02	2002-03	2003-04	2004-05	2005-06	2006-07	2007-08	2008-09	2009-10
Vehicle Excise Duties (CDDZ + EKED)	4,855,000	4,269,000	4,291,000	4,336,000	4,689,000	4,737,000	4,950,000	5,139,000	5,393,000	5,582,000	5,675,000
-Fuel duties (CUDG)	22,515,000	22,630,000	21,916,000	22,147,000	22,786,000	23,313,000	23,438,000	23,585,000	24,905,000	24,615,000	26,197,000
-VAT charged on Fuel duties (CUDG)	4,503,000	4,526,000	4,383,200	4,429,400	4,557,200	4,662,600	4,687,600	4,717,000	4,981,000	4,923,000	5,239,400
Excluding the VAT charge on Fuel duties	27,370,000	26,899,000	26,207,000	26,483,000	27,475,000	28,050,000	28,388,000	28,724,000	30,298,000	30,197,000	31,872,000
This does not include the VAT on the fuel											
Including the VAT on Fuel Duty	31,873,000	31,425,000	30,590,200	30,912,400	32,032,200	32,712,600	33,075,600	33,441,000	35,279,000	35,120,000	37,111,400
		From PESA Table 3.6 (2005 edition)						From PESA Table 5.2			
All Government Spending on Transport - £'000	8,764,000	8,987,000	11,250,000	13,566,000	16,551,000	16,023,000	17,039,000	19,885,000	20,530,000	20,978,000	22,972,000
4.5 of which: local roads	2,854,000	3,180,000	3,829,000	4,353,000	4,382,000	2,352,000	2,705,000	3,313,000	3,231,000	3,487,000	4,131,000
4.5 of which: national roads	1,943,000	2,106,000	2,312,000	2,614,000	2,501,000	4,599,000	4,963,000	4,946,000	5,115,000	5,668,000	5,993,000
4.5 of which: local public transport	2,073,000	2,102,000	2,670,000	3,569,000	5,473,000	2,223,000	2,573,000	2,909,000	3,150,000	3,527,000	3,898,000
4.5 of which: railway	1,212,000	1,044,000	1,792,000	2,437,000	3,348,000	6,055,000	5,921,000	7,826,000	7,909,000	7,152,000	7,728,000
4.5 of which: other transport	681,000	555,000	646,000	593,000	846,000	794,000	877,000	891,000	1,125,000	1,144,000	1,222,000
Non-transport transfer to HM Treasury	23,109,000	22,438,000	19,340,200	17,346,400	15,481,200	16,689,600	16,036,600	13,556,000	14,749,000	14,142,000	14,139,400
All Road Spending - £'000	4,797,000	5,286,000	6,141,000	6,967,000	6,883,000	6,951,000	7,668,000	8,259,000	8,346,000	9,155,000	10,124,000
% of Motorist Revenue spent on Roads	15.1%	16.8%	20.1%	22.5%	21.5%	21.2%	23.2%	24.7%	23.7%	26.1%	27.3%
Increase in Road Transport Spending		489,000	855,000	826,000	-84,000	68,000	717,000	591,000	87,000	809,000	969,000
% Increase		10.2%	16.2%	13.5%	-1.2%	1.0%	10.3%	7.7%	1.1%	9.7%	10.6%
OBR GDP Deflator (2020 = 100)	62.5	63.6	64.6	66.0	67.4	69.4	71.2	73.3	75.3	77.3	78.6
Real Revenue from the Motorist - £'000	50,994,467	49,374,074	47,364,422	46,818,469	47,494,147	47,159,226	46,456,763	45,649,785	46,856,429	45,417,018	47,237,603
Real Increase in Motorist Revenue		-1,620,392	-2,009,652	-545,954	675,679	-334,921	-702,463	-806,979	1,206,645	-1,439,412	1,820,585
Real % Increase in Real Motorist Revenue		-3.2%	-4.1%	-1.2%	1.4%	-0.7%	-1.5%	-1.7%	2.6%	-3.1%	4.0%
Real Road Spending - £'000	7,674,849	8,305,214	9,508,435	10,551,891	10,205,425	10,020,719	10,770,189	11,274,231	11,084,888	11,839,203	12,886,431
Real Increase in Road Transport Spending		630,365	1,203,220	1,043,456	-346,466	-184,706	749,470	504,042	-189,344	754,315	1,047,228
Real % Increase Road Spending		8.2%	14.5%	11.0%	-3.3%	-1.8%	7.5%	4.7%	-1.7%	6.8%	8.8%
Billions of miles driven per annum	290.2	289.7	293.7	300.6	302.4	306.9	306.9	311.4	314.1	311.0	308.1
Real pounds spent per million mile driven - £'s	£26.45	£28.67	£32.37	£35.10	£33.75	£32.65	£35.09	£36.20	£35.29	£38.07	£41.83
Real Increase in Road Transport Spending		£2.22	£3.71	£2.73	-£1.35	-£1.10	£2.44	£1.11	-£0.91	£2.78	£3.76
Real % Increase Road Spending		8.4%	12.9%	8.4%	-3.9%	-3.2%	7.5%	3.2%	-2.5%	7.9%	9.9%

Revenue raised from the motorist - £'000	2010-11	2011-12	2012-13	2013-14	2014-15	2015-16	2016-17	2017-18	2018-19	2019-20	2020-21
Vehicle Excise Duties (CDDZ + EKED)	5,773,000	5,921,000	5,987,000	6,105,000	5,894,000	5,906,000	5,981,000	6,362,000	6,651,000	6,984,000	6,948,000
-Fuel duties (CUDG)	27,256,000	26,798,000	26,571,000	26,882,000	27,156,000	27,622,000	27,937,000	27,878,000	27,993,000	27,572,000	20,909,000
-VAT charged on Fuel duties (CUDG)	5,451,200	5,359,600	5,314,200	5,376,400	5,431,200	5,524,400	5,587,400	5,575,600	5,598,600	5,514,400	4,181,800
Excluding the VAT charge on Fuel duties	33,029,000	32,719,000	32,558,000	32,987,000	33,050,000	33,528,000	33,918,000	34,240,000	34,644,000	34,556,000	27,857,000
This does not include the VAT on the fuel											
Including the VAT on Fuel Duty	38,480,200	38,078,600	37,872,200	38,363,400	38,481,200	39,052,400	39,505,400	39,815,600	40,242,600	40,070,400	32,038,800
All Government Spending on Transport - £'000	21,491,000	19,413,000	20,279,000	20,794,500	21,981,000	27,909,000	28,821,000	30,331,000	32,678,000	34,600,000	45,133,000
					From PESA Table 5.2						
4.5 of which: local roads	3,584,000	3,081,000	2,851,000	3,151,400	3,713,000	3,986,000	4,163,000	4,274,000	4,820,000	5,574,000	6,261,000
4.5 of which: national roads	5,861,000	5,095,000	4,813,000	5,024,700	5,302,000	5,159,000	5,224,000	5,766,000	5,304,000	5,619,000	5,646,000
4.5 of which: local public transport	3,631,000	2,893,000	2,634,000	2,397,600	2,519,000	2,438,000	2,495,000	2,503,000	2,484,000	2,403,000	3,920,000
4.5 of which: railway	7,399,000	7,315,000	8,669,000	9,020,200	9,329,000	14,794,000	15,484,000	16,173,000	18,219,000	18,466,000	27,149,000
4.5 of which: other transport	1,016,000	1,029,000	1,312,000	1,200,600	1,118,000	1,532,000	1,455,000	1,615,000	1,851,000	2,538,000	2,157,000
Non-transport transfer to HM Treasury	16,989,200	18,665,600	17,593,200	17,568,900	16,500,200	11,143,400	10,684,400	9,484,600	7,564,600	5,470,400	-13,094,200
All Road Spending - £'000	9,445,000	8,176,000	7,664,000	8,176,100	9,015,000	9,145,000	9,387,000	10,040,000	10,124,000	11,193,000	11,907,000
% of Motorist Revenue spent on Roads	24.5%	21.5%	20.2%	21.3%	23.4%	23.4%	23.8%	25.2%	25.2%	27.9%	37.2%
Increase in Road Transport Spending	-679,000	-1,269,000	-512,000	512,100	838,900	130,000	242,000	653,000	84,000	1,069,000	714,000
% Increase	-6.7%	-13.4%	-6.3%	6.7%	10.3%	1.4%	2.6%	7.0%	0.8%	10.6%	6.4%
OBR GDP Deflator (2020 = 100)	80.0	81.2	82.9	84.4	85.5	86.2	88.4	89.9	92.0	94.1	100.0
Real Revenue from the Motorist - £'000	48,097,499	46,884,947	45,703,861	45,468,119	44,985,645	45,290,008	44,712,093	44,272,192	43,734,561	42,594,289	32,038,800
Real Increase in Motorist Revenue	859,896	-1,212,552	-1,181,085	-235,743	-482,474	304,363	-577,915	-439,901	-537,631	-1,140,272	-10,555,489
Real % Increase in Real Motorist Revenue	1.8%	-2.5%	-2.5%	-0.5%	-1.1%	0.7%	-1.3%	-1.0%	-1.2%	-2.6%	-24.8%
Real Road Spending - £'000	11,805,575	10,066,844	9,248,853	9,690,275	10,538,798	10,605,677	10,624,178	11,163,785	11,002,487	11,898,007	11,907,000
Real Increase in Road Transport Spending	-1,080,856	-1,738,731	-817,991	441,422	848,523	66,879	18,502	539,607	-161,298	895,519	8,993
Real % Increase Road Spending	-8.4%	-14.7%	-8.1%	4.8%	8.8%	0.6%	0.2%	5.1%	-1.4%	8.1%	0.1%
Billions of miles driven per annum	305.8	308.2	309.0	311.9	322.2	329.6	338.2	345.2	349.5	356.5	280.5
Real pounds spent per million mile driven - £'s	£38.61	£32.66	£29.93	£31.07	£32.71	£32.18	£31.41	£32.34	£31.48	£33.37	£42.45
Real Increase in Road Transport Spending	-£3.22	-£5.94	-£2.73	£1.14	£1.64	-£0.53	-£0.76	£0.93	-£0.86	£1.89	£9.07
Real % Increase Road Spending	-7.7%	-15.4%	-8.4%	3.8%	5.3%	-1.6%	-2.4%	2.9%	-2.7%	6.0%	27.2%

Compare fuel/electricity car running costs for 2019

Estimating electricity cost per kWh, including share of the standing charge at 20%

	2019	Economical Petrol Car		Pence per kWh + std. @20%	14.90
Pump price p/l (from BEIS)	125.00				
Fuel Duty p/l	57.95	Assuming annual miles	10,000	Renewable subsidy	23%
VAT at 20% p/l	20.83	at mpg	55	VAT rate	5%
VAT on duty p/l	11.59	Estimated miles tank range	450	Tariff per kWh (ex. VAT)	14.19
VAT on fuel p/l	9.24	Fuel per year litres	825.45	Tariff per kWh (ex. subsidy)	11.55
Percent tax/duty	63.0%	Your fuel cost p/yr (inc. taxes)	£1,032	kWh Charge rate per hour	7
Total tax/duty p/l	78.78	Of which tax/duty	£650		
Percent excess tax/duty	157.6%	Cost per mile in p.	10.32		
		Annual Hours fuelling	7.33		
		Cost equiv to Elect.	£528		
Cost of fuel p/l (ex. taxes)	46.22	Cost per mile in p. (ex. taxes)	3.81		
Price if VAT were 5%, p/l	48.53	Cost per mile in p. (equ. Elec.)	5.28		

Renault ZOE		BMW i3		Nissan LEAF	
Assuming annual miles	10,000	Assuming annual miles	10,000	Assuming annual miles	10,000
kWh added	52	kWh added	42	kWh added	40
Miles added	233	Miles added	179	Miles added	160
Charging time (hours)	7.4	Charging time (hours)	6.0	Charging time (hours)	5.7
Charge cost (ex. taxes)	£6.00	Charge cost (ex. taxes)	£4.85	Charge cost (ex. taxes)	£4.62
Charge cost (inc. taxes)	£7.75	Charge cost (inc. taxes)	£6.26	Charge cost (inc. taxes)	£5.96

Note current absence of road charging

Renault ZOE		BMW i3		Nissan LEAF	
Annual hours charging	319	Annual hours charging	335	Annual hours charging	357
Additional electricity cost p/yr	£333	Additional electricity cost p/yr	£350	Additional electricity cost p/yr	£373
Cost per mile in p. (ex. taxes)	2.58	Cost per mile in p. (ex. taxes)	2.71	Cost per mile in p. (ex. taxes)	2.89
Cost per mile in p. (inc. taxes)	3.33	Cost per mile in p. (inc. taxes)	3.50	Cost per mile in p. (inc. taxes)	3.73

Estimating electricity cost per kWh, including share of the standing charge at 20%

	Pence per kWh + std. @20%	14.90
	Renewable subsidy	23%
	VAT rate	5%
	Tariff per kWh (ex. VAT)	14.19
	Tariff per kWh (ex. subsidy)	11.55
	kWh Charge rate per hour	7

Modern Family Petrol Car — 2019

Assuming annual miles	10,000
at mpg	45
Estimated miles tank range	420
Fuel per year litres	1,008.89
Your fuel cost p/yr (inc. taxes)	£1,261
Of which tax/duty	£795
Cost per mile in p.	12.61
Annual Hours fuelling	7.86
Cost equiv to Elect.	£490
Cost per mile in p. (ex. taxes)	4.66
Cost per mile in p. (equ. Elec.)	4.90

Petrol Sports Car

Assuming annual miles	10,000
at mpg	30
Estimated miles tank range	366
Fuel per year litres	1,513.33
Your fuel cost p/yr (inc. taxes)	£1,892
Of which tax/duty	£1,192
Cost per mile in p.	18.92
Annual Hours fuelling	9.02
Cost equiv to Elect.	£734
Cost per mile in p. (ex. taxes)	6.99
Cost per mile in p. (equ. Elec.)	7.34

Tesla Model S

Assuming annual miles	10,000
kWh added	100
Miles added	360
Charging time (hours)	14.3
Charge cost (ex. taxes)	£11.55
Charge cost (inc. taxes)	£14.90
Annual hours charging	397
Additional electricity cost p/yr	£414
Cost per mile in p. (ex. taxes)	3.21
Cost per mile in p. (inc. taxes)	4.14

Porsche Taycan

Assuming annual miles	10,000
kWh added	79
Miles added	239
Charging time (hours)	11.3
Charge cost (ex. taxes)	£9.12
Charge cost (inc. taxes)	£11.77
Annual hours charging	472
Additional electricity cost p/yr	£493
Cost per mile in p. (ex. taxes)	3.82
Cost per mile in p. (inc. taxes)	4.93

Audi e-tron Sportback

Assuming annual miles	10,000
kWh added	95
Miles added	232
Charging time (hours)	13.6
Charge cost (ex. taxes)	£10.97
Charge cost (inc. taxes)	£14.16
Annual hours charging	585
Additional electricity cost p/yr	£610
Cost per mile in p. (ex. taxes)	4.73
Cost per mile in p. (inc. taxes)	6.10

Note current absence of road charging

Part of a series - see also:

- UK Economic & Social Change – 1700-2019 – Three centuries of progress
  - UK Economy – 1700-1913 – An economy in transition
- UK Economy – 1900-2019 – Growth of the state & world war
- UK Economy – 1990-2019 – Quarter of a century of new changes
  - UK Economy – 1990-2019 – Stable income inequality
- UK Household Expenditure – 1700-2019 – Cost of Living
  - UK Housing – 1700-2019 – Growth of home ownership
- UK Pauperism, Poverty and Hardship – 1700-2019 – The Retreat of Real Poverty
  - UK Pollution (Air Quality), Cars – 1970-2019 – Continuous improvement
- UK Pollution (Air Quality), Energy – 1970-2019 – Continuous improvement
  - UK Population & Life Expectancy – 1970-2019 – Continuous Improvement

UK Pollution (Air Quality), Energy

1970–2019 or two generations

Continuous improvement

UK improvement of the quality of life

Growth of population and life expectancy,
primary energy per person,
primary energy consumption by fuel/source

1700-2019

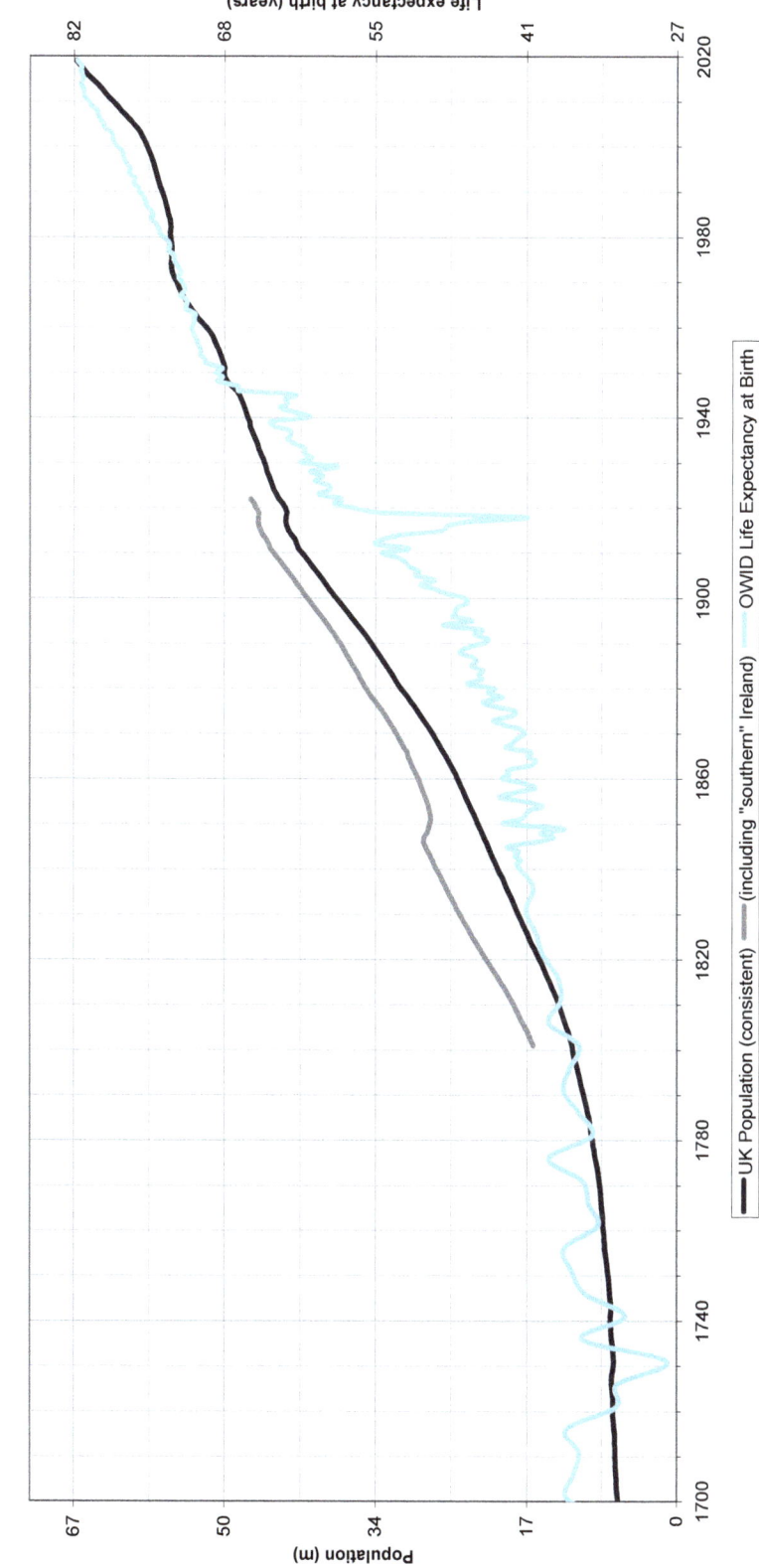

UK and England Long Term History of Population (Millions) and Life expectancy at birth (years)

— UK Population (consistent) —— (including "southern" Ireland) —— OWID Life Expectancy at Birth

73

BEIS (DUKES) & NIC - UK Total primary energy per person in tonnes of oil equivalent - correlated to calculated life expectancy

Legend: Energy per person — Energy per person (inc. imports) — OWID Life Expectancy at Birth

BEIS (DUKES) & NIC - UK Availability and consumption of primary energy in millions of tonnes of oil equivalent

Legend: Coal & solid fuels, Petroleum, Natural gas, Nuclear, Bioenergy, Thermal, Hydro, Wind, Solar, Net electricity imports, Other

75

BEIS (DUKES) & NIC - UK Availability and consumption of primary energy share - from millions of tonnes of oil equivalent

Share of primary energy by source

Coal & solid fuels ■ Petroleum ■ Natural gas ■ Nuclear ■ Bioenergy ■ Thermal ■ Hydro ■ Wind ■ Solar ■ Net electricity imports ■ Other

UK improvement of the quality of life

Growth of life expectancy and population,

reduction of living costs,

use of energy,

rise of the real cost of fuel and light in the 21st century,

after 2003

1900-2019

UK population (millions) and Life Expectancy at Birth (Years)

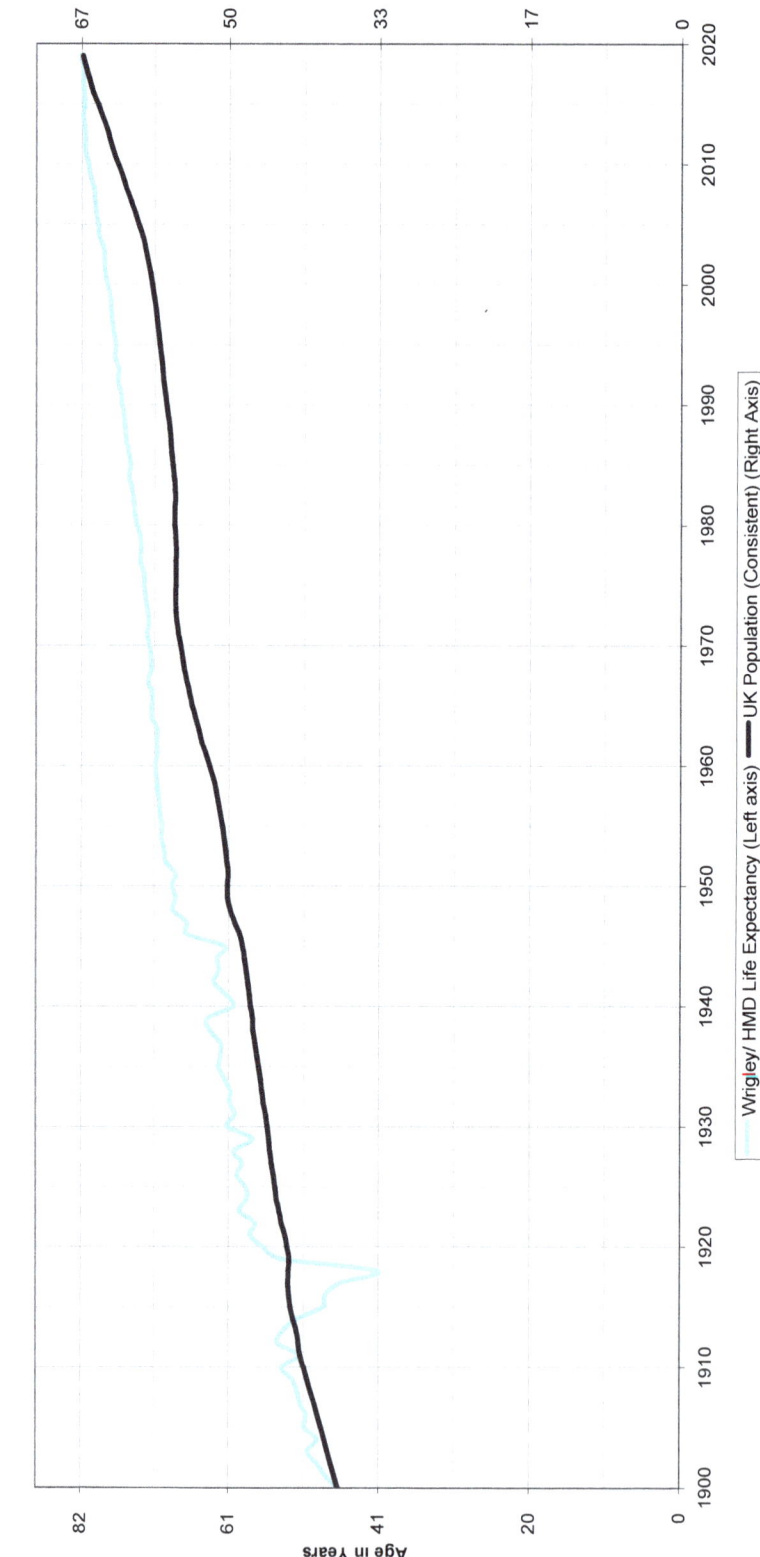

Wigley/ HMD Life Expectancy (Left axis) —— UK Population (Consistent) (Right Axis)

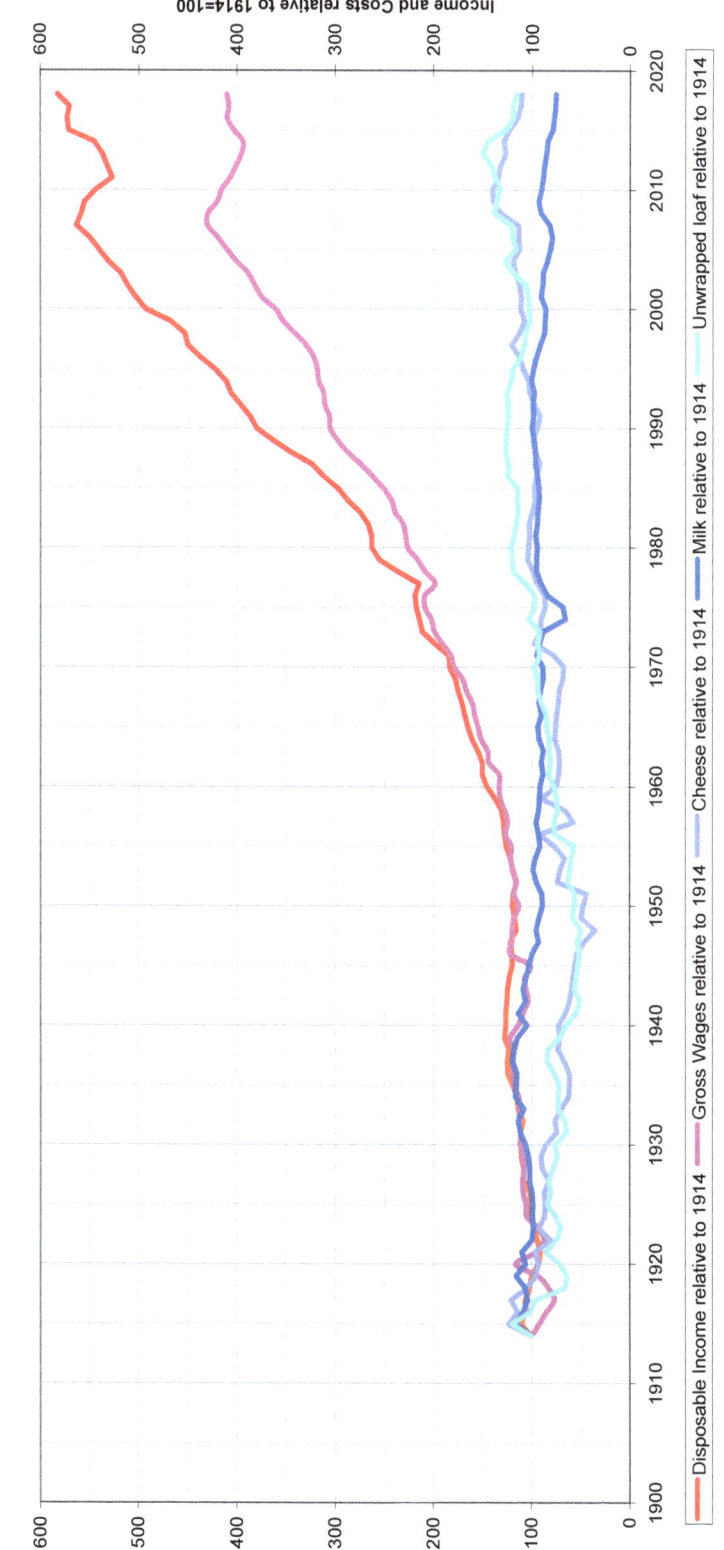

An index of the real value of key household income and expenditure relative to 1914.

Income and Food

(All metrics normalised to real current values before indexing.)

Income and Costs relative to 1914=100

Disposable Income relative to 1914 — Gross Wages relative to 1914 — Cheese relative to 1914 — Milk relative to 1914 — Unwrapped loaf relative to 1914

79

BEIS (DUKES) & NIC - Reported UK Energy usage in millions of tonnes of oil equivalent

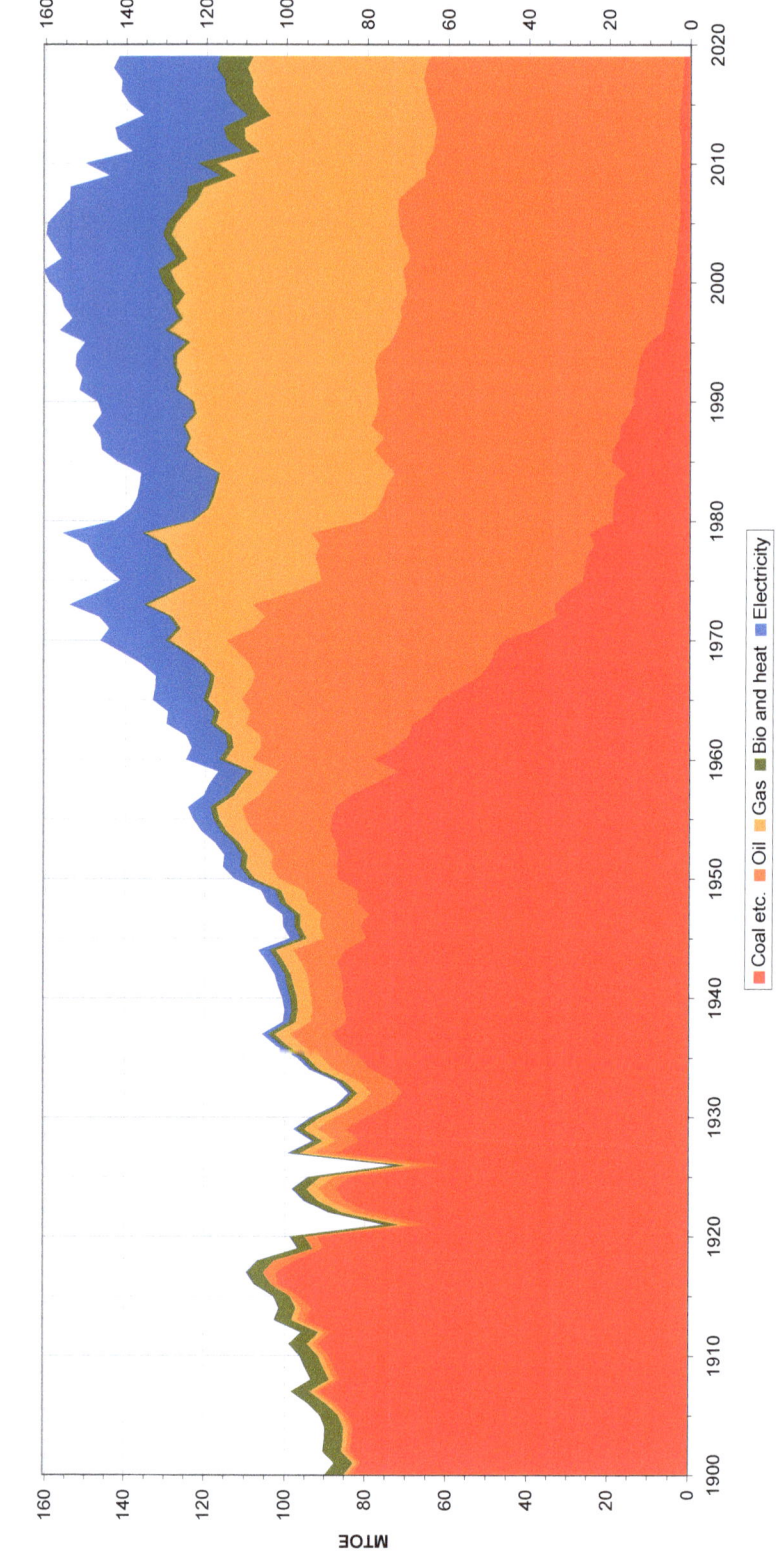

Coal etc. ■ Oil ■ Gas ■ Bio and heat ■ Electricity

Real (CPI) effective prices of Fuel & Light Relative to 1987

Fuel & Light Indexed to 1987 - Fouquet (2011) —— Fuel & Light Indexed to 1987 - Phelps-Brown & Hopkins (1981) —— Fuel & Light Indexed to 1987 - ONS (2020)

81

UK Improvement of Air Quality

Growth of life expectancy and population,

reduction of emissions,

use of energy,

rise of the real cost of fuel and light in the 21st century

1970-2019

UK Recent History of Life Expectancy at Birth and Growth in Population (Millions)

Legend: Wrigley/ HMD Life Expectancy (Left axis) —— UK Population (Consistent) (Right Axis)

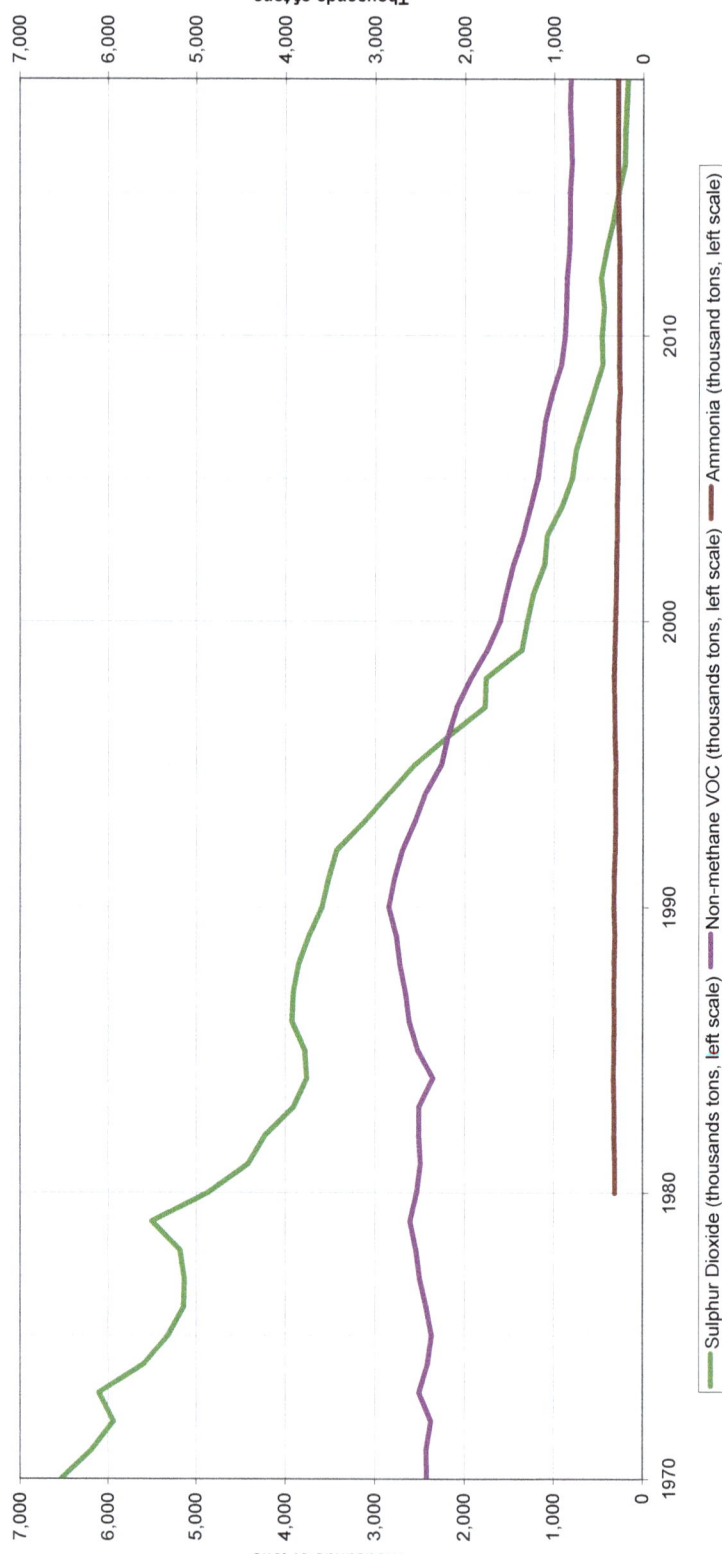

UK trend in weight of atmospheric pollutants (Defra)

Sulphur Dioxide, Non-methane volatile organic compounds and Ammonia

—— Sulphur Dioxide (thousands tons, left scale)   —— Non-methane VOC (thousands tons, left scale)   —— Ammonia (thousand tons, left scale)

UK trend in weight of atmospheric pollutants (Defra/BEIS(NAEI))
(Heating & Residential use contribution (NOx as NO2 - 20%), (PM10 - 28%) and (PM2.5 - 43%))

Thousands of tons

Nitrogen Oxides (thousands tons, left scale)
PM2.5 (thousand tons, right scale)
UK Heat/Resd. Use NOx (as NO2) Tonnage (K)
UK Heat/Resd. Use PM10 Tonnage (K)
PM10 (thousand tons, right scale)
UK Heat/Resd. Use PM2.5 Tonnage (K)

85

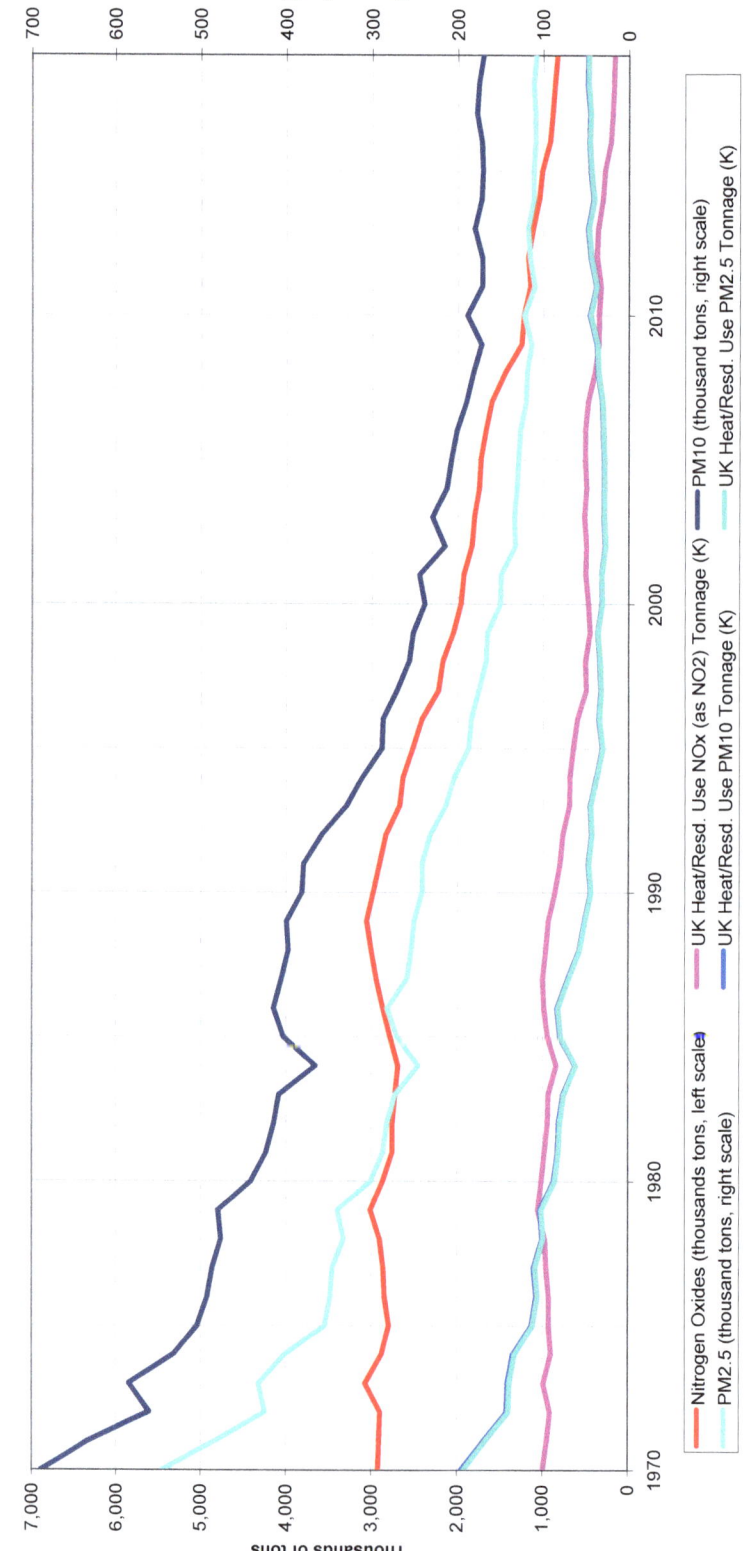

UK trend in weight of atmospheric pollutants (Defra/BEIS(NAEI))
(Heating & Residential use contribution (NOx as NO2 - 20%), (PM10 - 28%) and (PM2.5 - 43%))

Thousands of tons

Nitrogen Oxides (thousands tons, left scale)
PM2.5 (thousand tons, right scale)
UK Heat/Resd. Use NOx (as NO2) Tonnage (K)
UK Heat/Resd. Use PM10 Tonnage (K)
PM10 (thousand tons, right scale)
UK Heat/Resd. Use PM2.5 Tonnage (K)

UK trend in weight of atmospheric pollutants (Defra/BEIS(NAEI))
(Heating & Residential use contribution (NOx as NO2 - 20%), (PM10 - 28%) and (PM2.5 - 43%))

UK Heat/Resd. Use NOx (as NO2) Tonnage (K) —— UK Heat/Resd. Use PM10 Tonnage (K) —— UK Heat/Resd. Use PM2.5 Tonnage (K)

Thousands of tons

87

Non-pollutant emissions

CO2 (and it's Carbon content)

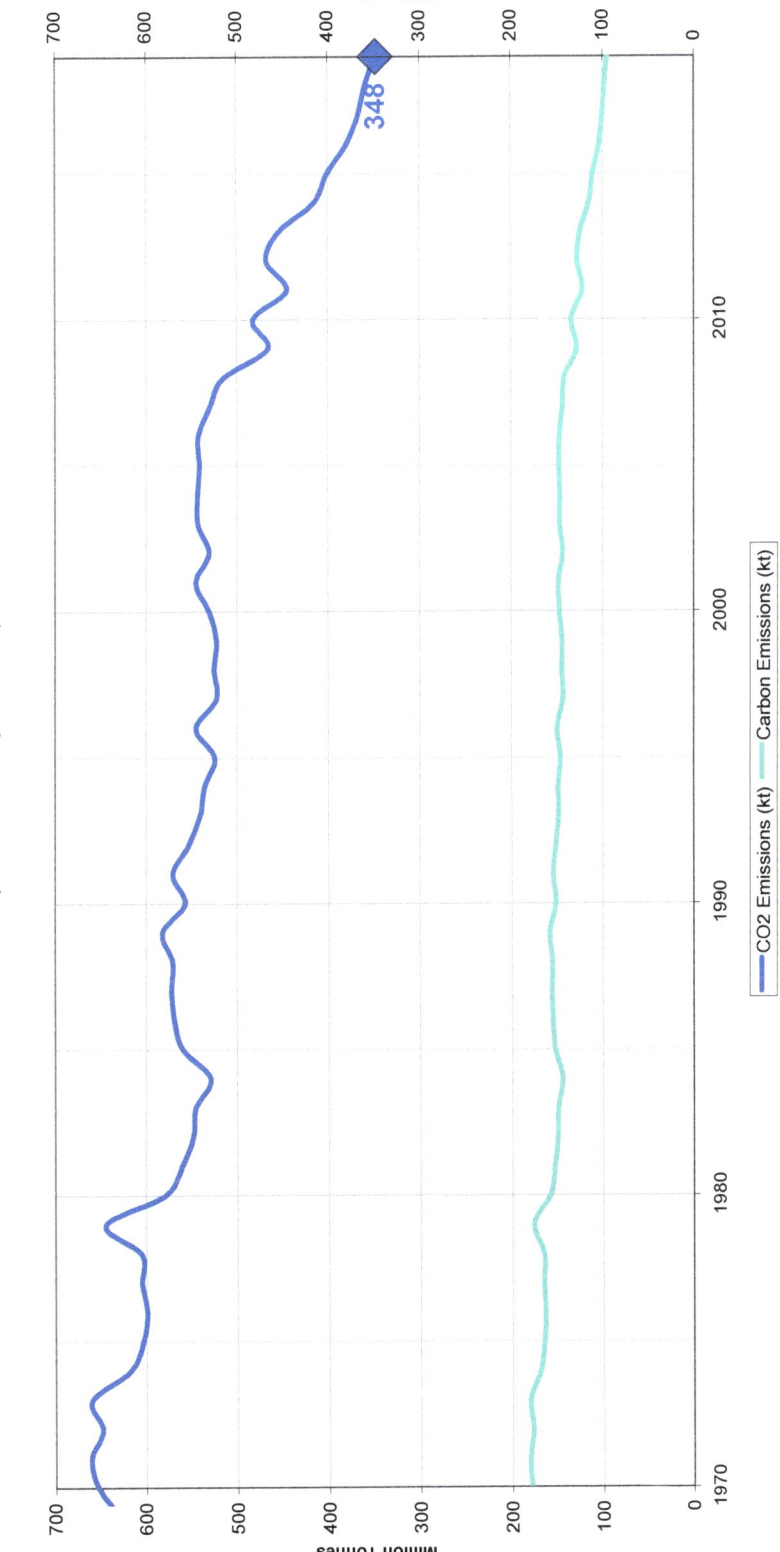

UK Carbon and CO2 emissions (million tonnes per annum) - 47% reduction since 1970

Million Tonnes

348

—— CO2 Emissions (kt) —— Carbon Emissions (kt)

89

UK CO2 emissions per capita (metric tonnes per annum) - 56% reduction since 1970

Energy for the UK and per household

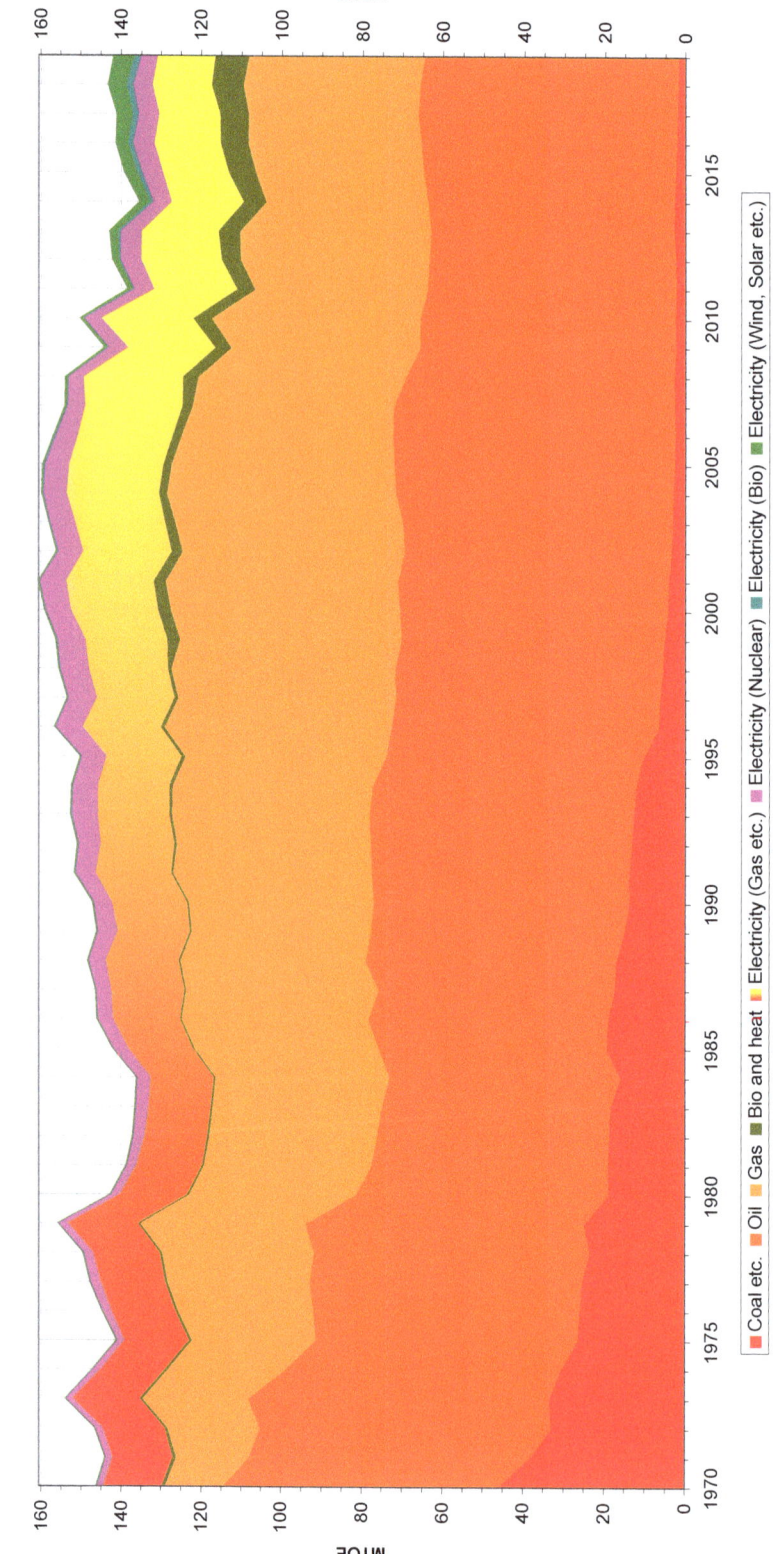

BEIS (DUKES) Reported UK Energy Usage in Millions of Tonnes of Oil Equivalent

■ Coal etc.　■ Oil　■ Gas　■ Bio and heat　■ Electricity (Gas etc.)　■ Electricity (Nuclear)　■ Electricity (Bio)　■ Electricity (Wind, Solar etc.)

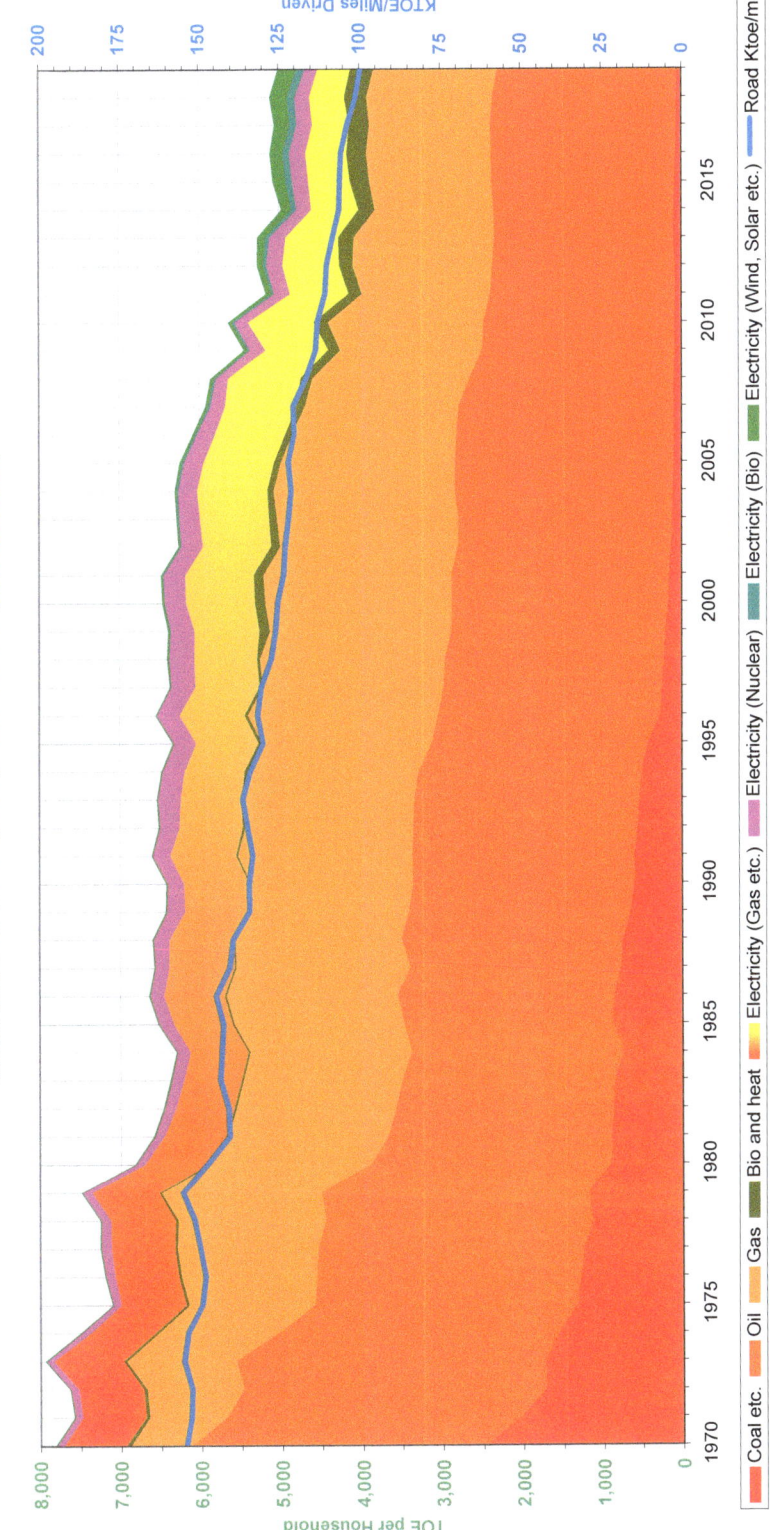

BEIS (DUKES) Reported UK Energy Usage in Tonnes of Oil Equivalent per Household (36% reduction) and Road transport Tonnes of Oil Equivalent per Million Miles driven (36% reduction)

93

Rise of the real cost of fuel and light in the 21st century after 2003

1970-2019

Real (CPI) effective prices of Fuel & Light Relative to 1987

Indexed to 1987

Fuel & Light Indexed to 1987 - Fouquet (2011) ——— Fuel & Light Indexed to 1987 - Phelps-Brown & Hopkins (1981) ——— Fuel & Light Indexed to 1987 - ONS (2020)

95

The first two decades of the 21st century before Coronavirus crash from 2020

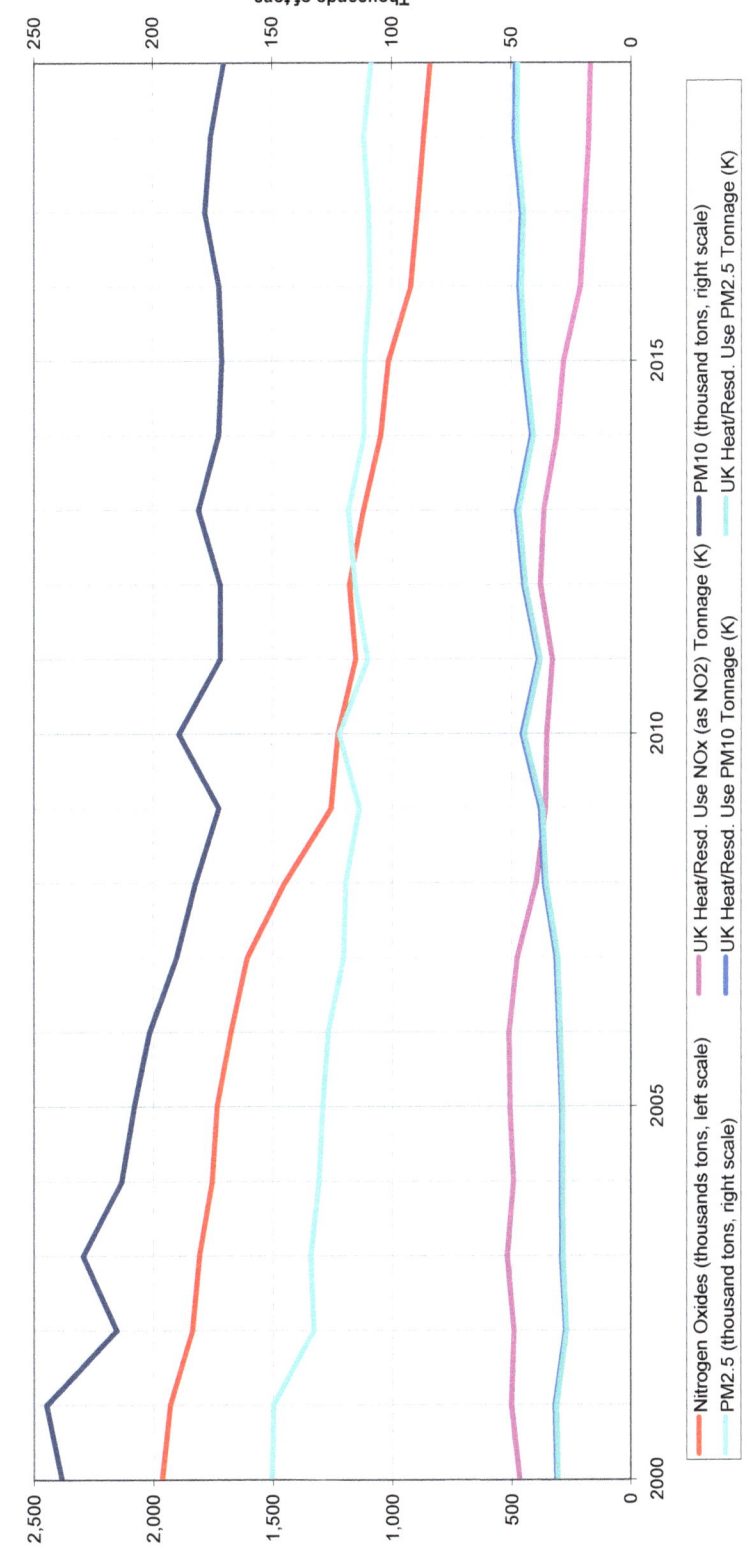

UK trend in weight of atmospheric pollutants (Defra/BEIS(NAEI))
(Heating & Residential use contribution (NOx as NO2 - 20%), (PM10 - 28%) and (PM2.5 - 43%))

Nitrogen Oxides (thousands tons, left scale)
PM2.5 (thousand tons, right scale)
UK Heat/Resd. Use NOx (as NO2) Tonnage (K)
UK Heat/Resd. Use PM10 Tonnage (K)
PM10 (thousand tons, right scale)
UK Heat/Resd. Use PM2.5 Tonnage (K)

Thousands of tons
Thousands of tons

97

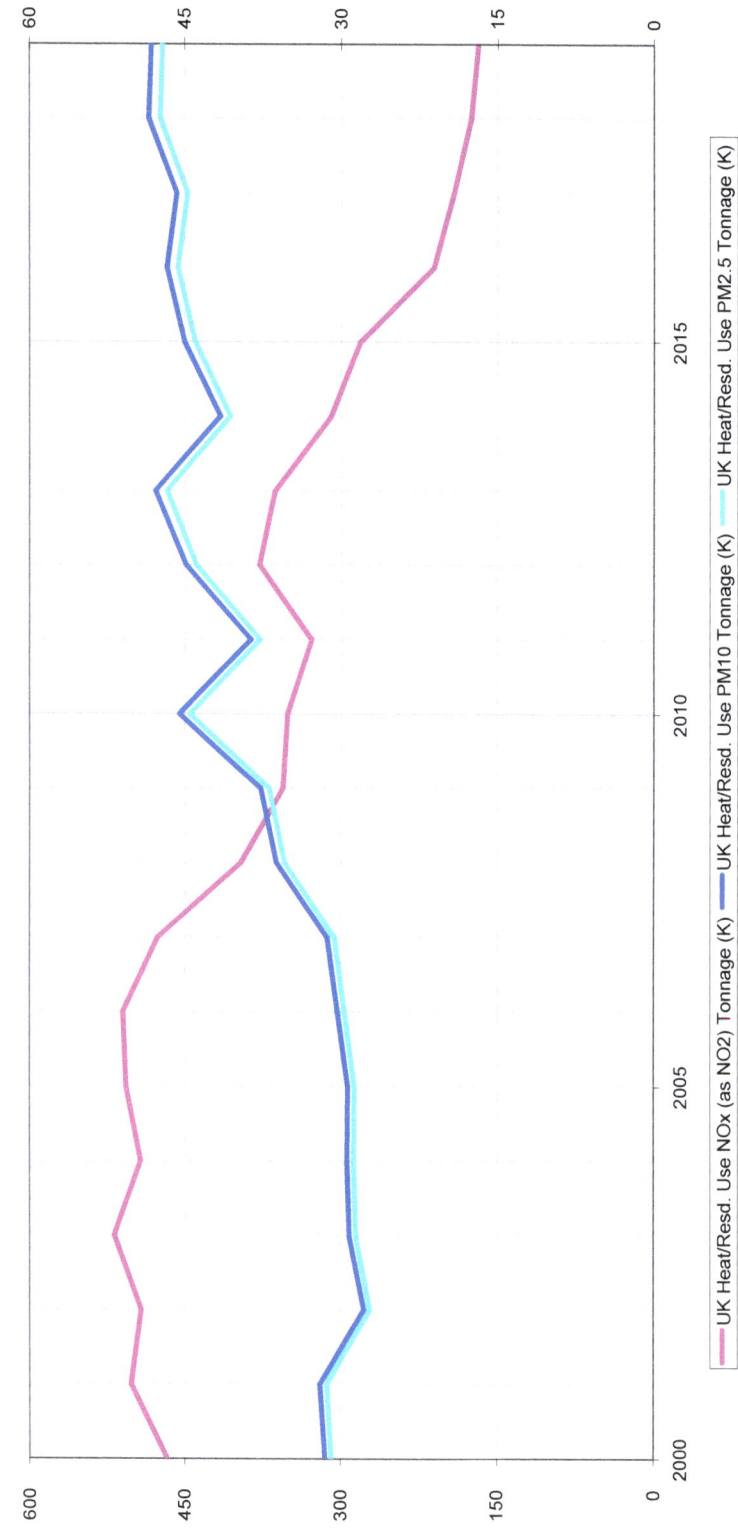

UK trend in weight of atmospheric pollutants (Defra/BEIS(NAEI))
(Heating & Residential use contribution (NOx as NO2 - 20%), (PM10 - 28%) and (PM2.5 - 43%))

BEIS (DUKES) Reported UK Energy Usage in Millions of Tonnes of Oil Equivalent

Coal etc. ■ Oil ■ Gas ■ Bio and heat ■ Electricity (Gas etc.) ■ Electricity (Nuclear) ■ Electricity (Bio) ■ Electricity (Wind, Solar etc.)

99

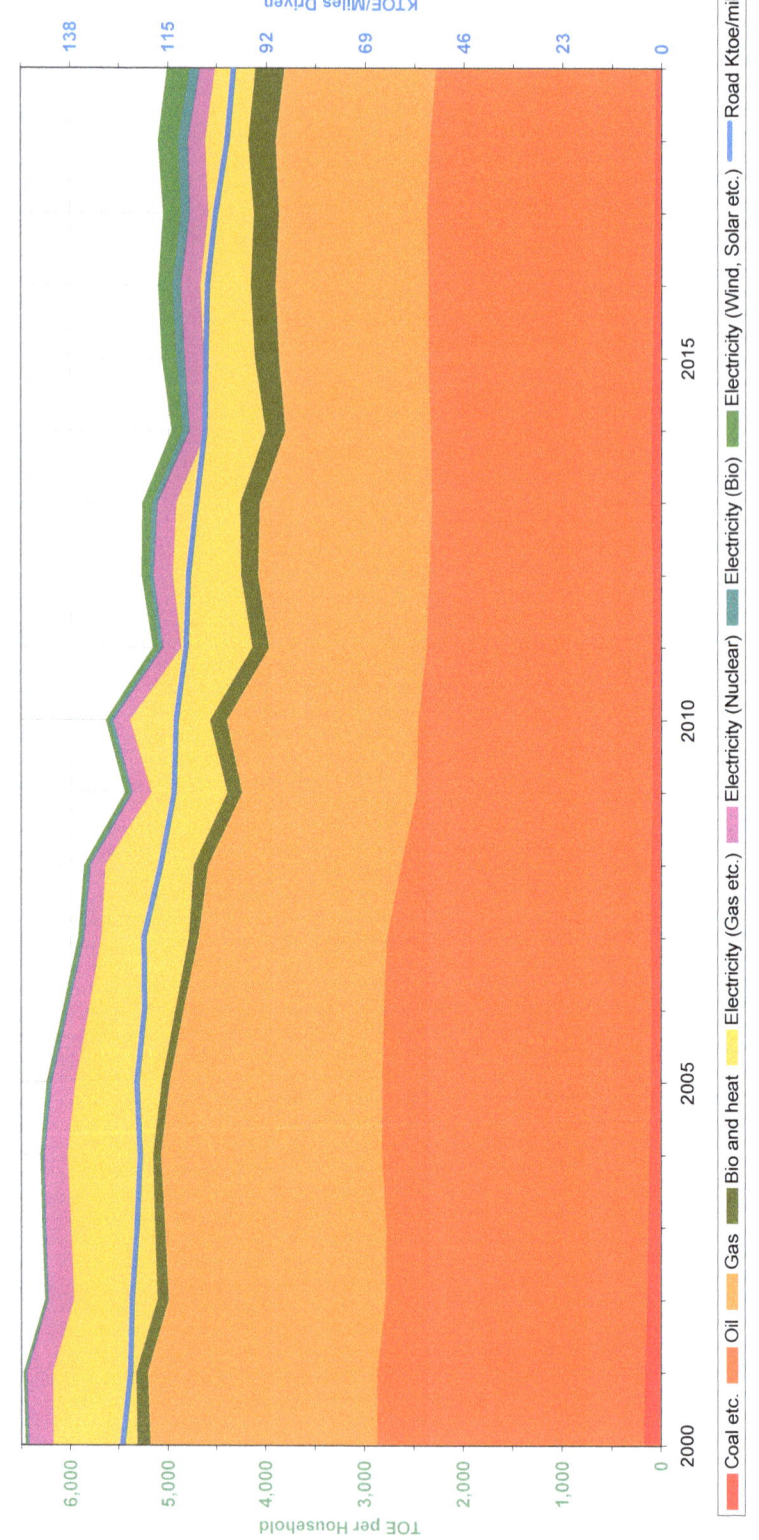

BEIS (DUKES) Reported UK Energy Usage in Tonnes of Oil Equivalent per Household (21% reduction)
and Road transport Tonnes of Oil Equivalent per Million Miles driven (23% reduction)

KTOE/Miles Driven

138
115
92
69
46
23
0

TOE per Household

6,000
5,000
4,000
3,000
2,000
1,000
0

2000   2005   2010   2015

Coal etc. Oil Gas Bio and heat Electricity (Gas etc.) Electricity (Nuclear) Electricity (Bio) Electricity (Wind, Solar etc.) Road Ktoe/mile

BEIS (DUKES) Reported UK Energy Usage by Share of Generation Source - 2019

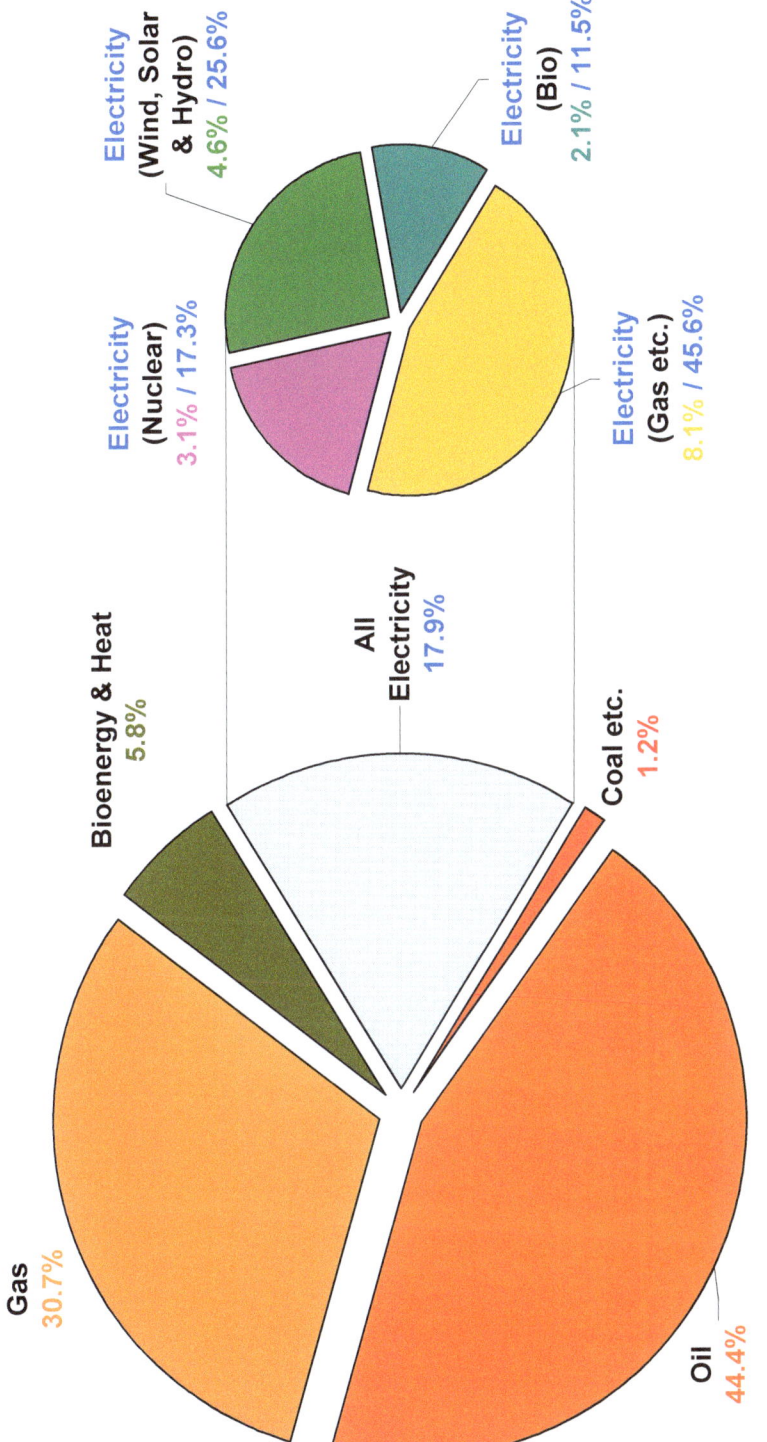

Electricity (Wind, Solar & Hydro)
4.6% / 25.6%

Electricity (Bio)
2.1% / 11.5%

Electricity (Nuclear)
3.1% / 17.3%

Electricity (Gas etc.)
8.1% / 45.6%

Bioenergy & Heat
5.8%

All Electricity
17.9%

Coal etc.
1.2%

Gas
30.7%

Oil
44.4%

Composition of "low carbon" energy and Electricity generation

"low" Carbon component UK Energy	Share Energy	Mtoe	TWh	Inst. GW	Inst. Share	2019 Ktoe	2019 TWh	Share Elec.	Load / Capacity
Wind	2.9%	5.536	64	21.2	22.4%	5,529	64.3	19.8%	34.6%
Solar	0.6%	1.166	14	13.1	13.8%	1,109	12.9	4.0%	11.2%
Hydro	0.3%	0.512	6	1.1	1.2%	507	5.9	1.8%	32.7%
Bio-energy	7.2%	13.689	159						
Transport	0.9%	1.725	20						
Other	0.9%	1.631	19						
Nuclear	3.1%	4.402	51	9.5	10.0%	4,832	56.2	17.3%	67.5%
Total "low" Carbon UK Energy	15.9%	28.661	333						
Landfill Gas and other Bio-Energy (75% Drax woodchip)				3.2	3.4%	3,207	37.3	11.5%	50.4%
Gas				28.1	29.6%	11,341	131.9	40.6%	53.6%
Oil & other				10.5	11.1%	791	9.2	2.8%	
Coal						593	6.9	2.1%	
Imports & Exports				5.0	5.3%				
Storage				3.1	3.3%				
Electricity Installed Q2 2019 (Drax report)/Delivered 2019				94.8		27,911	324.6		34.4%

The efficiency (load factor) of principal methods of electricity generation

UK electricity generation - Capacity load factors

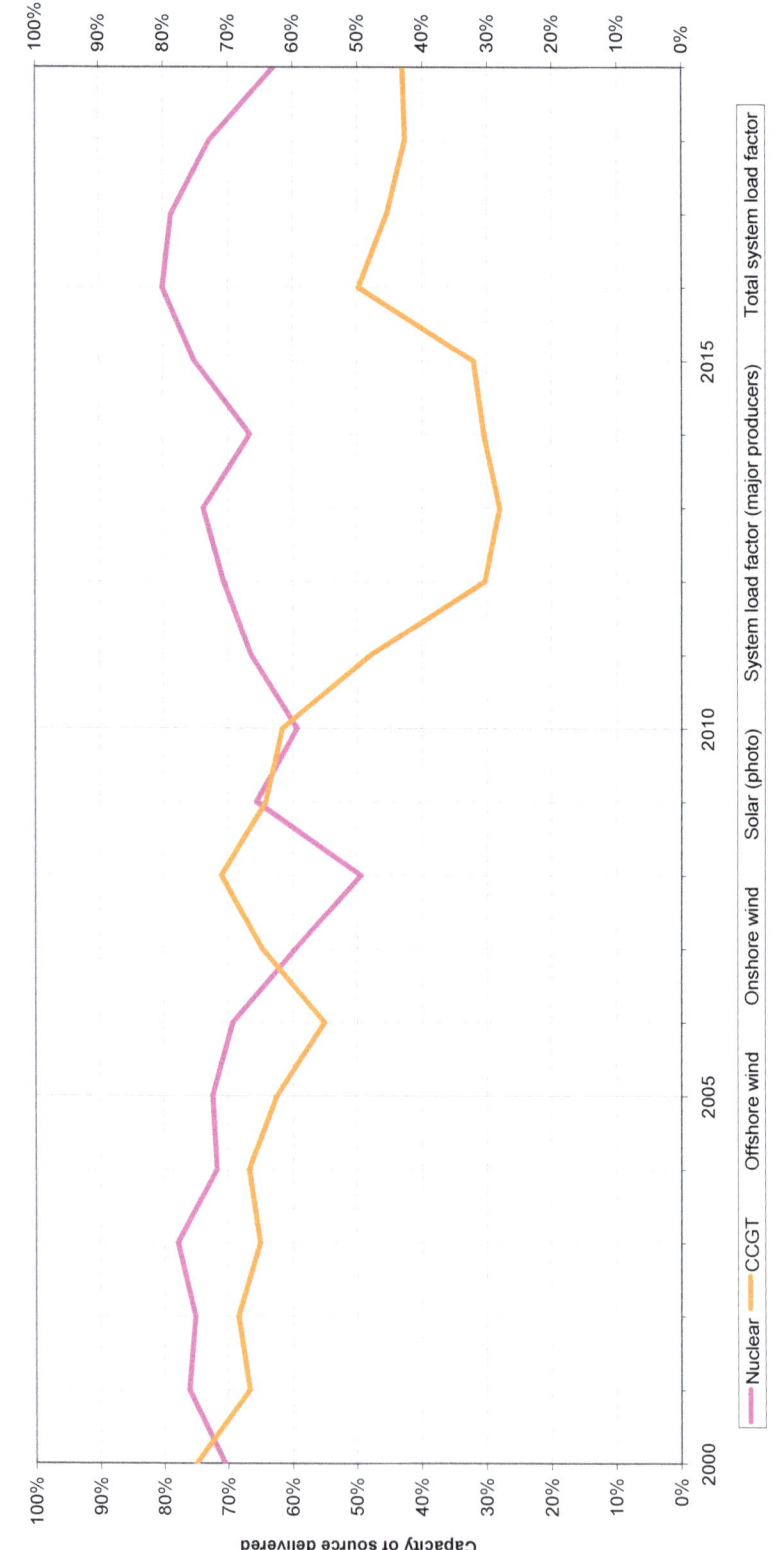

Capacity of source delivered

Nuclear — CCGT — Offshore wind — Onshore wind — Solar (photo) — System load factor (major producers) — Total system load factor

UK electricity generation - Capacity load factors

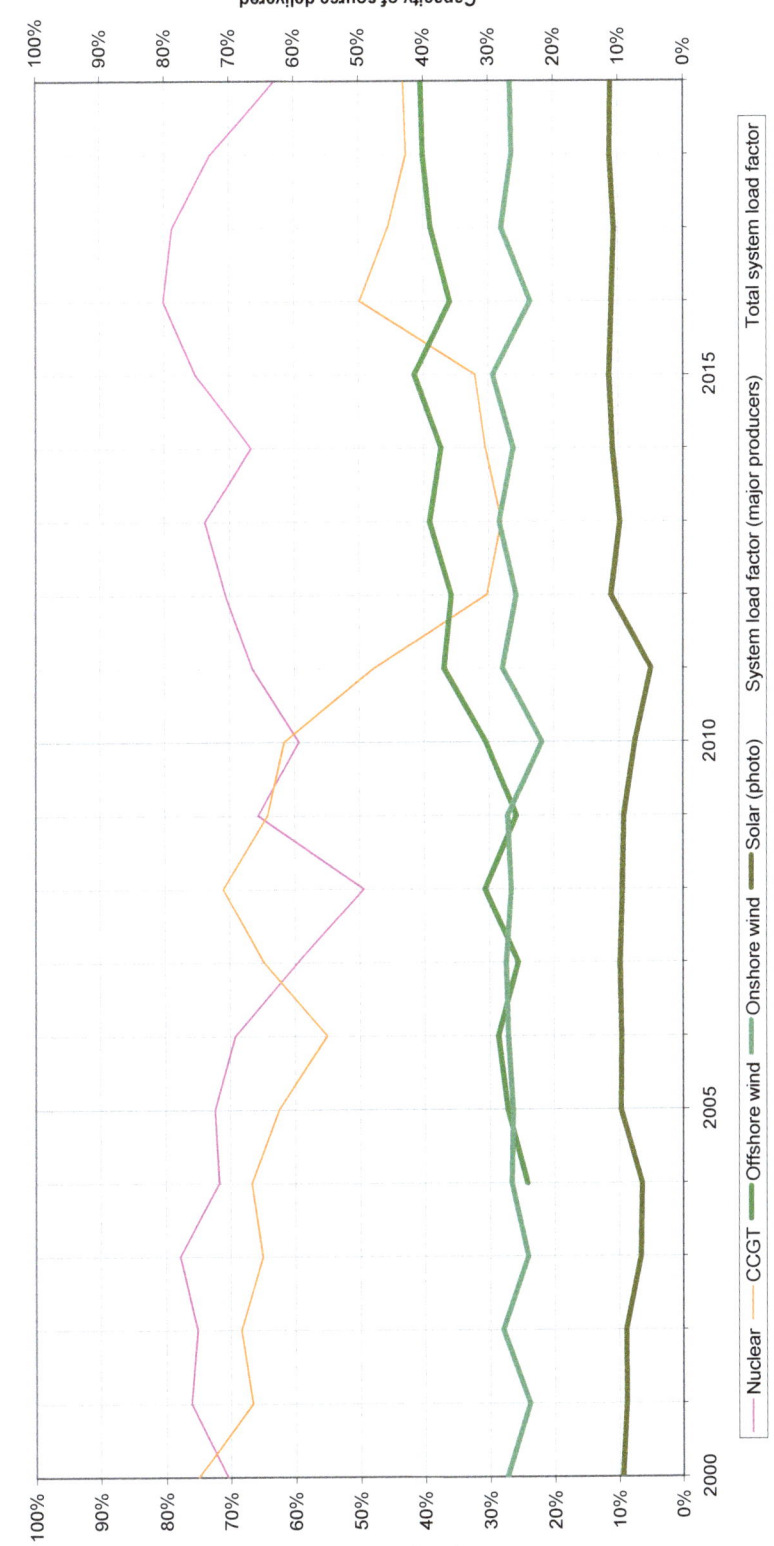

Nuclear — CCGT — Offshore wind — Onshore wind — Solar (photo) — System load factor (major producers) — Total system load factor

105

UK electricity generation - Capacity load factors

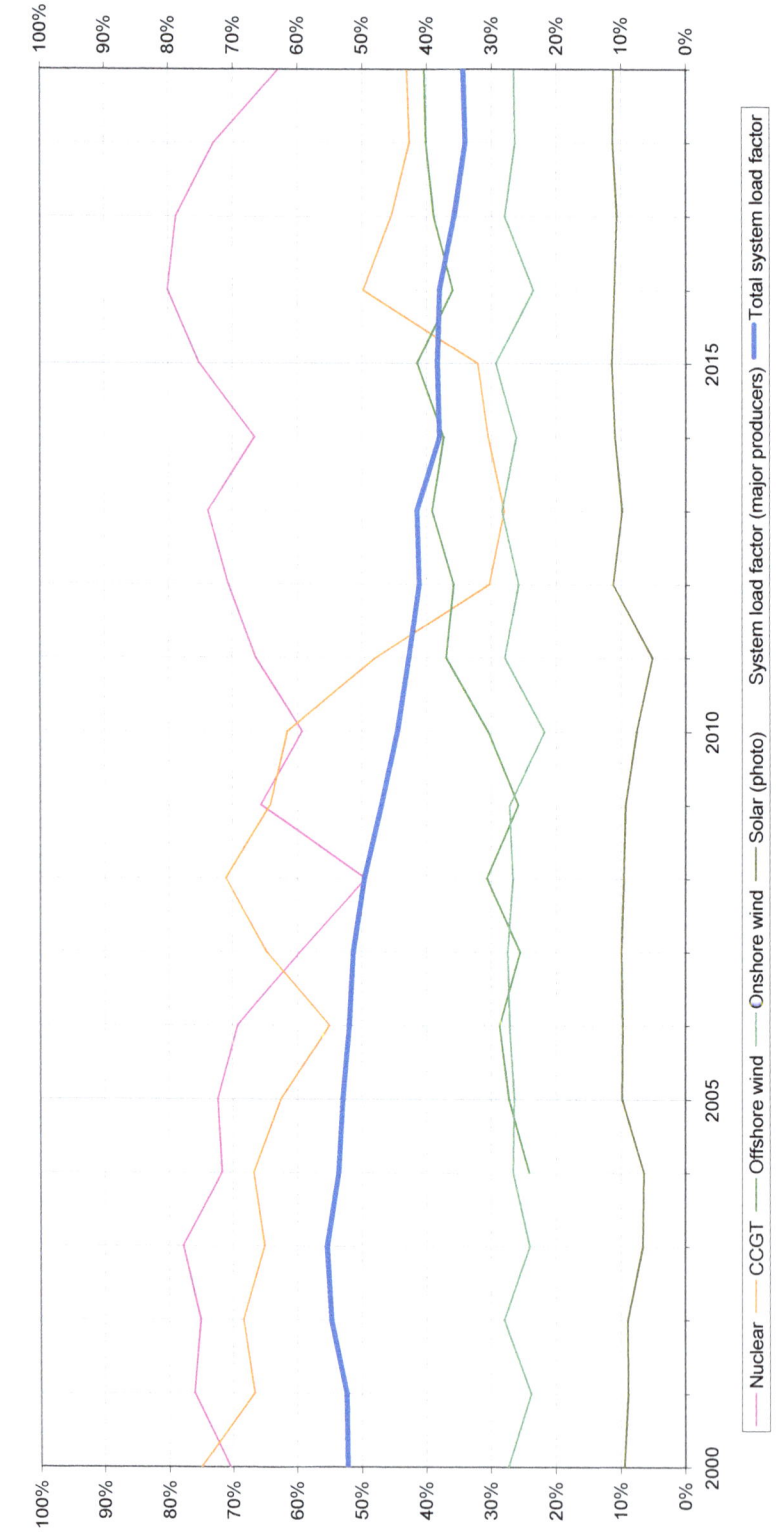

Rise of the real cost of Gas and Electricity

2000-2019

ONS Indexed Gas and Electricity Prices in Real (CPI) current (2019) pence per kWh
Correlated to reveal relative increase of electricity prices since 2014

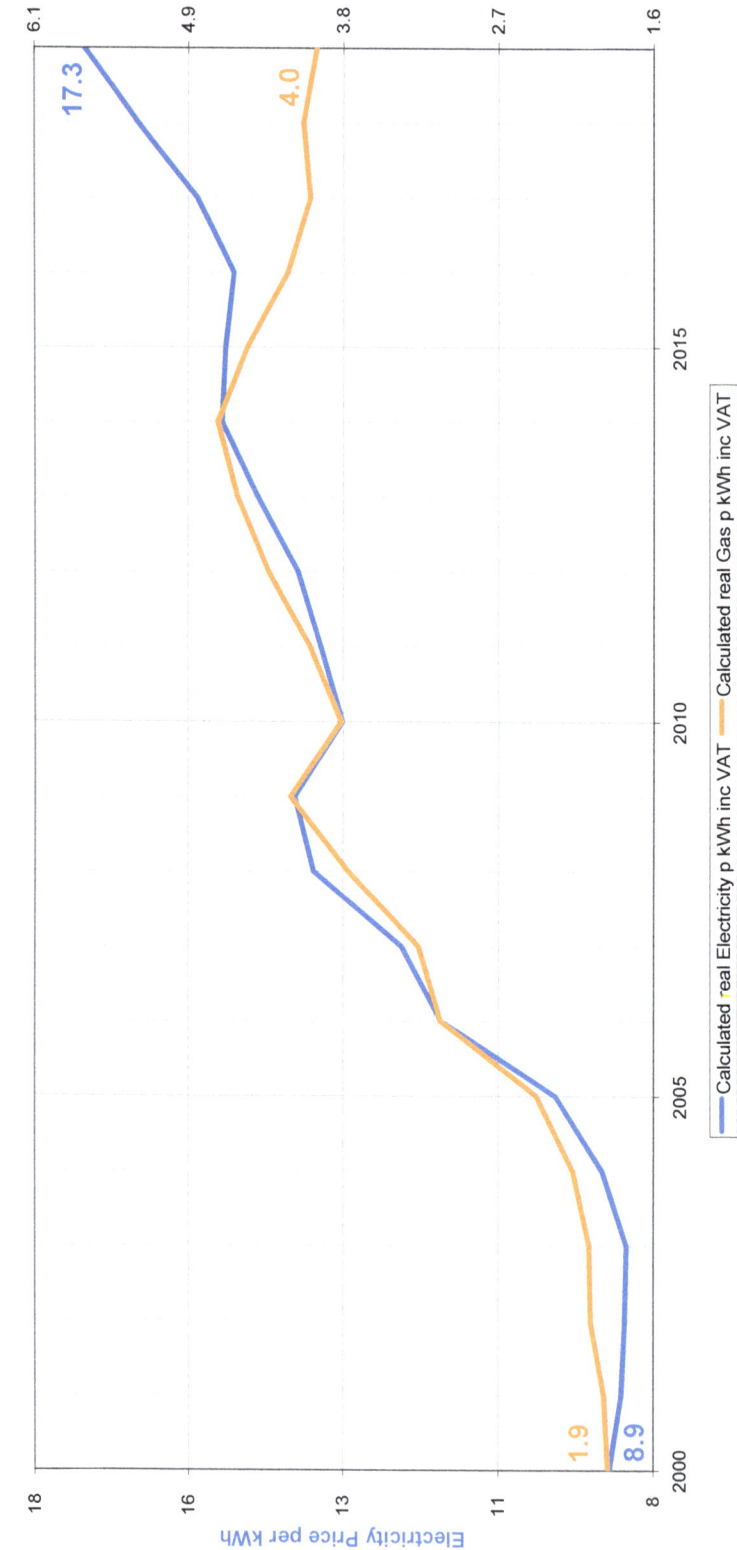

Calculated real Electricity p kWh inc VAT — Calculated real Gas p kWh inc VAT

Rise of the real cost of Gas

Mostly from exposure to the international market being driven by reduced exploration and supply due to ideological imposed policies.

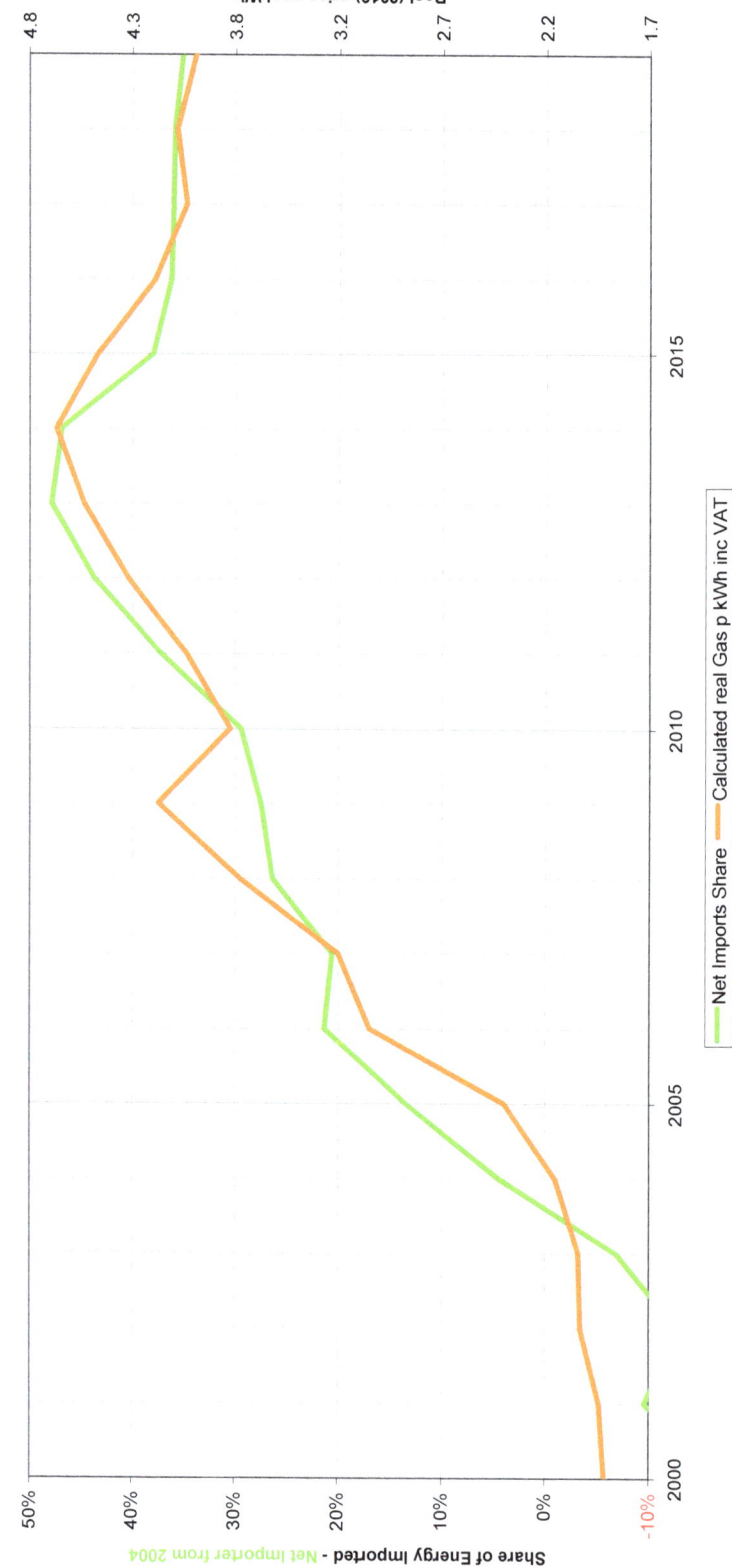

BEIS (DUKES) Reported UK Net Imported Energy as Share of All Energy Correlated to Real (CPI) pence per kWh for Consumer Gas Prices

110

— Net Imports Share — Calculated real Gas p kWh inc VAT

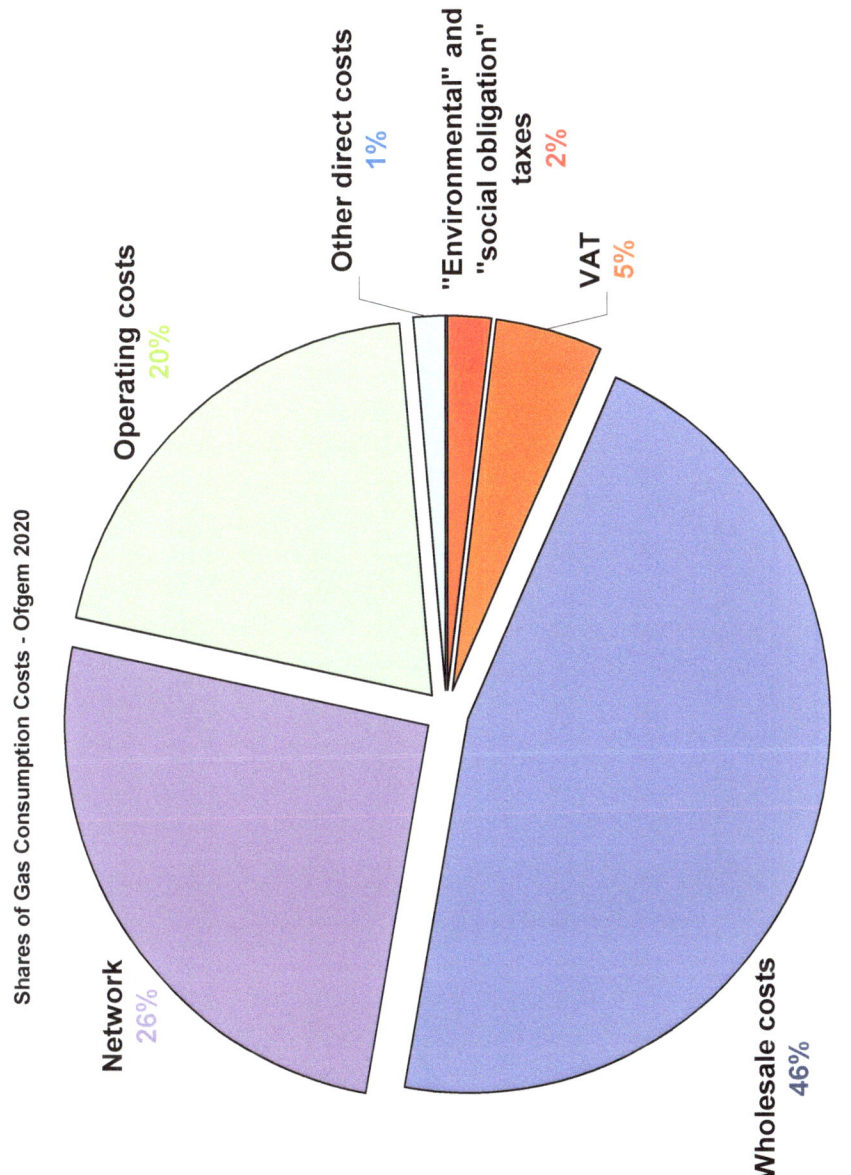

Shares of Gas Consumption Costs - Ofgem 2020

Other direct costs
1%

"Environmental" and "social obligation" taxes
2%

VAT
5%

Operating costs
20%

Network
26%

Wholesale costs
46%

111

Rise of the real cost of Electricity

Influenced by the exposure to wholesale gas market from 2004.

But the main driver is the imposition of so-called "green" taxes and subsidies for wind and solar from 2001 (CCL), plus "environmental and social obligation tax" from 2012 etc.

Especially 7 fold growth of Wind, Solar, plus Drax woodchip from just 5% of electricity generation (0.7% all energy) in 2010 to 27% of electricity generation (4.8% of all energy) in 2019

BEIS (DUKES) Reported UK Net Imported Energy as Share of All Energy Correlated to Real (CPI) pence per kWh for Consumer Consumer Electricity Prices

113

Share of electricity generation by source/fuel type

Correlated to show increase of energy imports, net importer from 2004, plus growth of wind and solar from 2010

Share of Energy Imported - Net Importer from 2004

Share of electricity generation

Electricity (Gas etc.) Electricity (Nuclear) Electricity (Bio) Electricity (Wind, Solar etc.) Net Imports Share

BEIS (DUKES) Reported UK Electricity Usage by Source in Millions of Tonnes of Oil Equivalent
(Wind, Solar, Hydro & Bio - currently less than 5% of all energy consumed and 27% of electricity consumed)

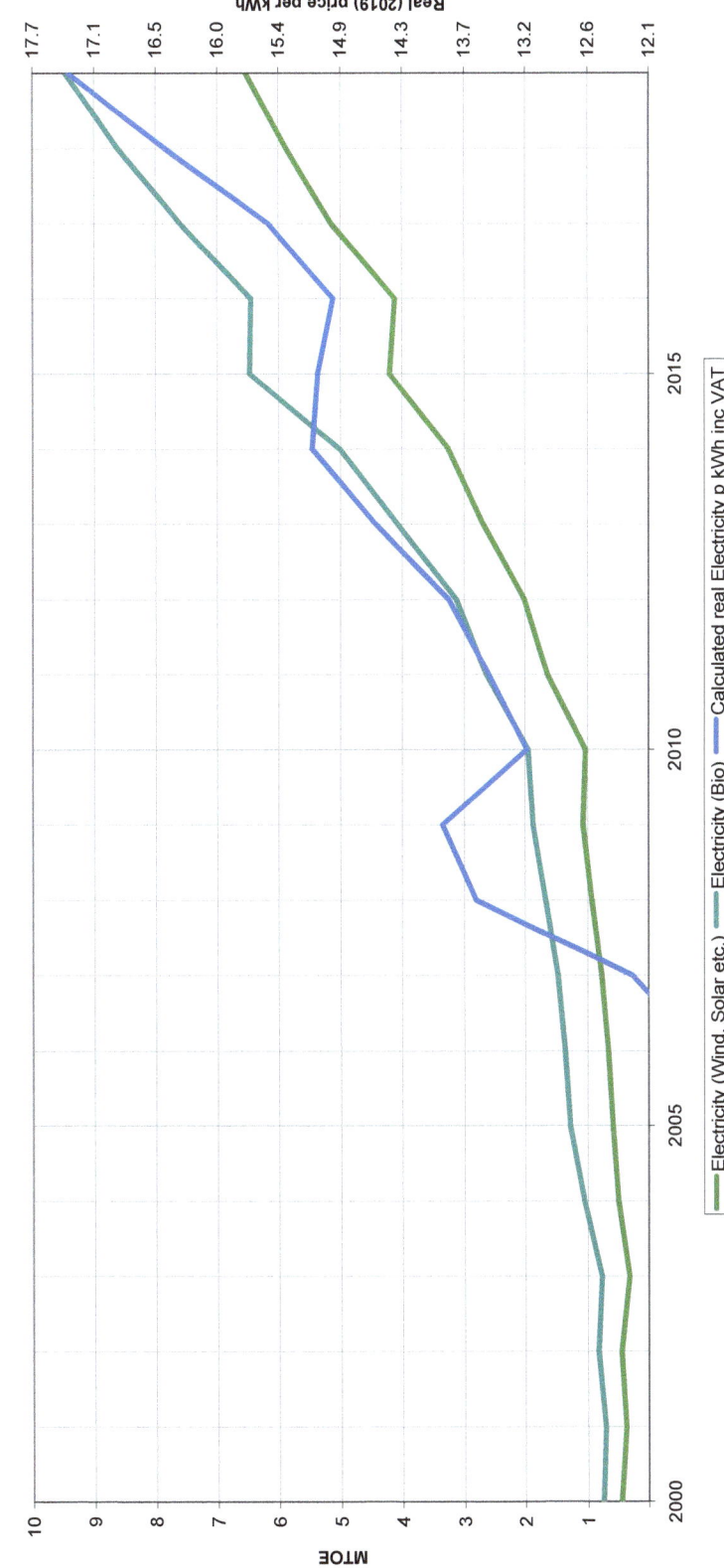

115

116

Shares of Electricity Generation Costs - Ofgem 2020

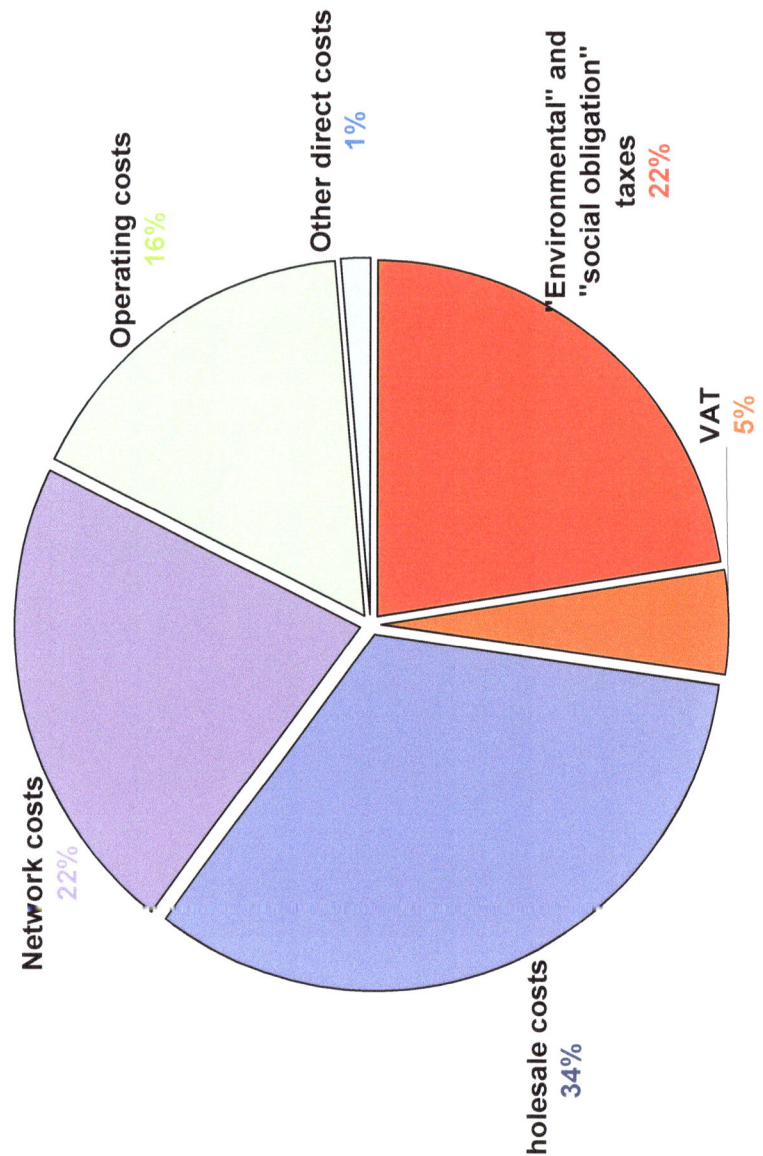

The combined cost of
Gas and Electricity
for the consumer – Ofgem

2010-2019

Wholesale price component of customer dual fuel bill falls by 25 percent from 2010 to 2019 - from 53% of bill to 40%

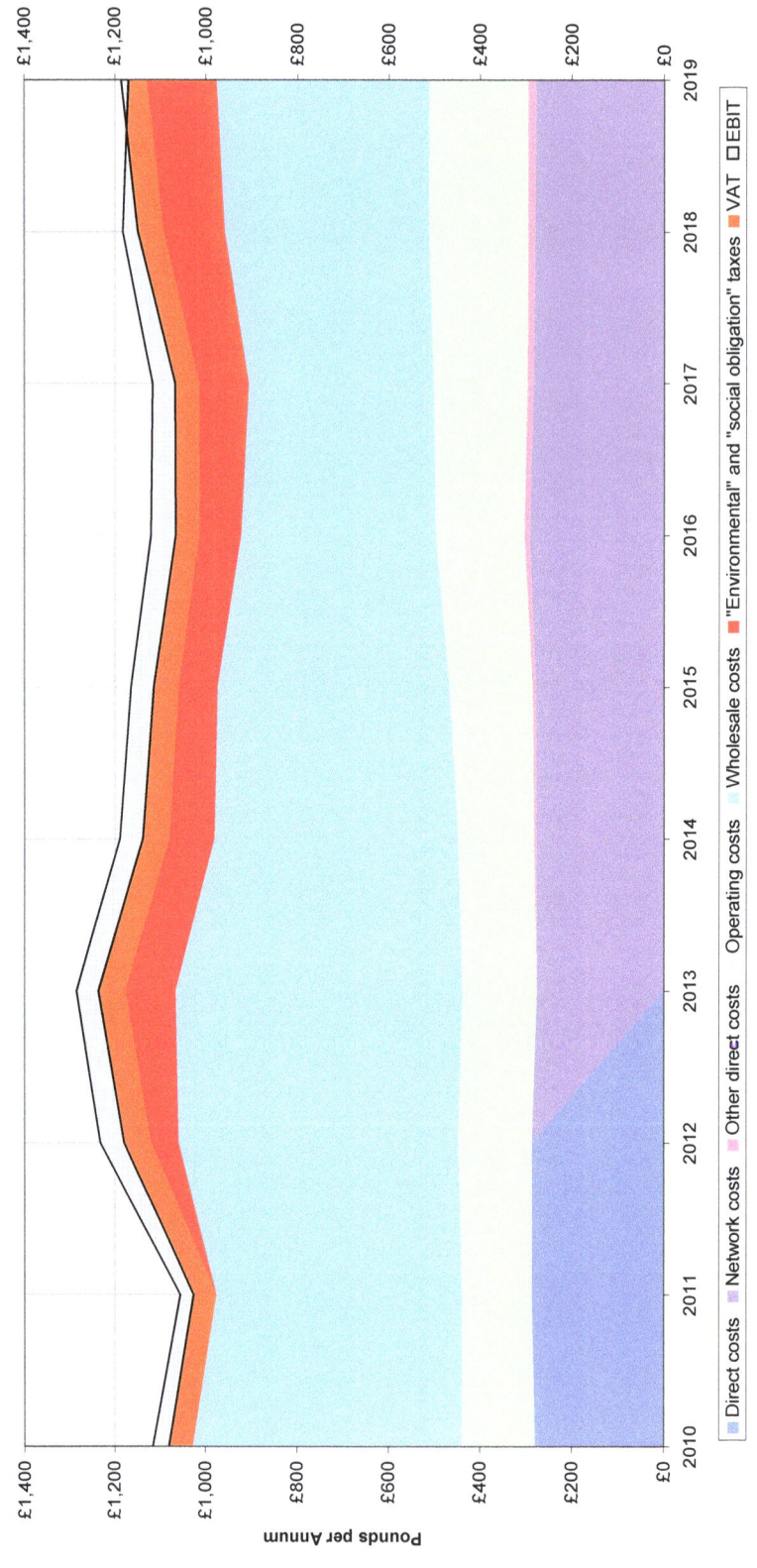

Components of Electricity and Gas Generation Costs for an average Dual Fuel Bill - Ofgem

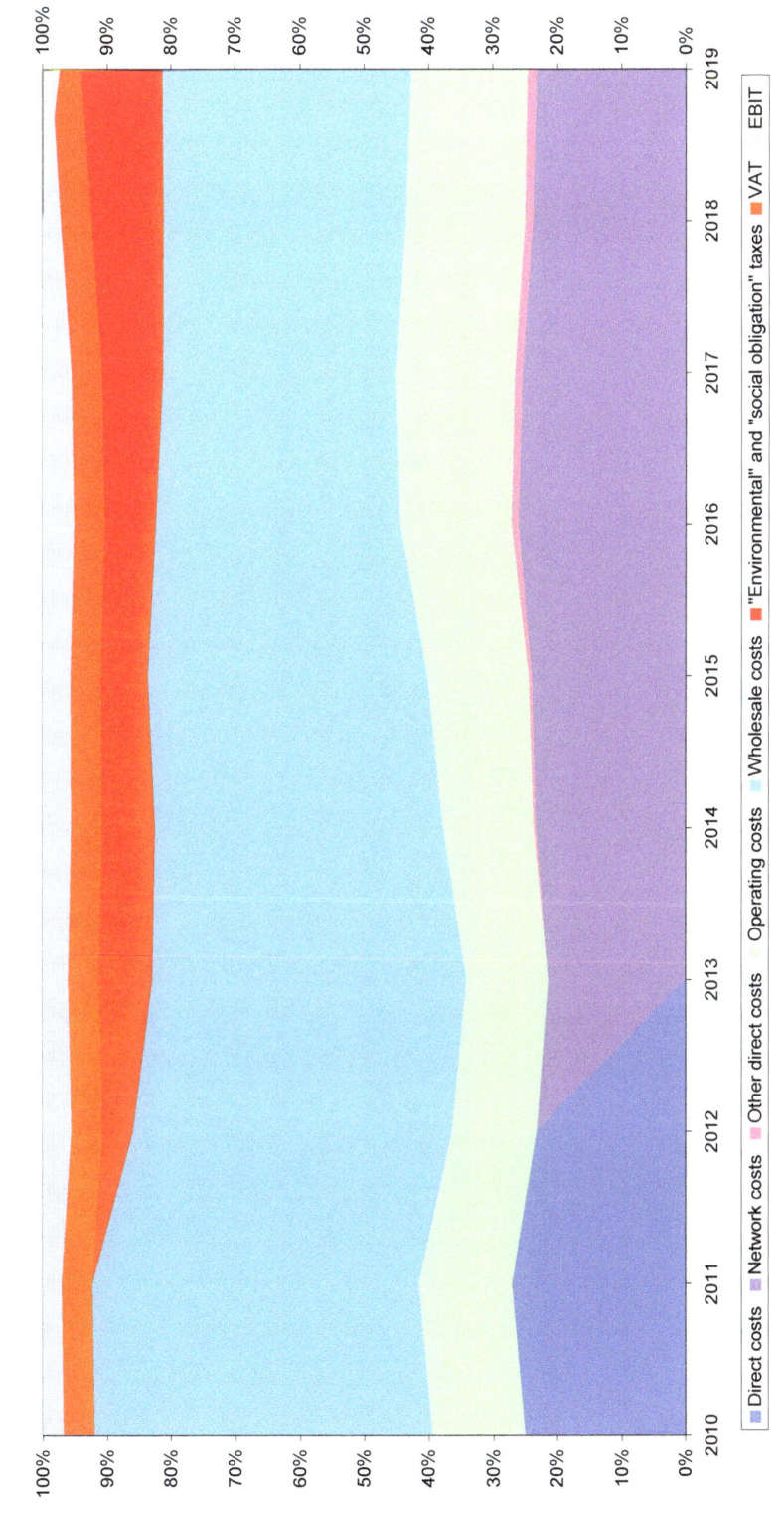

Shares of Electricity and Gas Generation Costs for an average Dual Fuel Bill - Ofgem

■ Direct costs ■ Network costs ■ Other direct costs ■ Operating costs ■ Wholesale costs ■ "Environmental" and "social obligation" taxes ■ VAT ■ EBIT

119

Part of a series - see also:

- UK Economic & Social Change – 1700-2019 – Three centuries of progress
  - UK Economy – 1700-1913 – An economy in transition
  - UK Economy – 1900-2019 – Growth of the state & world war
  - UK Economy – 1990-2019 – Quarter of a century of new changes
    - UK Economy – 1990-2019 – Stable income inequality
    - UK Household Expenditure – 1700-2019 – Cost of Living
    - UK Housing – 1700-2019 – Growth of home ownership
- UK Pauperism, Poverty and Hardship – 1700-2019 – The Retreat of Real Poverty
  - UK Pollution (Air Quality), Cars – 1970-2019 – Continuous improvement
  - UK Pollution (Air Quality), Energy – 1970-2019 – Continuous improvement
  - UK Population & Life Expectancy – 1970-2019 – Continuous Improvement

UK Pollution (Air Quality), Energy

2000-2019 or one generations

The imposition of "renewable" energy

122

Electricity Supplied (TWh), Installed Capacity (GW), ROC's and Capacity Load Factor - (www.ref.org.uk)

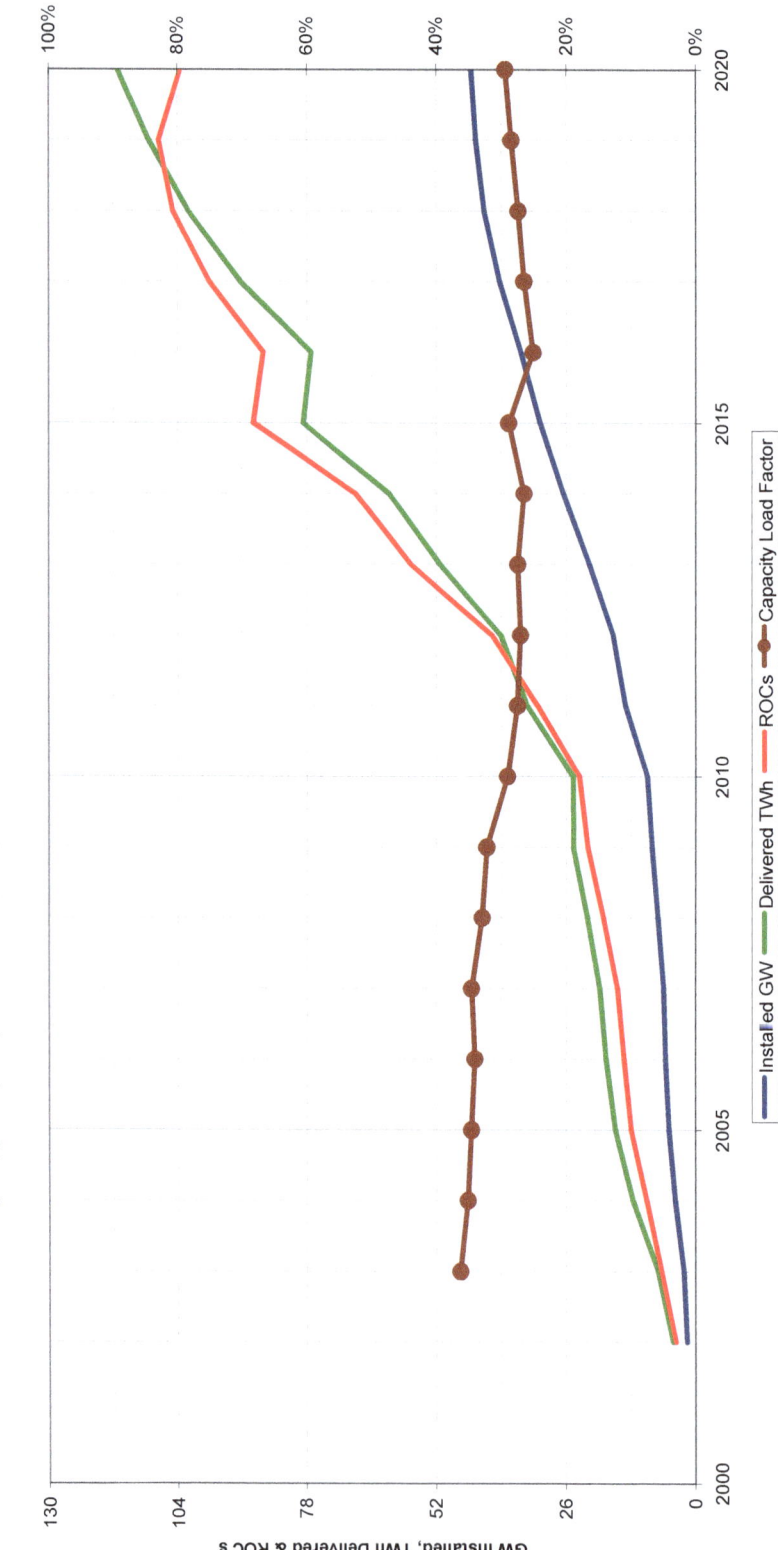

Installed GW — Delivered TWh — ROCs — Capacity Load Factor

Load Factors for top 5 renewable sources (93%) and total renewable load factor as percent of Capacity

Off-shore wind — On-shore wind — Photovoltaic — Hydro — Dedicated biomass — All

123

Installed Renewable Electricity Generating Capacity in Giga-Watts - (www.ref.org.uk)

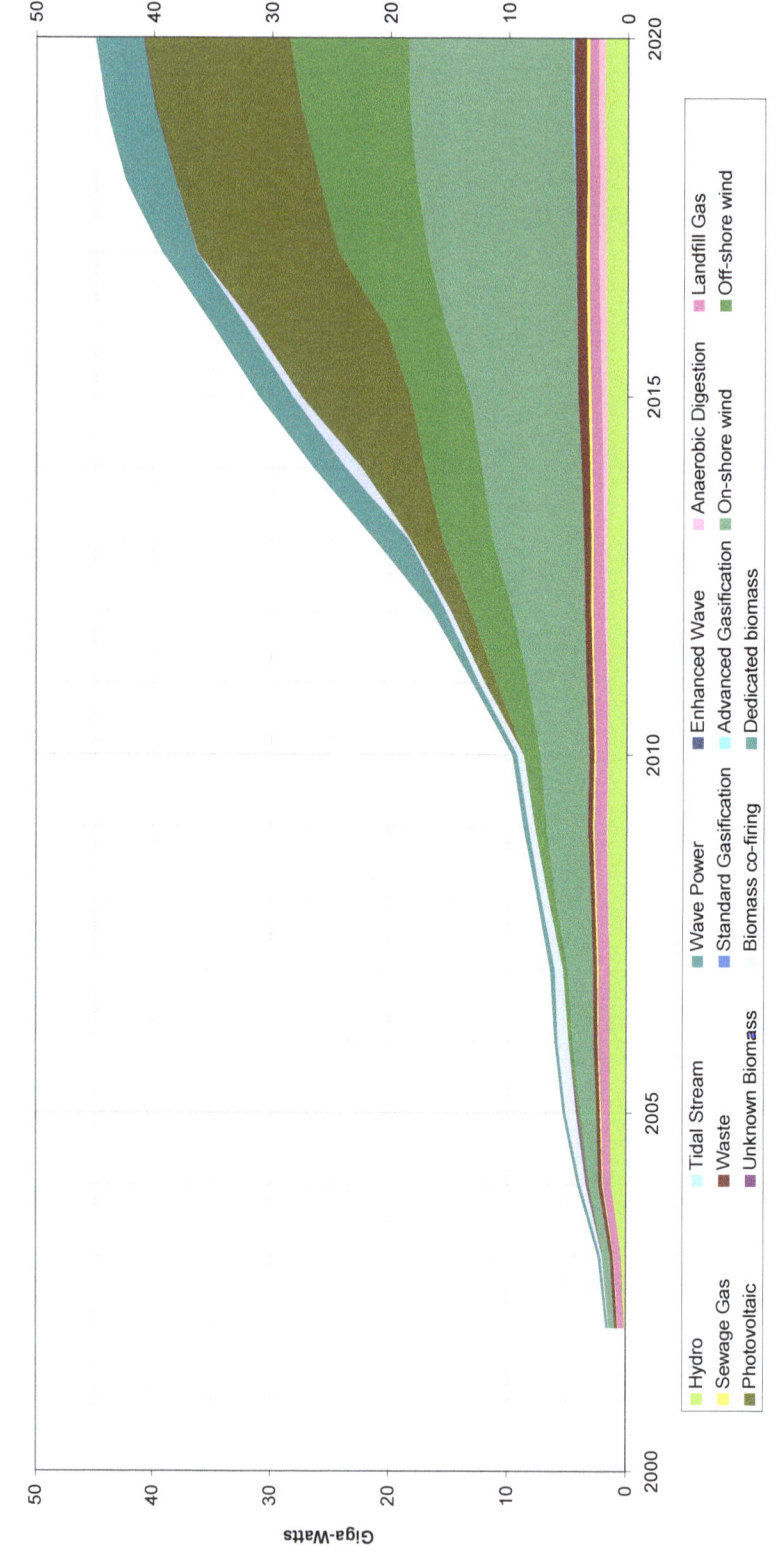

Hydro
Sewage Gas
Photovoltaic

Tidal Stream
Waste
Unknown Biomass

Wave Power
Standard Gasification
Biomass co-firing

Enhanced Wave
Advanced Gasification
Dedicated biomass

Anaerobic Digestion
On-shore wind

Landfill Gas
Off-shore wind

Electricty Energy Output in Tera-Watt Hours by Renewable Source - (www.ref.org.uk)

Hydro
Sewage Gas
Photovoltaic
Tidal Stream
Waste
Unknown Biomass
Wave Power
Standard Gasification
Biomass co-firing
Enhanced Wave
Advanced Gasification
Dedicated biomass
Anaerobic Digestion
On-shore wind
Landfill Gas
Off-shore wind

125

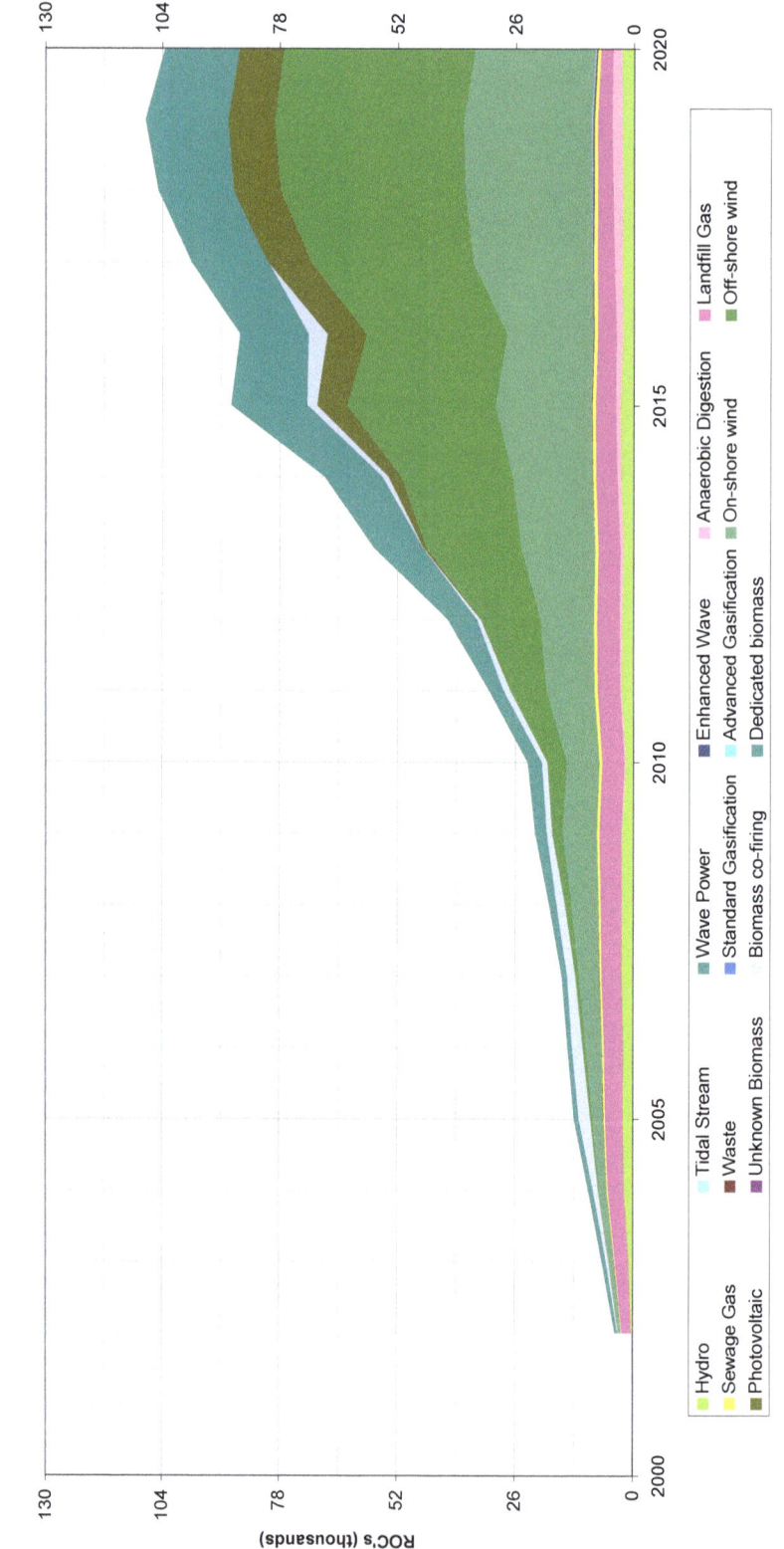

Tax-payer subsidies in the form of Renewable Obligation Certificates (thousands) - (www.ref.org.uk)

Subsidy in GBP per MWh for Offshore Wind - (www.ref.org.uk)

£112

£66

Nominal Pounds   "Real" (2020) Pounds

127

Part of a series - see also:

- UK Economic & Social Change – 1700-2019 – Three centuries of progress
  - UK Economy – 1700-1913 – An economy in transition
- UK Economy – 1900-2019 – Growth of the state & world war
- UK Economy – 1990-2019 – Quarter of a century of new changes
  - UK Economy – 1990-2019 – Stable income inequality
- UK Household Expenditure – 1700-2019 – Cost of Living
- UK Housing – 1700-2019 – Growth of home ownership
- UK Pauperism, Poverty and Hardship – 1700-2019 – The Retreat of Real Poverty
- UK Pollution (Air Quality), Cars – 1970-2019 – Continuous improvement
- UK Pollution (Air Quality), Energy – 1970-2019 – Continuous improvement
- UK Population & Life Expectancy – 1970-2019 – Continuous Improvement

UK Population & Life Expectancy

1970-2019 or two generations

Continuous improvement

Historical context

Death rates by age, Life expectancy by age

1700-2019

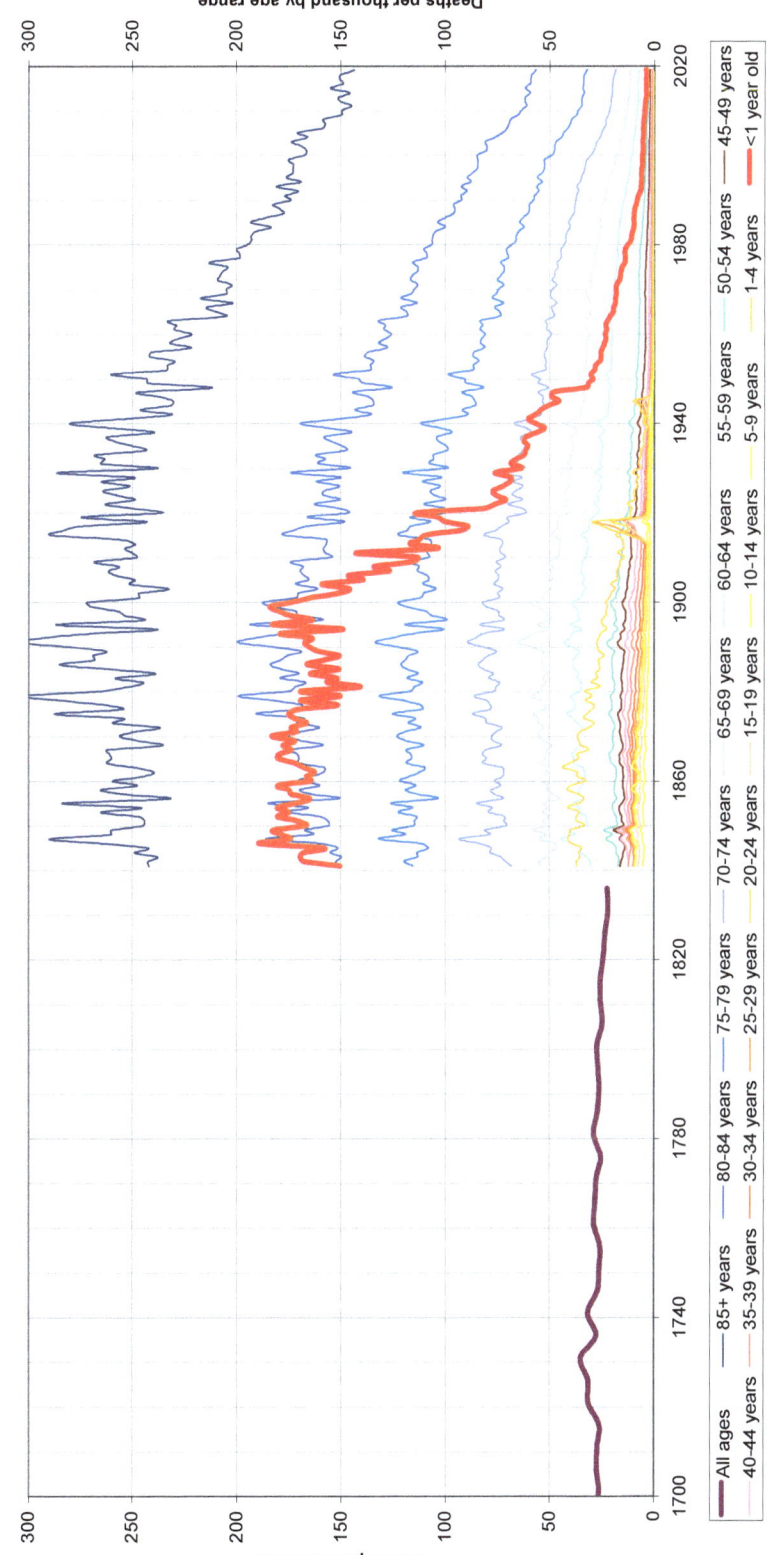

Death Rates per Thousand Population England all ages (Wrigley & Schofield to 1836) & England & Wales by age range from 1841 (ONS/HMD)

131

132

Life Expectancy at Decadal Age for England (Wrigley & Schofield before 1840) & England & Wales (ONS/HMD after Our World in Data/Max Roser)

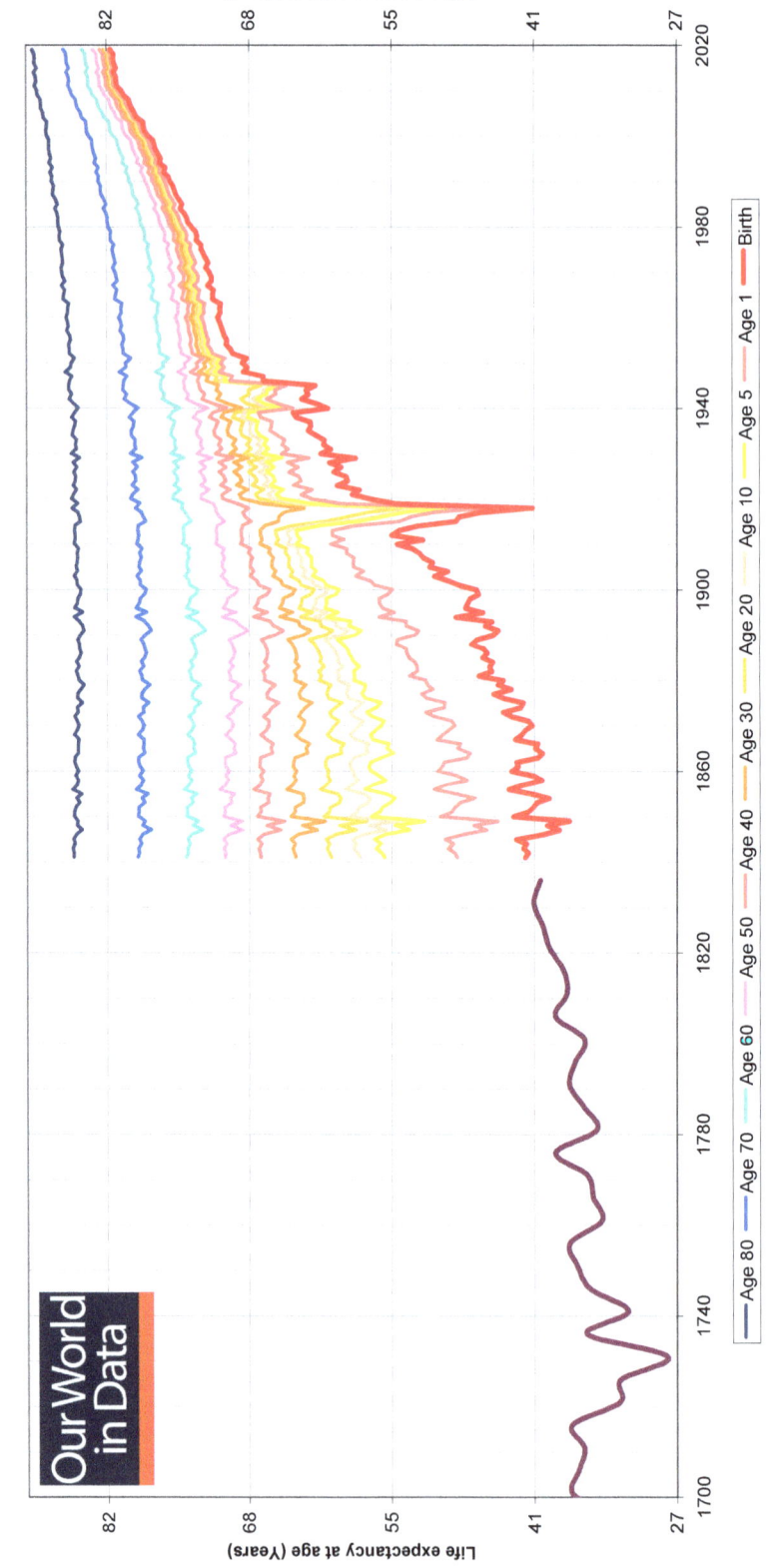

UK Population & Life Expectancy

World Comparison and Mortality Rates

1970-2019

Life Expectancy from World Bank/HMD/ONS (for major and comparable selected countries)

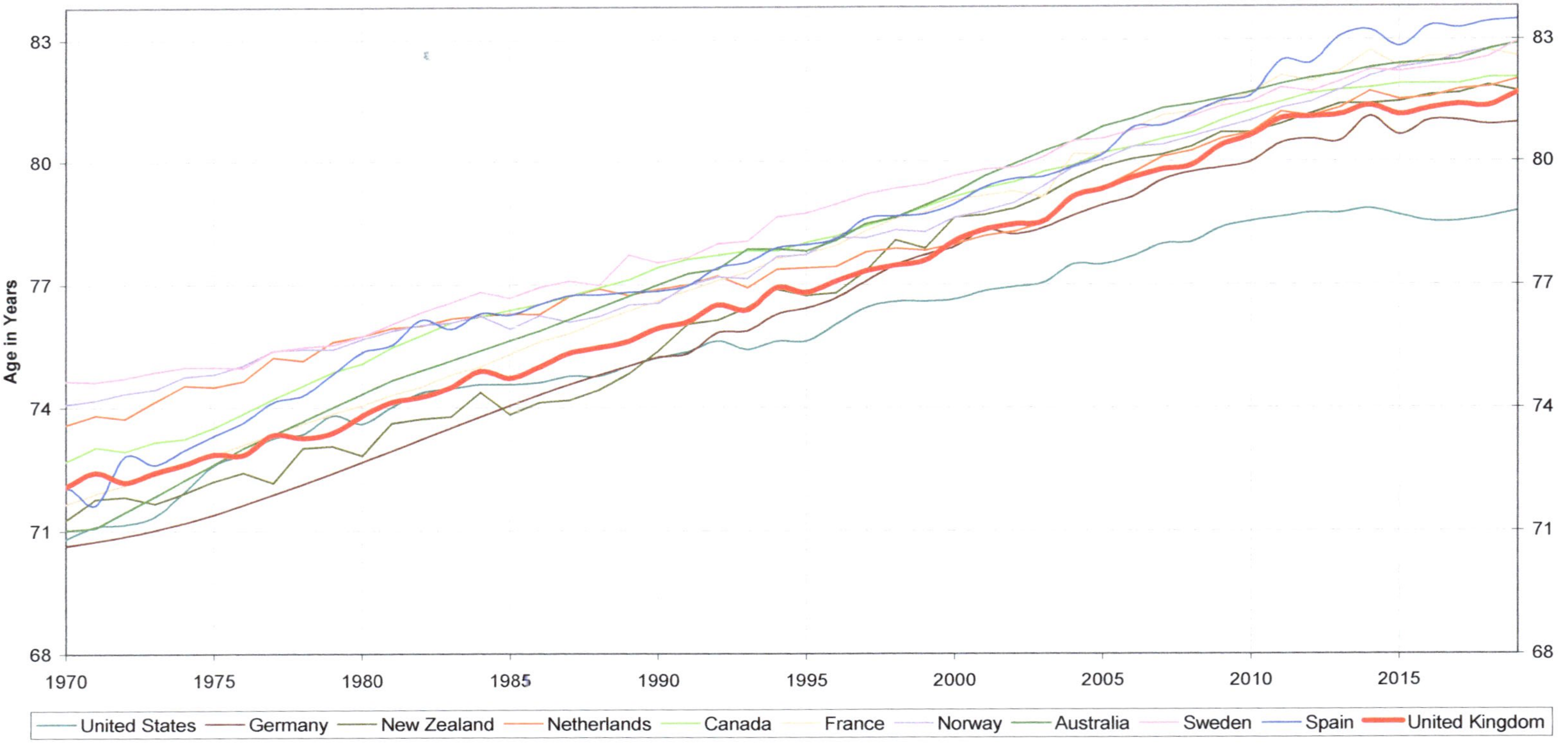
83
80
77
74
71
68
Age in Years
1970
1975
1980
1985
1990
1995
2000
2005
2010
2015
United States
Germany
New Zealand
Netherlands
Canada
France
Norway
Australia
Sweden
Spain
United Kingdom

UK Recent History of Life Expectancy at Birth and Growth in Population (Millions)

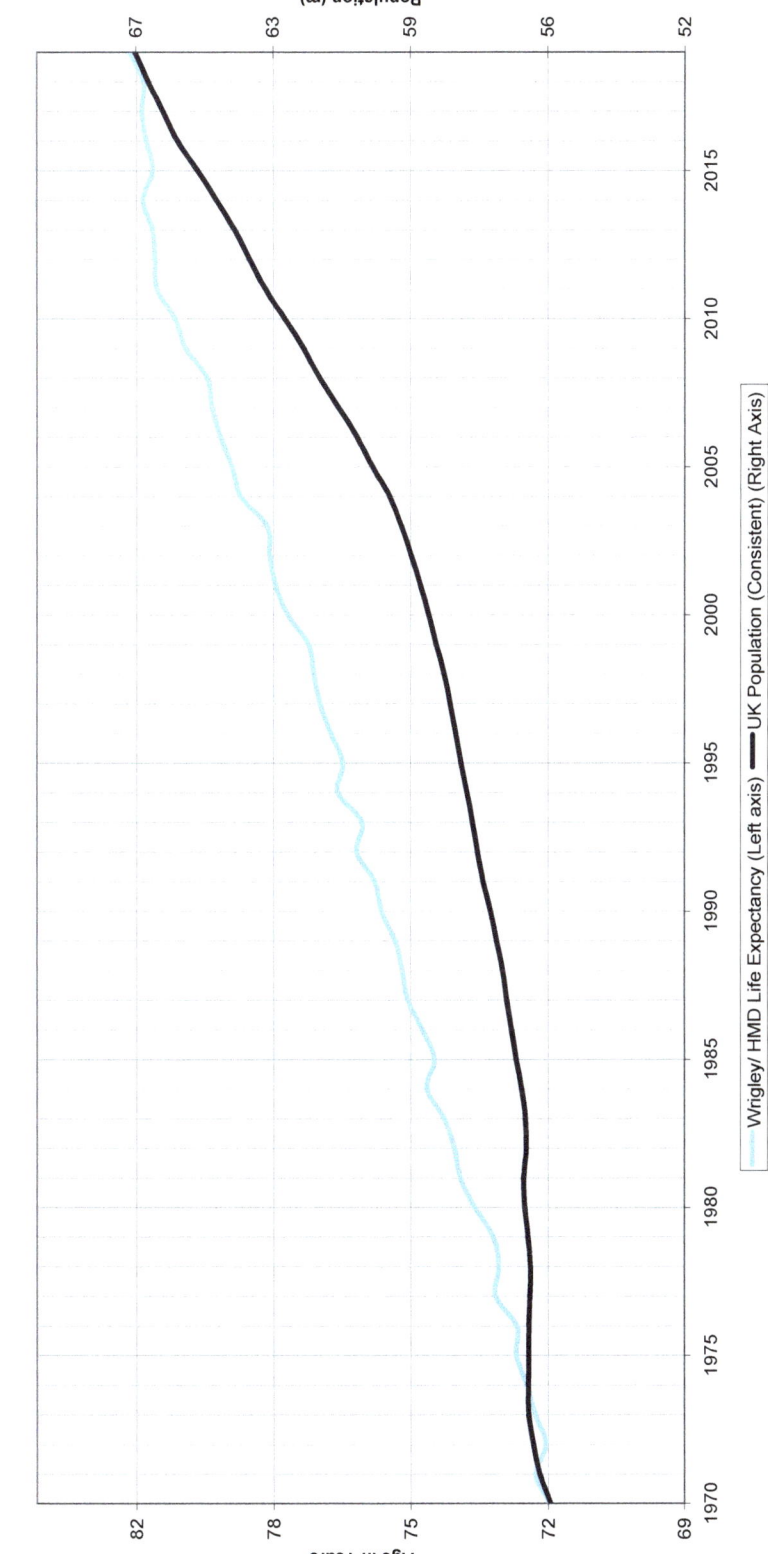

Wrigley/ HMD Life Expectancy (Left axis) — UK Population (Consistent) (Right Axis)

135

UK Recent History of Life Expectancy and Population Birth/Mortality Rates

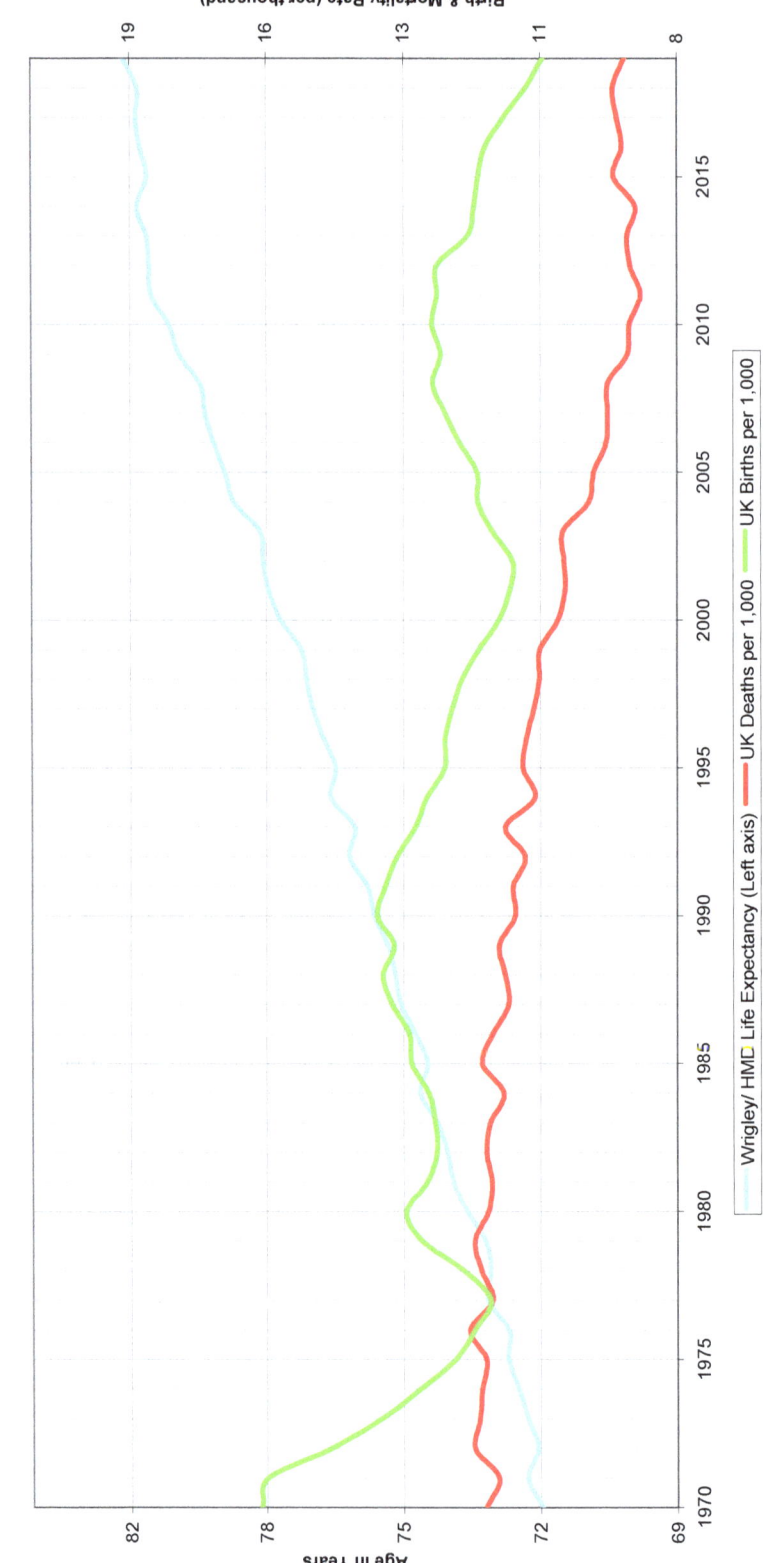

Wrigley/ HMD Life Expectancy (Left axis) — UK Deaths per 1,000 — UK Births per 1,000

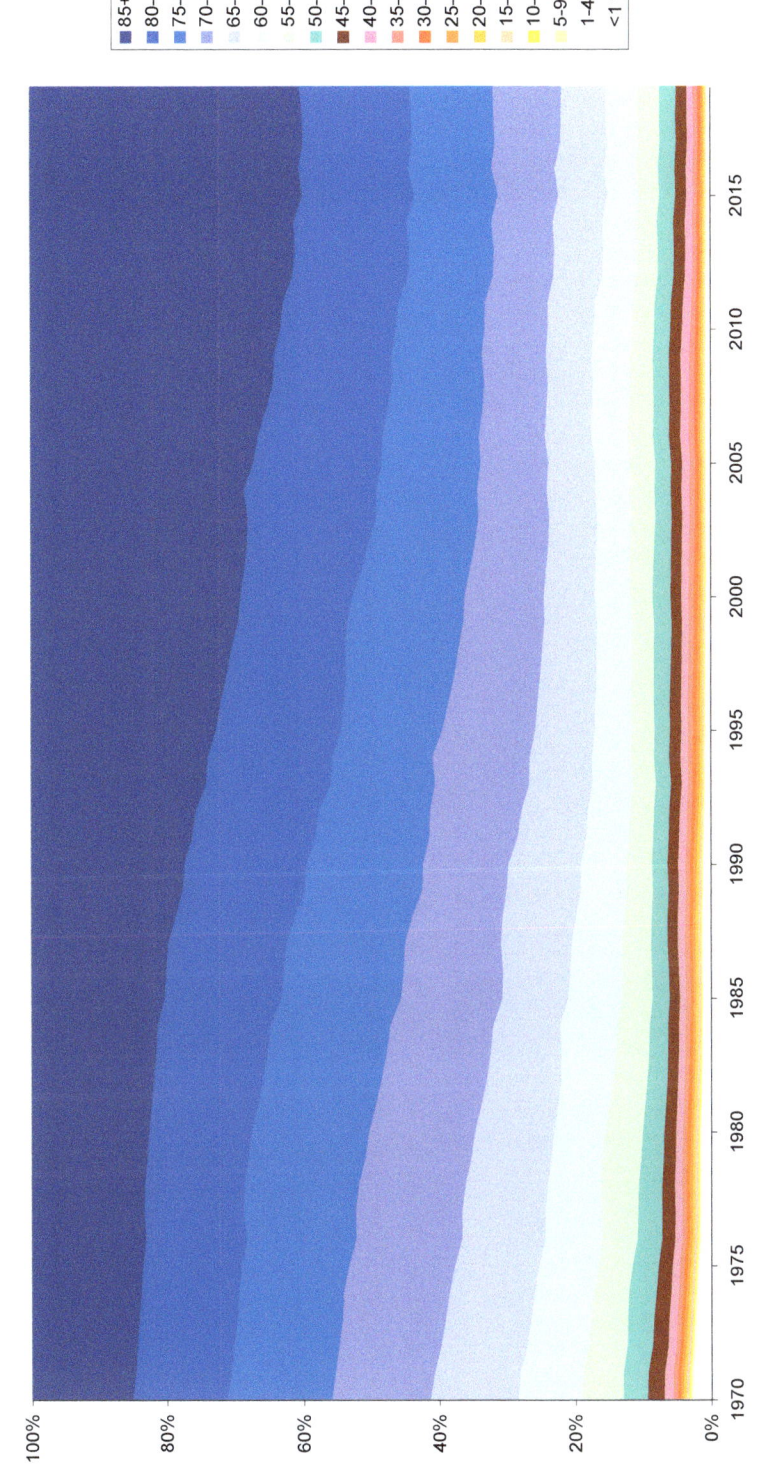

Deaths per annum by Age Range for England & Wales (Human Mortality Database)

Share of annual deaths by age range

85+ years
80-84 years
75-79 years
70-74 years
65-69 years
60-64 years
55-59 years
50-54 years
45-49 years
40-44 years
35-39 years
30-34 years
25-29 years
20-24 years
15-19 years
10-14 years
5-9 years
1-4 years
<1 year old

Death Rates per Thousand Population by Age Range for England & Wales (Human Mortality Database)

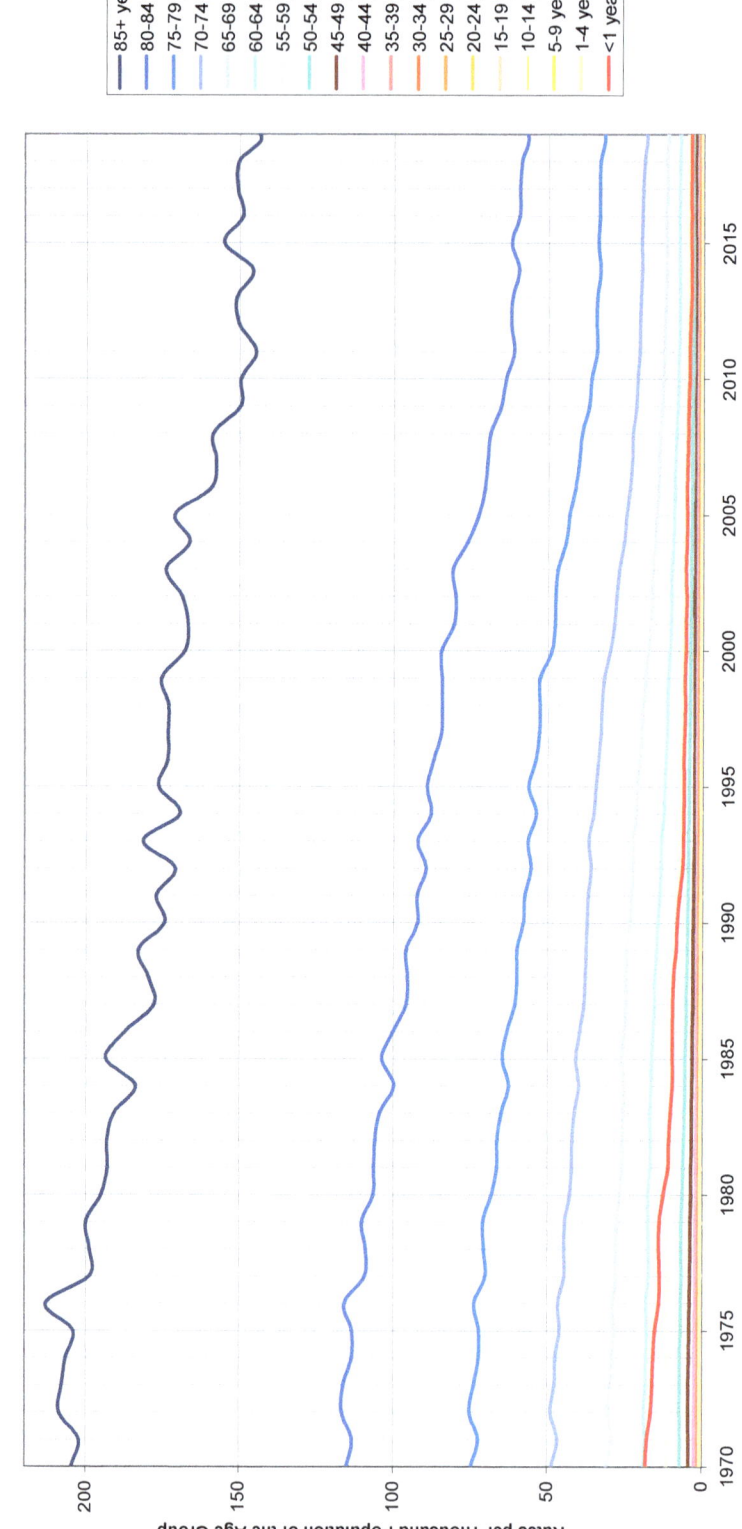

Life Expectancy at Decadal Age (ONS/Human Mortality Database)

Legend: Age 80, Age 70, Age 60, Age 50, Age 40, Age 30, Age 20, Age 10, Age 5, Age 1, Birth

Y-axis: Age in Years (89, 86, 83, 80, 77, 74, 71, 68)

X-axis: 1970, 1975, 1980, 1985, 1990, 1995, 2000, 2005, 2010, 2015

Focussing on the 21st Century

Slowing of the rate of increase of life expectancy

And return to rate of growth in 2019

UK Life Expectancy (ONS Life Tables) by age for Males

141

UK Life Expectancy (ONS Life Tables) by age for Females

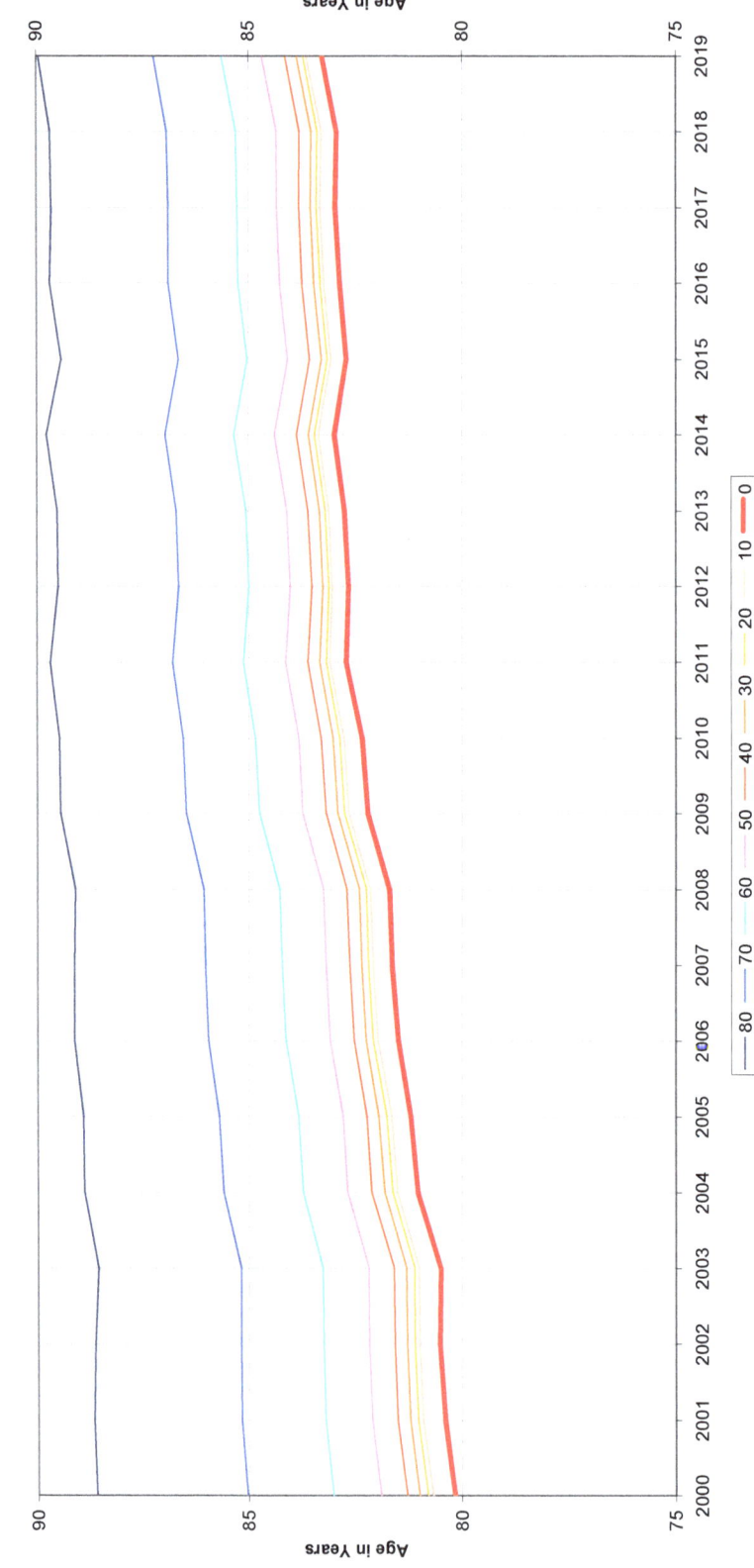

Relative annual change to UK Life Expectancy by age decade (ONS Life Tables) - Males

143

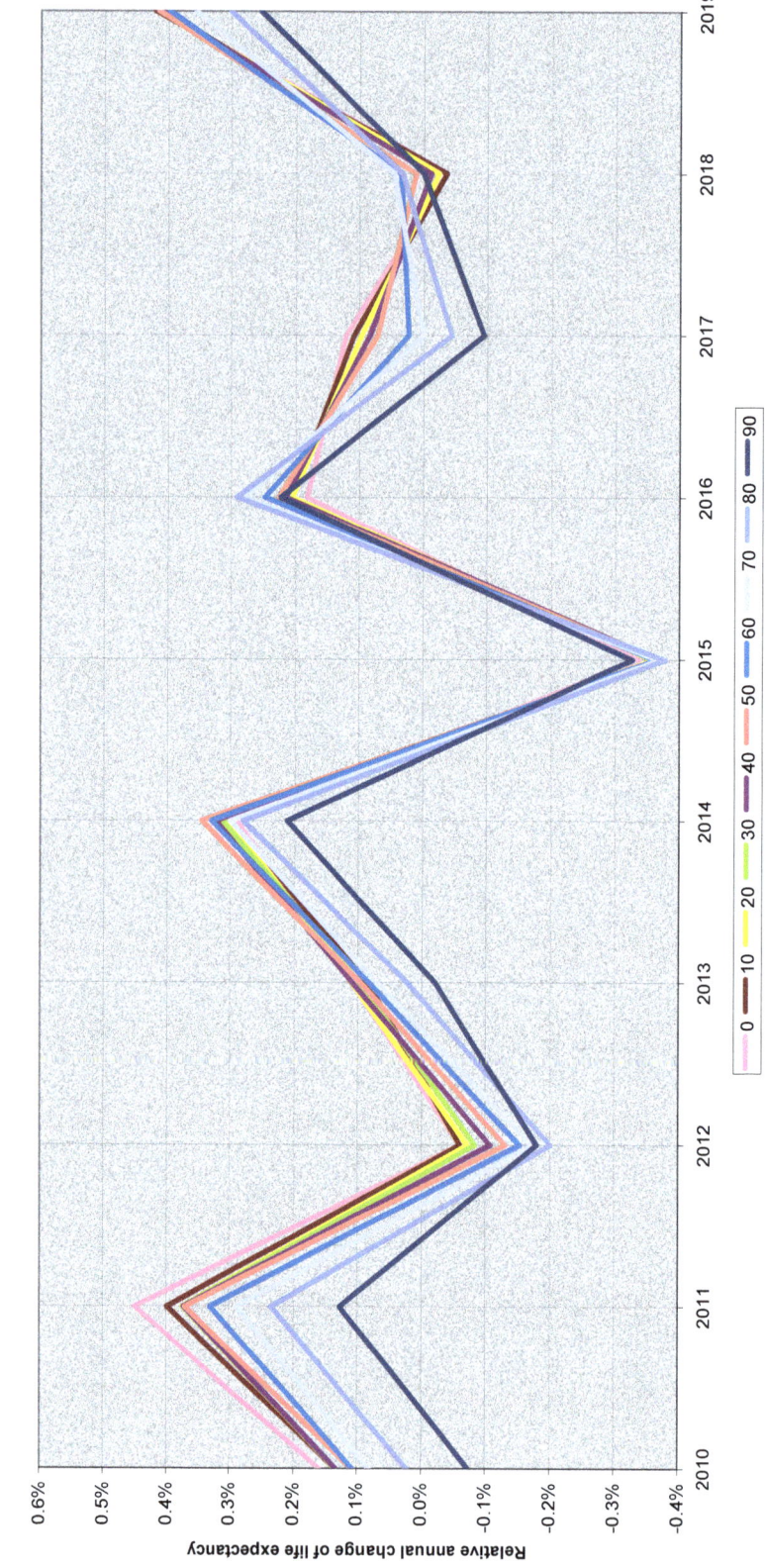

Relative annual change to UK Life Expectancy by age decade (ONS Life Tables) - Females

Death rates
(contribution by decadal age range)

Annual rate of UK deaths per thousand population - contribution from each decadal age range

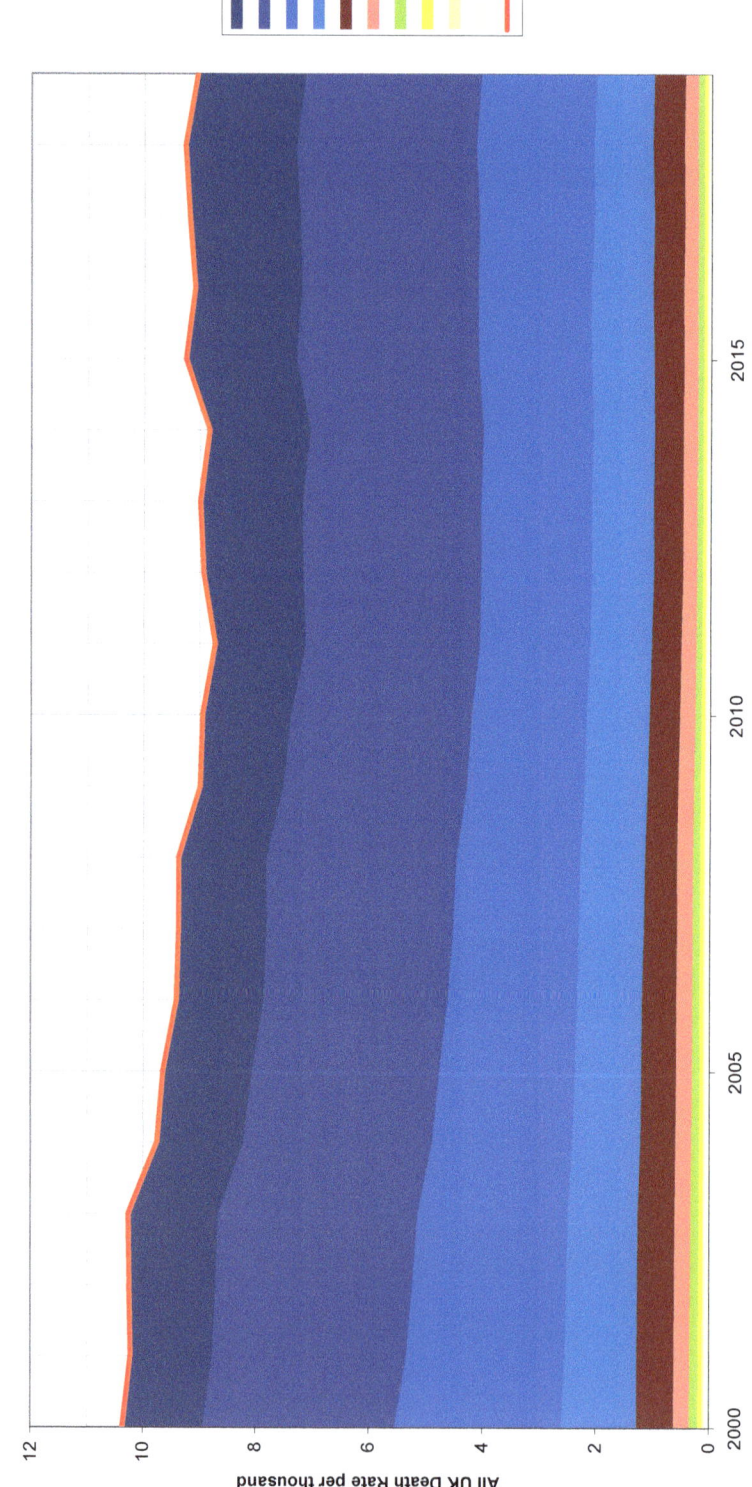

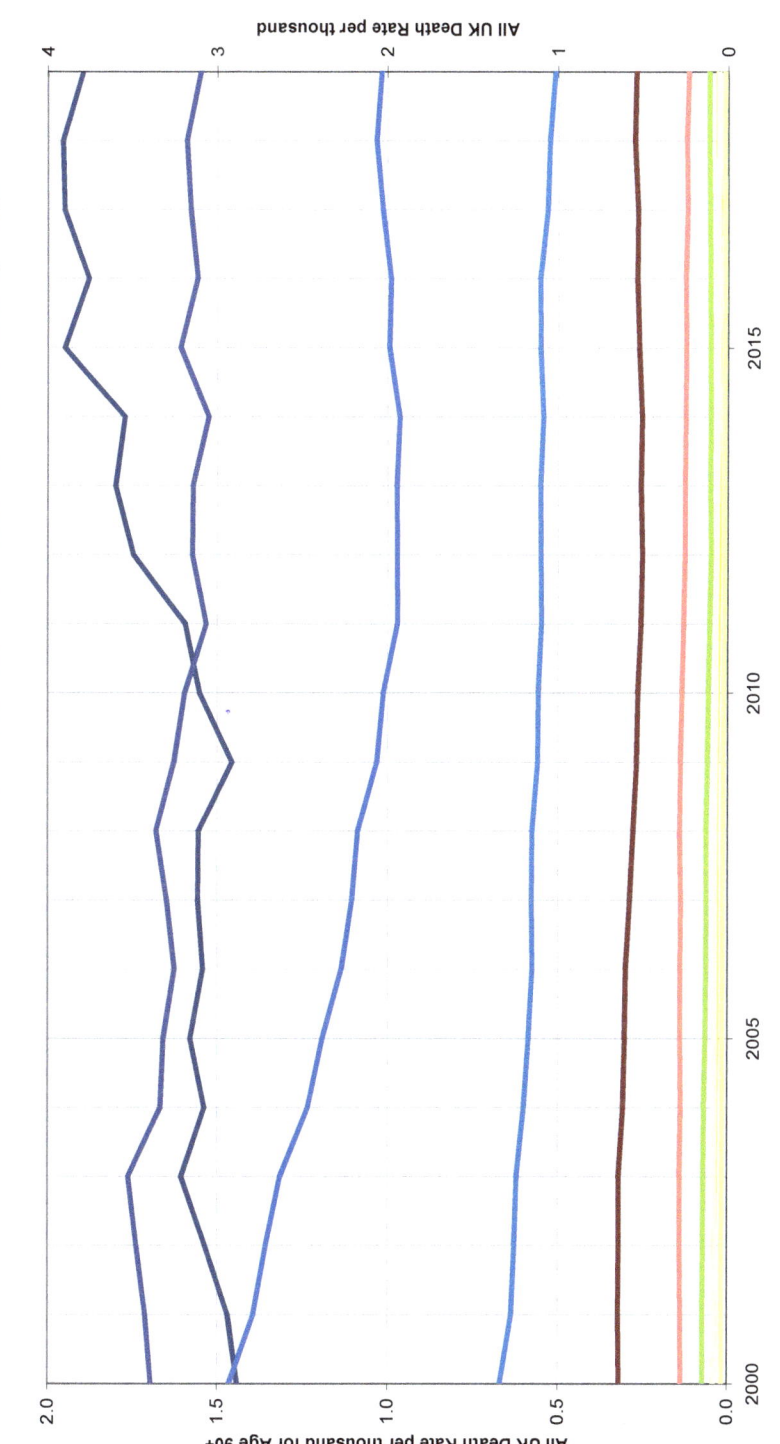

Annual rate of UK deaths per thousand population - contribution from each decadal age range

All UK Death Rate per thousand

Age 90+
Age 80-89
Age 70-79
Age 60-69
Age 50-59
Age 40-49
Age 30-39
Age 20-29
Age 10-19
Age 0-9

All UK Death Rate per thousand for Age 90+

147

ONS Health Inequalities Analysis

By "national indices of deprivation deciles"

UK Life Expectancy including low and high "deprivation" decile (ONS Life Tables) Males

Age in Years

Males   Females   Males Low Decile   Males High Decile   Females Low Decile   Females High Decile

149

150

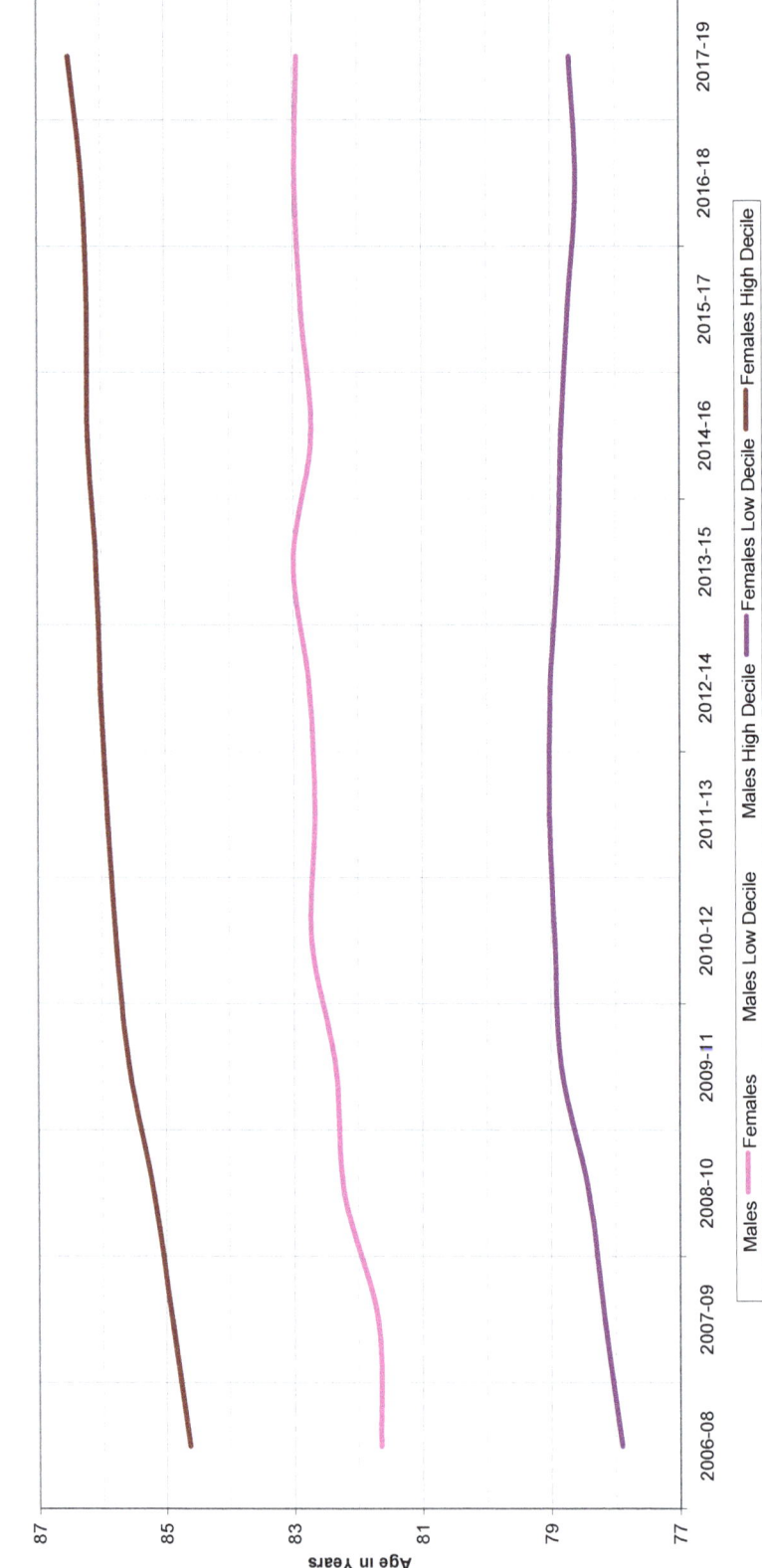

UK Life Expectancy including low and high "deprivation" decile (ONS Life Tables) - Females

UK Life Expectancy by "deprivation" decile (ONS Life Tables) - Males

151

152

UK Life Expectancy by "deprivation" decile (ONS Life Tables) - Females

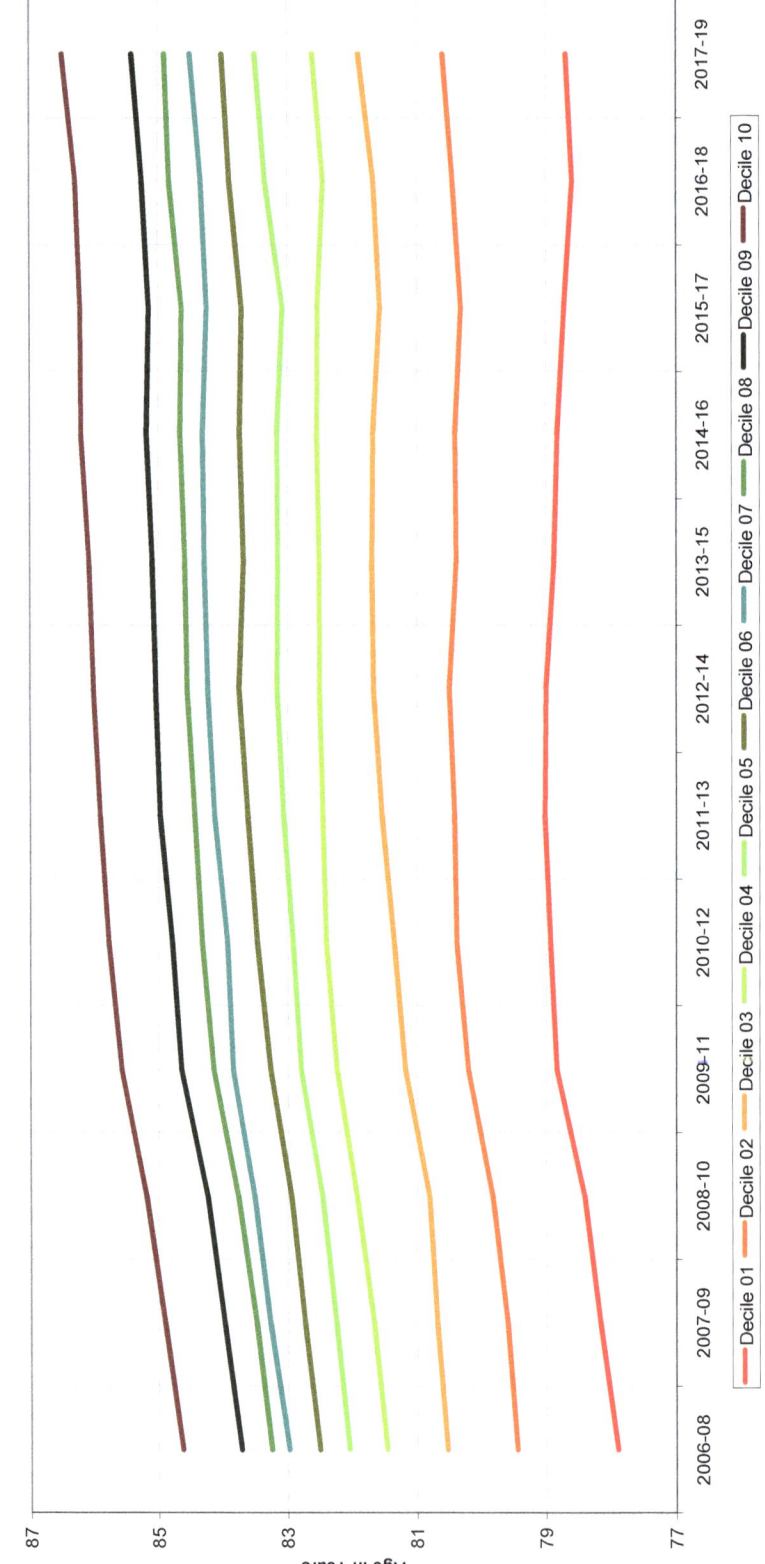

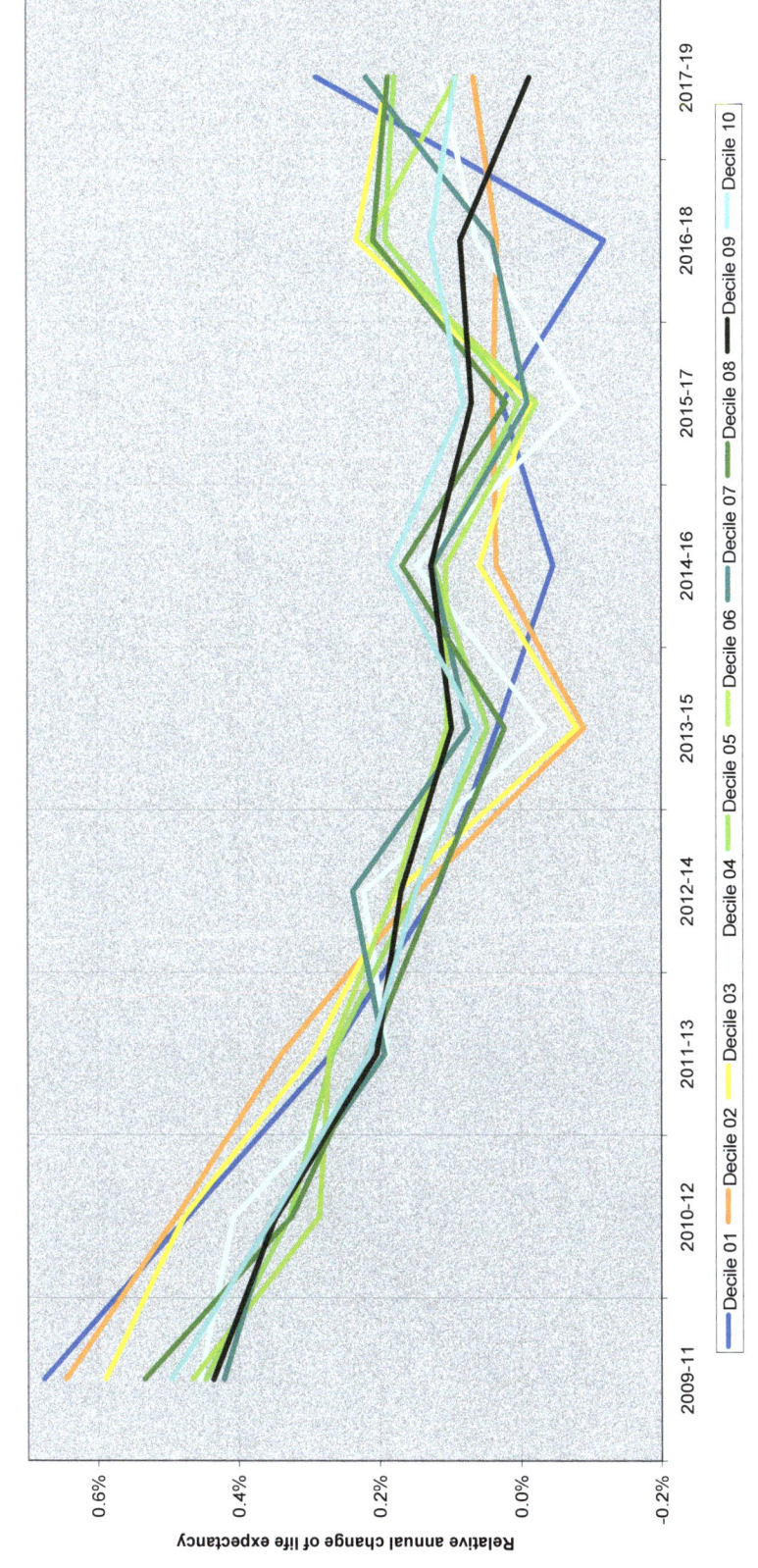

Relative annual change to UK Life Expectancy by "deprivation" decile (ONS Life Tables) - Males

153

Relative annual change to UK Life Expectancy by "deprivation" decile (ONS Life Tables) - Females

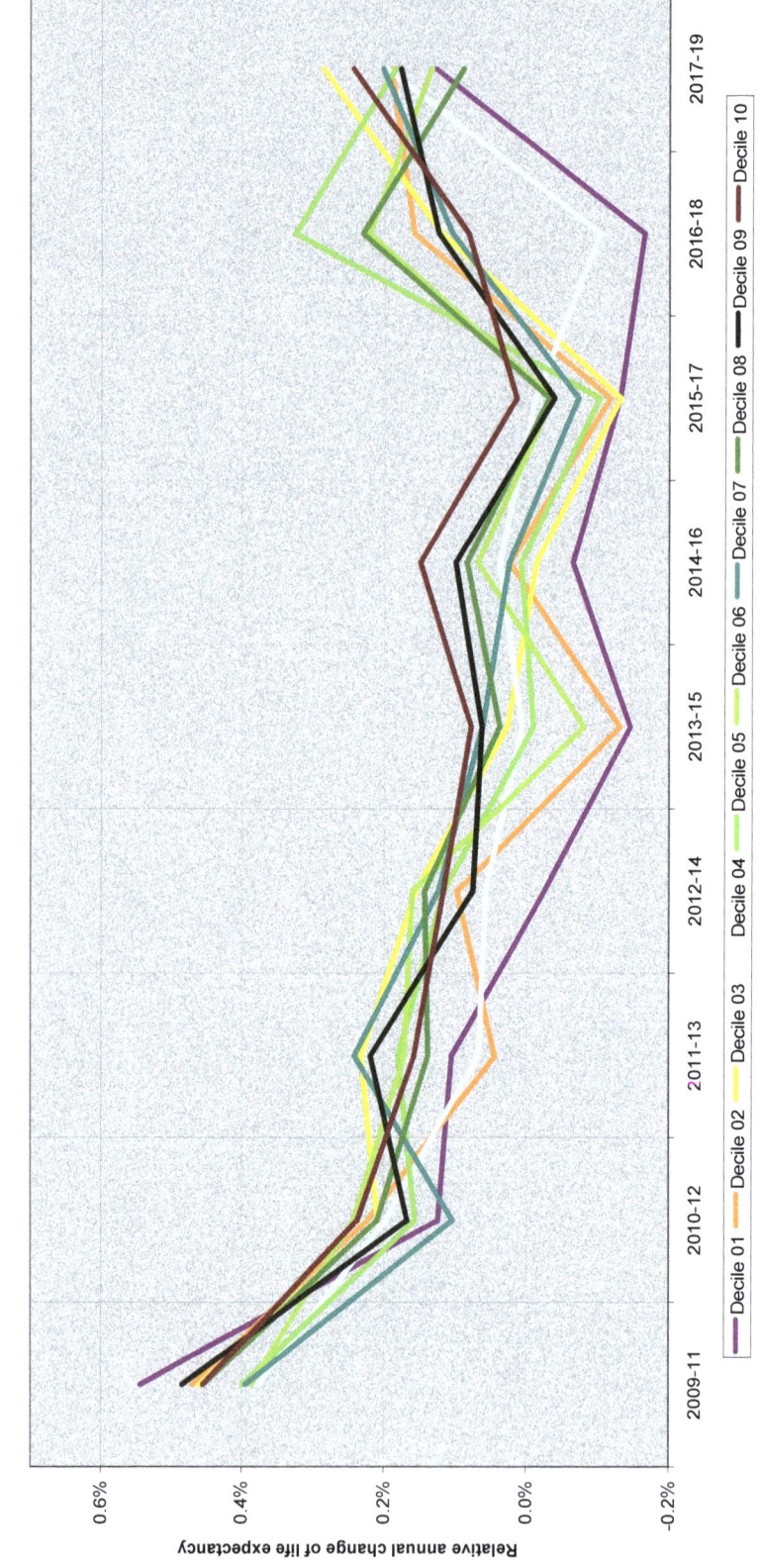

ONS analysis

By Nation and "Region"

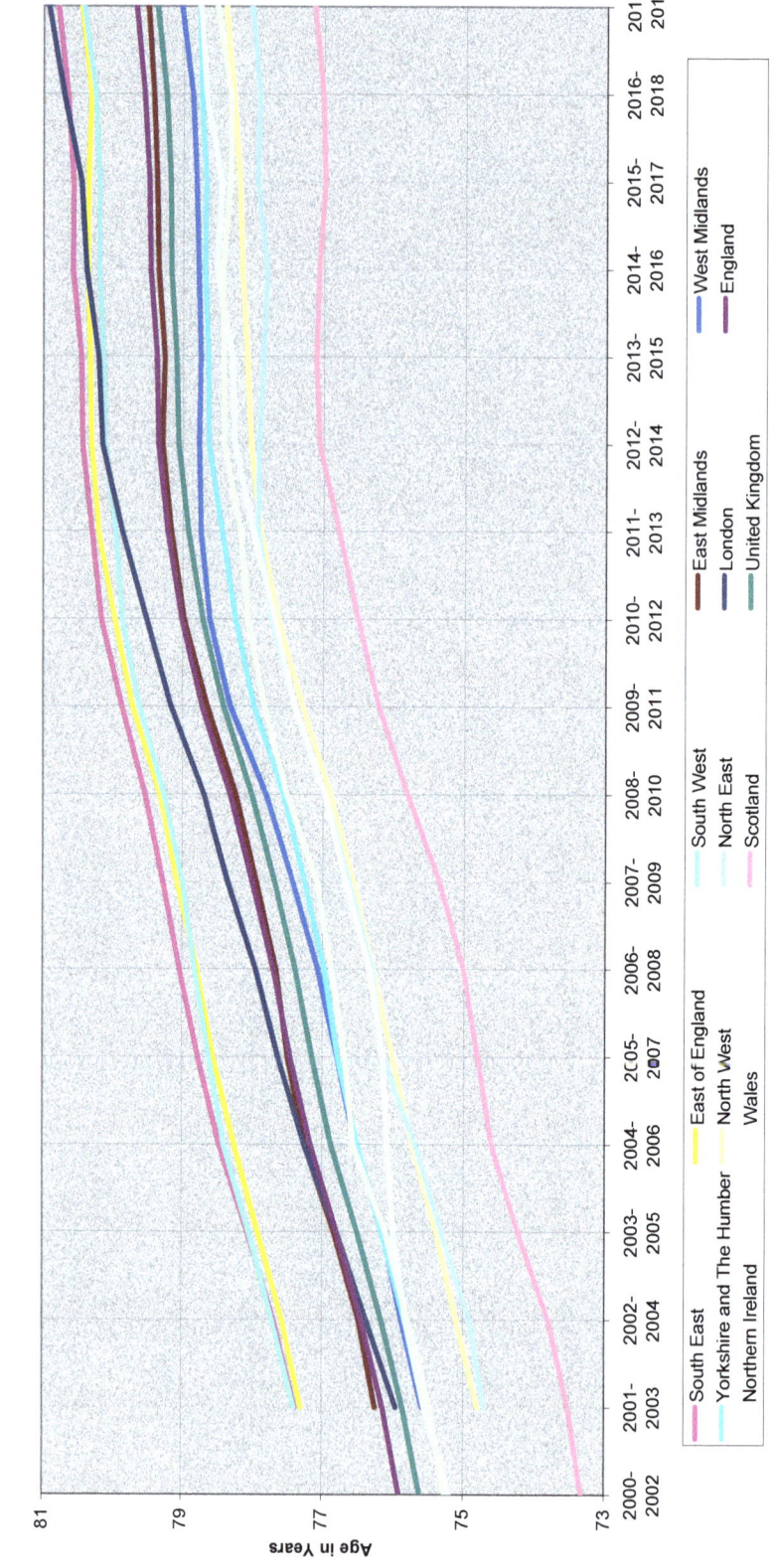

UK Life Expectancy (ONS Life Tables) - Males

Age in Years

South East
Yorkshire and The Humber
Northern Ireland

East of England
North West
Wales

South West
North East
Scotland

East Midlands
London
United Kingdom

West Midlands
England

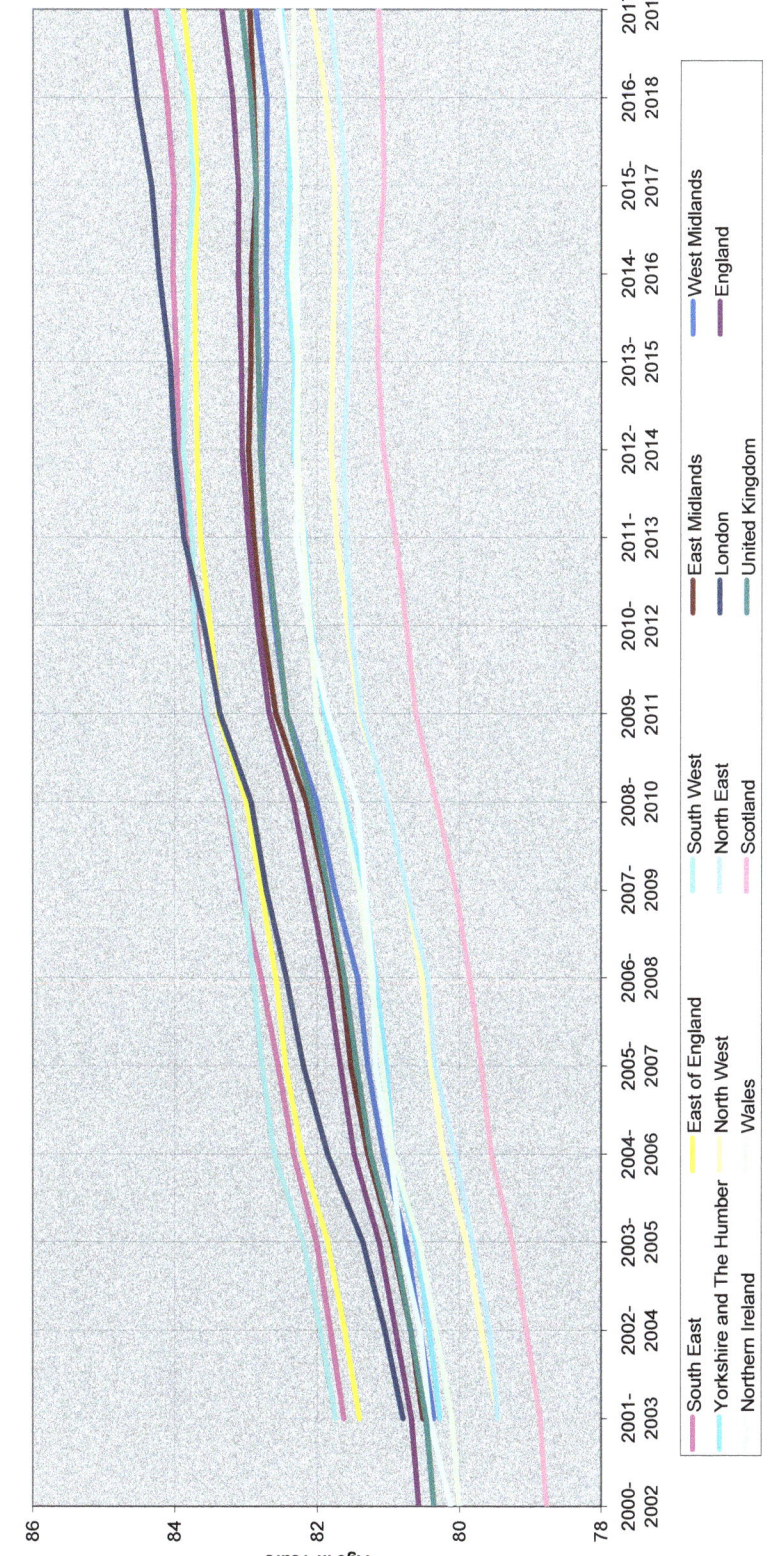

UK Life Expectancy (ONS Life Tables) - Females

Age in Years

Legend:
South East
Yorkshire and The Humber
Northern Ireland
East of England
North West
Wales
South West
North East
Scotland
East Midlands
London
United Kingdom
West Midlands
England

157

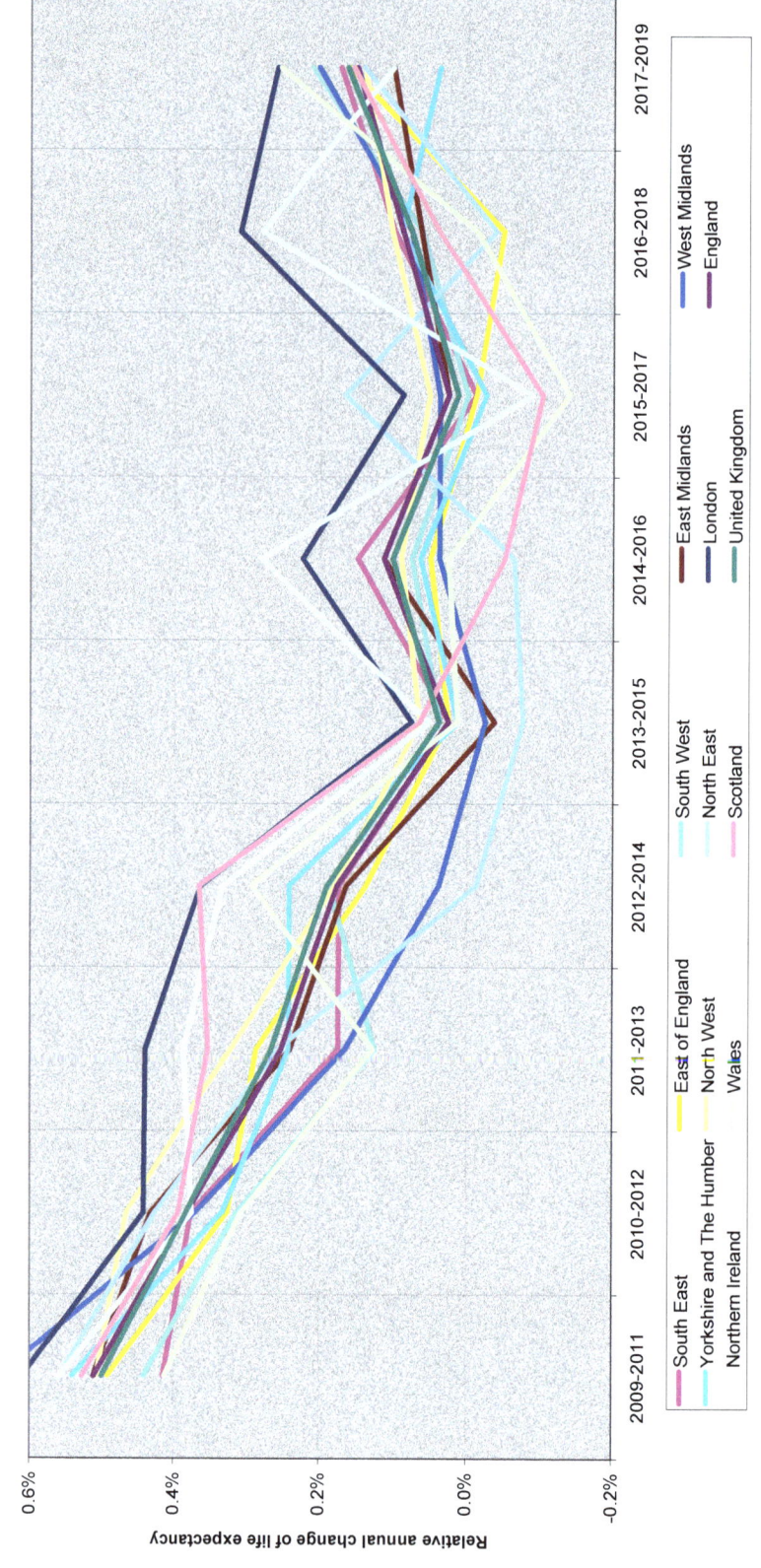

Relative annual change to UK Life Expectancy by UK nation/region (ONS Life Tables) - Males

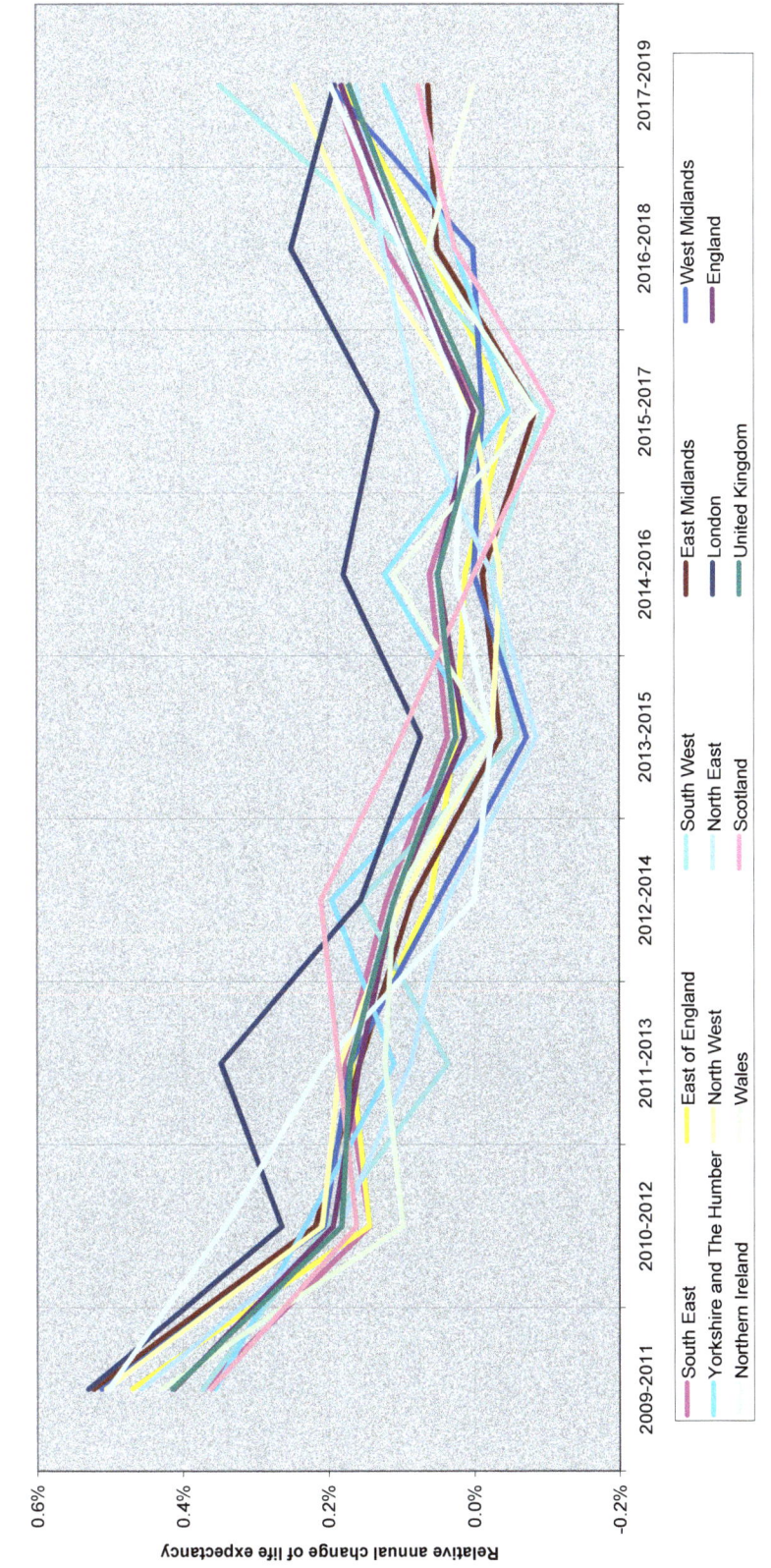

Relative annual change to UK Life Expectancy by UK nation/region (ONS Life Tables) - Females

159

ONS analysis

Life Expectancy for Londoners

The region with strongest continuing improvement

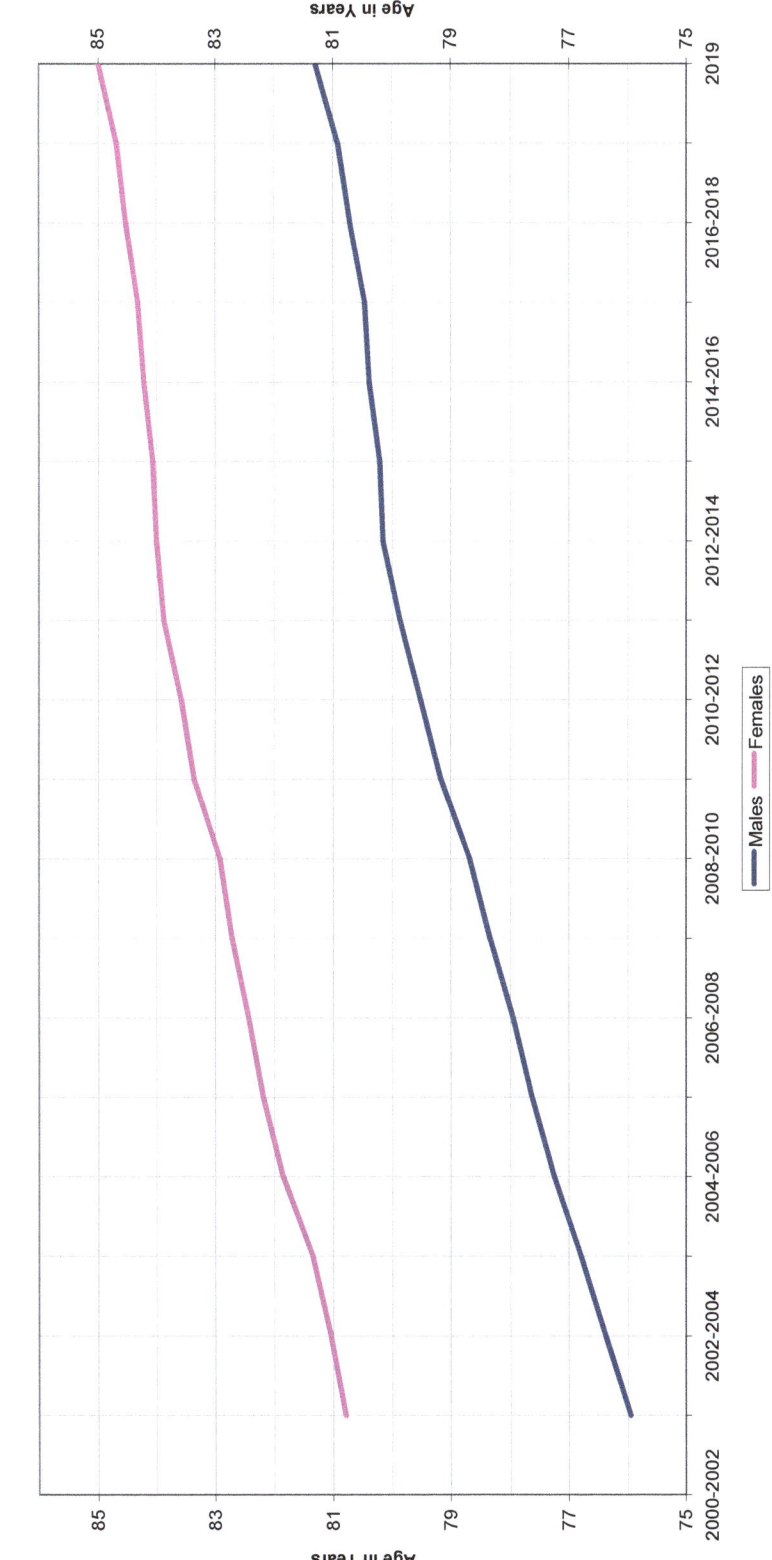

London Life Expectancy (ONS Life Tables, 2001-2003 to 2017-2019 + PHE WICH Mortality, 2018 & 2019)

Males   Females

161

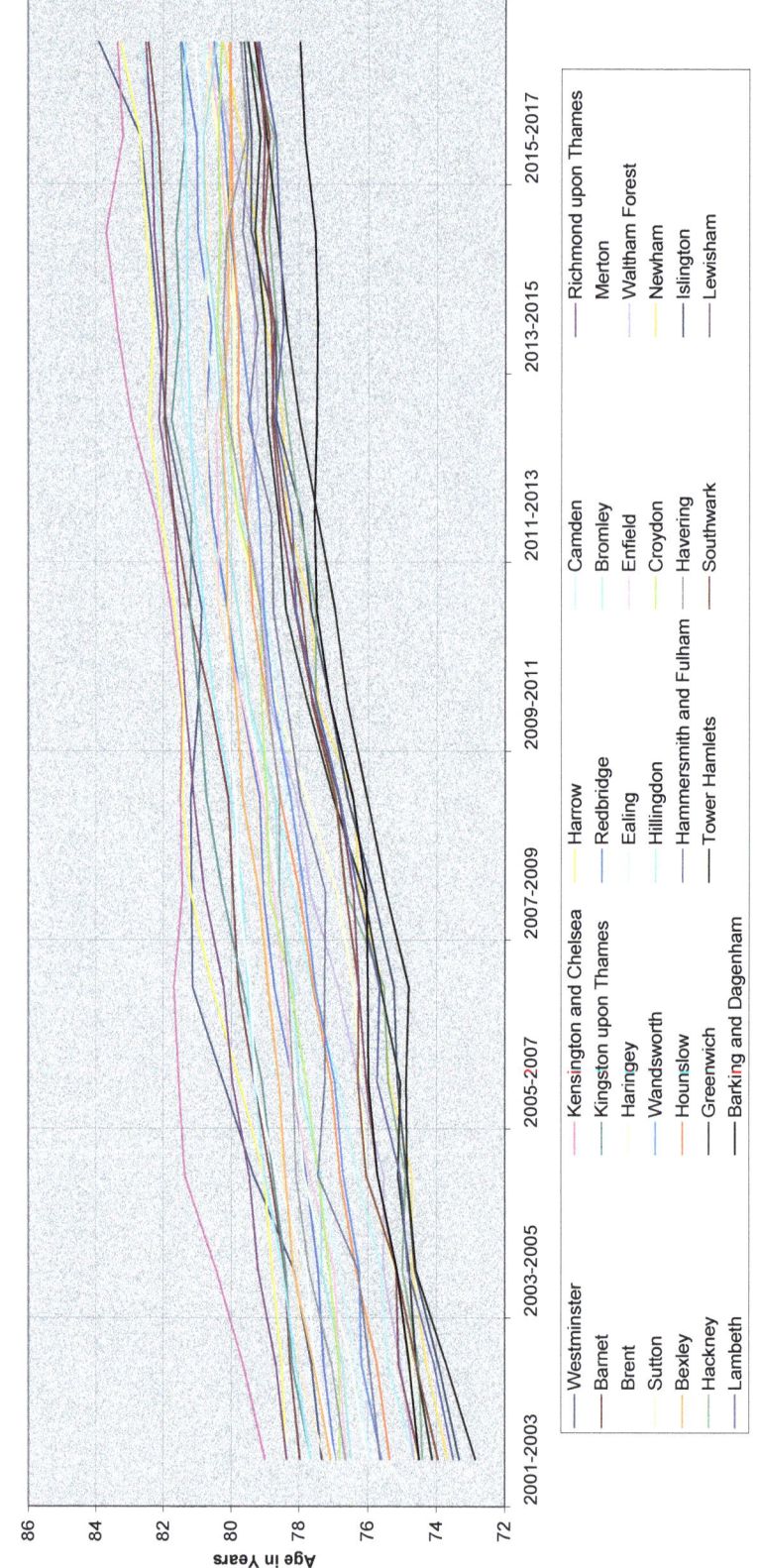

London Life Expectency (ONS Life Tables) by Borough - Males

London Life Expectancy (ONS Life Tables) by Borough - Females

163

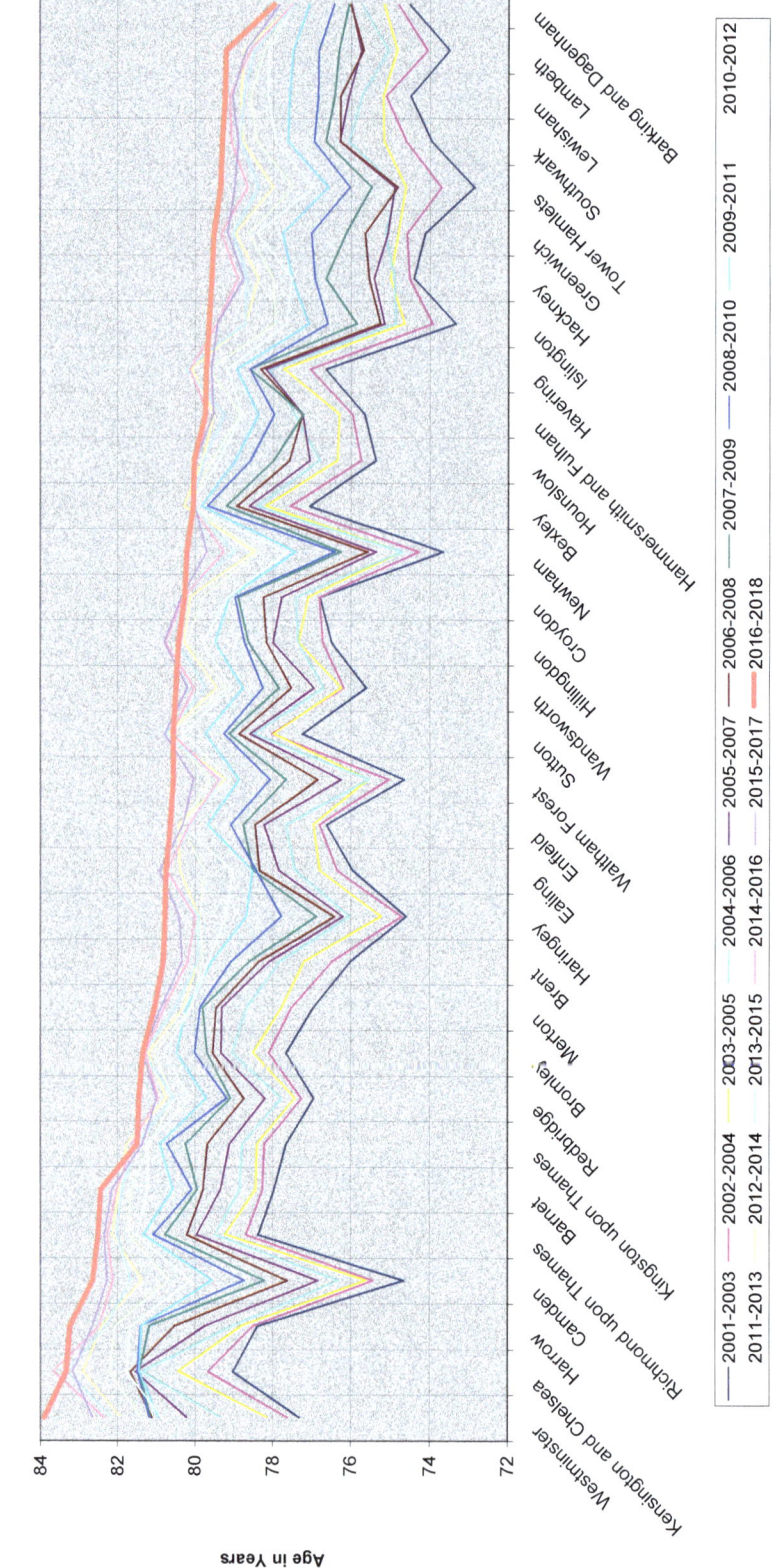

London Life Expectancy (ONS Life Tables) by Borough - Males

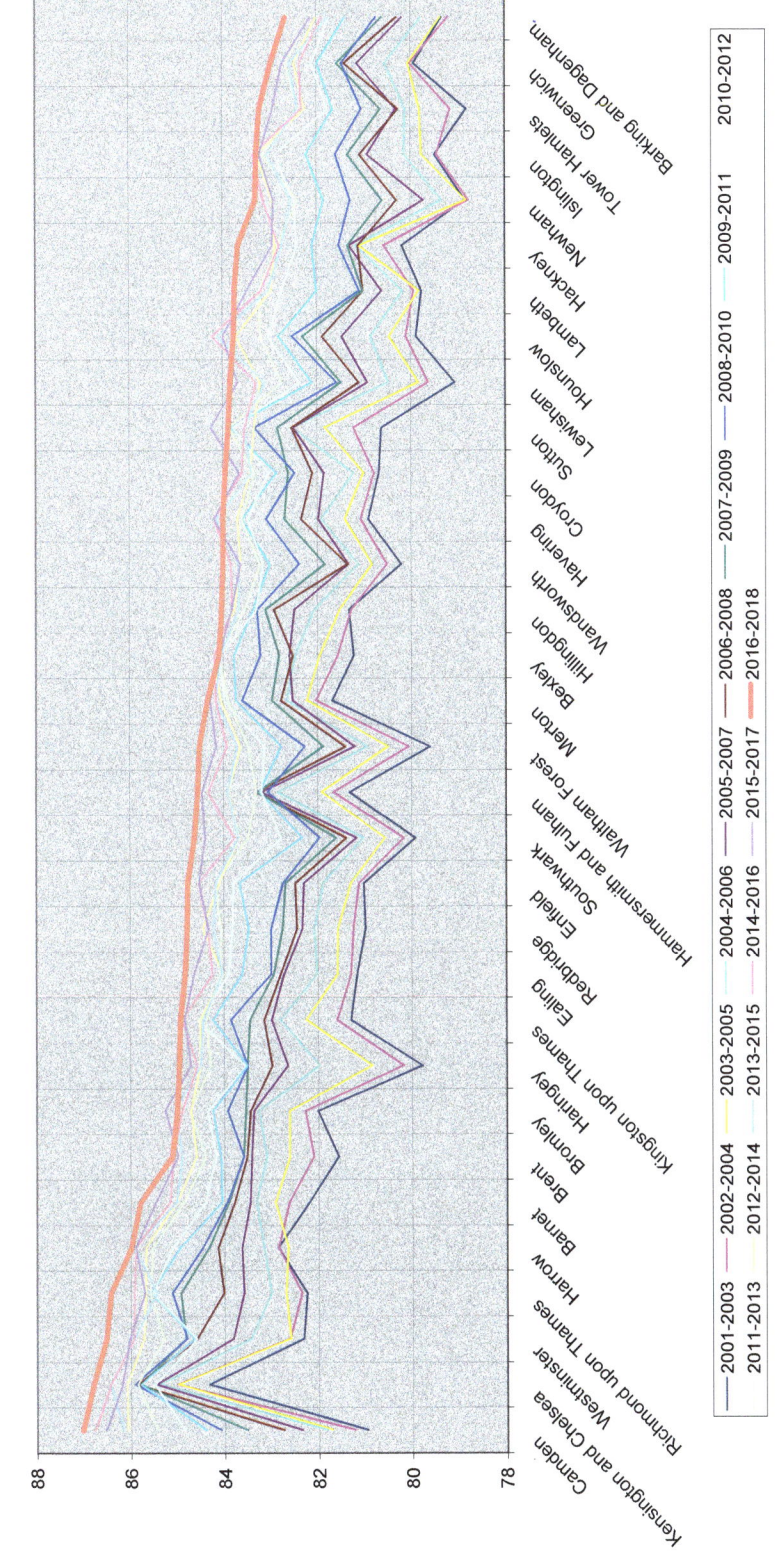

London Life Expectency (ONS Life Tables) by Borough - Females

Age in Years

88
86
84
82
80
78

Kensington and Chelsea
Westminster
Richmond upon Thames
Harrow
Barnet
Brent
Bromley
Haringey
Kingston upon Thames
Ealing
Redbridge
Enfield
Southwark
Hammersmith and Fulham
Waltham Forest
Merton
Bexley
Hillingdon
Wandsworth
Havering
Croydon
Sutton
Lewisham
Hounslow
Lambeth
Hackney
Newham
Islington
Tower Hamlets
Greenwich
Barking and Dagenham

2001-2003 2002-2004 2003-2005 2004-2006 2005-2007 2006-2008 2007-2009 2008-2010 2009-2011 2010-2012
2011-2013 2012-2014 2013-2015 2014-2016 2015-2017 2016-2018

165

Part of a series - see also:

- UK Economic & Social Change – 1700-2019 – Three centuries of progress
  - UK Economy – 1700-1913 – An economy in transition
  - UK Economy – 1900-2019 – Growth of the state & world war
- UK Economy – 1990-2019 – Quarter of a century of new changes
  - UK Economy – 1990-2019 – Stable income inequality
  - UK Household Expenditure – 1700-2019 – Cost of Living
  - UK Housing – 1700-2019 – Growth of home ownership
- UK Pauperism, Poverty and Hardship – 1700-2019 – The Retreat of Real Poverty
  - UK Pollution (Air Quality), Cars – 1970-2019 – Continuous improvement
  - UK Pollution (Air Quality), Energy – 1970-2019 – Continuous improvement
  - UK Population & Life Expectancy – 1970-2019 – Continuous Improvement

Bibliography, Selected Reading and Internet Data

"For out of old fields, as men saith,
Cometh all this new corn from year to year;
And out of old books, in good faith,
Cometh all this new science that men learn."

Geoffrey Chaucer:
Parliament of Foules,
1381-1382

Bibliography and Selected Reading

Adelino, N, Schoar, A and Severino, F	(2013) 'Credit Supply and House Prices: Evidence from Mortgage Market Segmentation' National Bureau of Economic Research Working Paper 17832
Adler, Professor M.	(2017) 'Extreme Poverty in the Midst of Unprecedented Affluence - Summary' University of Edinburgh
Adler, Professor M.	(2017) 'Extreme Poverty in the Midst of Unprecedented Affluence' University of Edinburgh
Adler, Professor M.	(2018) 'Cruel, Inhuman or Degrading Treatment? Benefit Sanctions in the UK' Palgrave Macmillan ISBN: 978-3-319-90355-2
Ainsworth, R. B.	(1949) 'Earnings and Working Hours of Manual Wage-Earners the United Kingdom in October, 1938' Wiley DOI: 10.2307/2984178

Akhtar, Galaiya and Reynolds	(2014) 'Residential mortgages: a comparison of the Bank of England's published statistical and regulatory data collections' Bank of England
Allen, Professor R. C.	(1994) 'Real Incomes in the English Speaking World, 1879-1913 (from Labour Market Evolution)' Routledge ISBN: 978-0-415-10865-2
Allen, Professor R. C.	(2007) 'Pessimism Preserved: Real Wages in the British Industrial Revolution' University of Oxford Working Paper 314
Allen, Professor R. C.	(2009) 'Engels' pause: Technical change, capital accumulation, and inequality in the British Industrial Revolution' Science Direct DOI: 10.1016/j.eeh.2009.04.004
Allen, Professor R. C.	(2009) 'The British Industrial Revolution in Global Perspective' Cambridge University Press ISBN: 978-0-521-68785-0
Allen, Professor R. C.	(2016) 'Revising England's Social Tables Once Again' University of Oxford Discussion Paper Number: 146
Allen, Professor R. C.	(2018) 'Class structure and inequality during the industrial revolution: lessons from England's social tables, 1688–1867' Wiley DOI: 10.1111/ehr.12661
Alvaredo, F., Atkinson, A. B., Morelli, S.	(2018) 'Top wealth shares in the UK over more than a century' Science Direct DOI: 10.1016/j.jpubeco.2018.02.008
Anon.	(1823/1828) 'A New System of Practical Domestic Economy'
Arkell, T.	(2006) 'Illuminations and Distortions, Gregory King's Scheme Calculated for the Year 1688' Wiley DOI: 10.1111/j.1468-0289.2005.00330.x
Armstrong, W. A.	(1981) 'The Influence of Demographic Factors on the Position of the Agricultural Labourer in England and Wales, c1750-1914' British Agricultural History Society The Agricultural History Review, Vol. 29, No. 2 (1981), pp. 71-82
Ashworth, H.	(1842) 'Statistics of the Present Depression of Trade in Bolton' Wiley DOI: 10.2307/2337951
Atkinson, Professor A. B.	(1997) 'Distribution of Income and Wealth in Britain over the Twentieth Century (from Twentieth Century British Social Trends)' Springer ISBN: 978-0-333-72149-0
Atkinson, Professor A. B.	(2002) 'Top Incomes in the United Kingdom over the Twentieth Century' University of Oxford Discussion Paper No 13
Atkinson, Professor A. B.	(2005) 'Top Incomes in the United Kingdom over the Twentieth Century' Wiley DOI: 10.1111/j.1467-985X.2005.00351.x
Atkinson, Professor A. B.	(2007) 'The Distribution of Top Incomes in the United Kingdom 1908–2000 (from Top Incomes over the 20th Century)' Oxford University Press ISBN: 978-0-199-28688-1
Atkinson, Professor A. B.	(2013) 'Wealth and Inheritance in Britain from 1896 to the Present' London School of Economics CASE/178
Atkinson, Professor A. B.	(2016) 'Pareto and the upper tail of the income distribution in the UK: 1799 to the present' London School of Economics CASE papers (198)
Atkinson, Professor A. B. and Jenkins, S. P.	(2019) 'A different perspective on the evolution of UK income inequality' London School of Economics Working Paper 01-19

Atkinson, Professor A. B., Piketty, T. and Saez, E.	(2011) 'Top Incomes in the Long Run of History' American Economic Association DOI: 10.1257/jel.49.1.3
Ayres, Professor J. G. (Chair) and Hurley J. F. (Chair)	(2010) 'The Mortality Effects of Long-Term Exposure to Particulate Air Pollution in the United Kingdom' COMEAP ISBN: 978-0-85951-685-3
Banks, J. and Johnson, P.	(1998) 'How Reliable is the Family Expenditure Survey' Institute for Fiscal Studies ISBN: 978-1-873357-70-2
Baxter, R. D.	(1868) 'National Income. The United Kingdom' MacMillan and Co.
Baxter, R. D.	(1869) 'The Taxation of the United Kingdom' MacMillan and Co.
Belfield et al.	(2017) 'Two decades of income inequality in Britain: the role of wages, household earnings and redistribution' The Institute for Fiscal Studies Working Paper W17/01
Belfield, Chandler and Joyce	(2015) 'Housing: Trends in Prices, Costs and Tenure' Institute for Fiscal Studies ISBN: 978-1-909463-79-0
Berry, Harrison, Ryland & de Weymarn	(2007) 'Interpreting movements in broad money' Bank of England BofE Quarterly Bulletin
Block, F. and Somers, M.	(2003) 'In the shadow of Speenhamland Social Policy and the Old Poor Law' Sage Publications DOI: 10.1177/0032329203252272
Bogdanor, Professor V. B.	(2016) 'The IMF Crisis, 1976: Transcript' Gresham College, Oxford
Bolton	(2019) 'Student Loan Statistics' House of Commons Library Briefing Paper 1079
Booth, C.	(1892) 'Life and Labour of the People in London' MacMillan and Co.
Booth, C.	(1904) 'Life and Labour of the People in London' MacMillan and Co.
Bosanquet, S. R.	(1841) 'The Rights of the Poor and Christian Alms Giving Vindicated'
Boulter, Thorpe, Harrison and Allen	(2005) 'Road vehicle non-exhaust particulate matter: final report on emission modelling' TRL Limited
Bourquin and Waters	(2019) 'The effect of taxes and benefits on UK inequality' The Institute for Fiscal Studies Briefing Note No 249
Bourquin, Cribb, Waters and Xu	(2019) 'Living standards, poverty and inequality in the UK: 2019' The Institute for Fiscal Studies ISBN: 978-1-912-80527-3
Bowley, Professor Sir A. L.	(1900) 'Wages in the United Kingdom in the Nineteenth Century' Cambridge University Press
Bowley, Professor Sir A. L.	(1920) 'The Change in the distribution of National Income 1880-1913' Clarenden Press (Oxford)
Bowley, Professor Sir A. L.	(1937) 'Wages and Income in the United Kingdom Since 1860' Cambridge University Press ISBN: 978-1-316-50960-9
Boyer, Professor G. R.	(2019) 'The Winding Road to the Welfare State - Economic Insecurity & Social Welfare Policy in Britain' Princeton University Press ISBN: 978-0-691-17873-8
Boyer, Professor G. R. and Hatton, Professor T. J.	(1994) 'Regional Labour Market Integration in England and Wales, 1850-1913 (from Labour Market Evolution)' Routledge ISBN: 978-0-415-10865-2
Boyer, Professor G. R. and Hatton, Professor T. J.	(2002) 'New Estimates of British Unemployment, 1870-1913' Cambridge University Press DOI: 10.1017/S0022050702001031

Bradshaw, Professor J.	(2001) 'Methodologies to Measure Poverty: More Than One is Best!' University of York
Brewer, Goodman and Leicester	(2006) 'Household spending in Britain What can it teach us about poverty?' Joseph Rowntree Foundation ISBN: 978-1-861-34855-5
Brewer, Sibieta and Wren-Lewis	(2008) 'Racing away? Income inequality and the evolution of high incomes' The Institute for Fiscal Studies Briefing Note No 76
Broadberry, Professor S. N. et al.	(2015) 'British Economic Growth, 1270-1870' Cambridge University Press ISBN: 978-1-107-67649-7
Broadberry, Professor S. N. and Burhop, Professor C.	(2009) 'Real wages and labour productivity in Britain and Germany, 1871-1938: a unified approach to the international comparison of living standards' Max Planck Society DOI: 10.1017/S0022050710000331
Broadberry, Professor S. N. et al.	(2011) 'British Economic Growth and the Business Cycle 1700-1850' Broadberry et al. AnnualGDP10a
Broadberry, Professor S. N. et al.	(2011) 'British Economic Growth, 1270-1870: An Output Based Approach' Broadberry et al. BritishGDPLongRun16a.docx
Broadberry, Professor S. N. et al.	(2011) 'The Sectoral Distribution of the Labour Force and Labour Productivity of Britain, 1381-1951' Broadberry et al. SectoralSharesGB10b
Brundage, Professor A.	(2002) 'The English Poor Laws, 1700-1930' Palgrave Macmillan ISBN: 978-0-333-68271-8
BSA	(2014) 'Extract from BSA Yearbook 2013/14 - Interest Rates' Building Societies Association
Bunn and Rostom	(2014) 'Household debt and spending' Bank of England BofE Quarterly Bulletin
Burkhauser, Professor R. V. et al.	(2018) 'Top incomes and inequality in the UK: reconciling estimates from household survey and tax return data' Oxford University Press DOI: 10.1093/oep/gpx041
Burrell, Older, Watmough, Ripley and Hopkins	(2018/2020) 'The financial lives of consumers across the UK' Financial Conduct Authority
Carrington and Madsen	(2010) 'House Prices, Credit and Willingness to Lend' Monash University JEL: E44; E51
Chadwick, D.	(1849) 'Poor Rates Principle of Rating Letter to the Mayor of Salford'
Chadwick, D.	(1860) 'On the Rate of Wages in Manchester and Salford, and the Manufacturing Districts of Lancashire, 1839-59' Wiley DOI: 10.2307/2338478
Chalmers, G.	(1782/1804) 'An Estimate of the Comparative Strength of Great Britain'
Chapman, L. (revised)	(1977/1988) 'Roget's International Thesaurus - Fourth Edition' Harper Collins ISBN: 978-0-004-33176-1
Clark, Professor G.	(1999) 'Housing Rents, Housing Quality, and Living Standards in England and Wales, 1640-1909' University of California Davis
Clark, Professor G.	(2001) 'Farm Wages and Living Standards in the Industrial Revolution England, 1670-1850' University of California Davis
Clark, Professor G.	(2001) 'Land Rental Values and the Agrarian Economy - England and Wales 1500-1912' University of California Davis

Clark, Professor G.	(2002) 'The Agricultural Revolution and the Industrial Revolution, 1500-1912' University of California Davis
Clark, Professor G.	(2003) 'The Price History of English Agriculture, 1209-1914' University of California Davis
Clark, Professor G.	(2005) 'The Condition of the Working Class in England, 1209–2004' The University of Chicago Press DOI: 10.1086/498123
Clark, Professor G.	(2007) 'The Long March of History Farm Labourers Wages in England, 1208-1850' University of California Davis
Clark, Professor G.	(2011) 'Average Earnings and Retail Prices, UK, 1209-2010' University of California Davis
Clark, Professor G.	(2014) 'The Industrial Revolution' University of California Davis
Clark, Professor G.	(2018) 'Average Earnings and Retail Prices, UK, 1209-2017' University of California Davis
Clark, Professor G.	(2020) 'What Were British Earnings and Prices Then? A Question-and-Answer Guide' MeasuringWorth
Cobbett, W.	(1830/2001) 'Rural Rides' Penguin Classics ISBN: 978-0-140-43579-4
Colquhoun, P.	(1806) 'A Treatise on Indigence'
Colquhoun, P.	(1815) 'Treatise on the Wealth, Power and Resources of the British Empire'
Corlett, A. et al.	(2019) 'The Living Standards Audit 2019' Resolution Foundation
Corlett, A. and Judge, L.	(2017) 'HOME AFFRONT: Housing across the generations' Resolution Foundation
Coulson, R. L.	(2017) 'Clarifying Income Distribution' Policy Exchange ID report mon-2347
Crafts, Professor N. F. R.	(1985) 'British Economic Growth during the Industrial Revolution' Oxford University Press ISBN: 978-0-198-73067-5
Crafts, Professor N. F. R.	(1995) 'Recent research on the national accounts of the UK, 1700–1939' Routledge DOI: 10.1080/03585522.1995.10415893
Crafts, Professor N. F. R.	(1997) 'Some Dimensions of the Quality of Life during the British Industrial Revolution' London School of Economics ISBN: 978-0-85328-387-7
Crafts, Professor N. F. R.	(2020) 'Slow Real Wage Growth during the Industrial Revolution: Productivity Paradox or Pro-Rich Growth?' CAGE Working paper no. 474
Crafts, Professor N. F. R. and Harley, Professor C. K.	(1992) 'Output Growth and the British Industrial Revolution: A Restatement of the Crafts-Harley View' Wiley DOI: 10.2307/2597415
Crafts, Professor N. F. R. and Harley, Professor C. K.	(2002) 'Precocious British Industrialization: A General Equilibrium Perspective (from British Exceptionalism)' Cambridge University Press ISBN: 978-0-511-52383-0
Crafts, Professor N. F. R. and Mills, Professor T. C.	(2017) 'Six centuries of British economic growth: a time-series perspective' Oxford University Press DOI: 10.1093/ereh/hew020
Crafts, Professor N. F. R. and Mills, Professor T. C.	(2020) 'The Race between Population and Technology: Real Wages in the First Industrial Revolution' University of Warwick ISSN: 2059-4283

Crafts, Professor N. F. R., Gazeley and Newell (Ed.)	(2007) 'Work and Pay in Twentieth-Century Britain' Oxford University Press ISBN: 978-0-199-21266-8
Cribb, J. et al.	(2017) 'Living standards, poverty and inequality in the UK: 2017' Institute for Fiscal Studies ISBN: 978-1-911102-56-4
Darton, D. and Streilitz, J. (Ed.)	(2003) 'Tackling UK poverty and disadvantage in the twenty-first century' Joseph Rowntree Foundation ISBN: 978-1-85935-090-9
Davenant, C.	(1695) 'An Essay of the Ways and Means of Supplying the War'
Davies, Rev. D.	(1795) 'The Case of Labourers in Husbandry, Stated and Considered'
Deane, Professor P. M.	(1979) 'The First Industrial Revolution' Cambridge University Press ISBN: 978-0-521-29609-0
Deane, Professor P. M. and Cole, Professor W. A.	(1962/1969) 'British Economic Growth 1688-1959 (Second Edition)' Cambridge University Press 978-0-521-09569-7
DEFRA	(2019) 'Defra National Statistics Release: Air quality statistics in the UK 1987 to 2018' DEFRA
DEFRA	(2020) 'Air Pollution in the UK 2019' DEFRA
DEFRA	(2020) 'Air Pollution in the UK 2019: Compliance Assessment Summary' DEFRA
DEFRA	(2022) 'Air quality statistics in the UK - https://www.gov.uk/government/statistics/air-quality-statistics' DEFRA
Department of Employment	(1978) 'British Labour Statistics, Year Book 1976' Her Majesty's Stationery Office SBN 11 360695 8
Department of Employment and Productivity	(1971) 'British Labour Statistics, Historical Abstract 1886-1968' Her Majesty's Stationery Office
Devine	(2020) 'Poverty in the UK: Statistics' House of Commons Library Briefing Paper 7096
Devine	(2021) 'Income inequality in the UK' House of Commons Library Briefing Paper 7484
Devlin, S.	(2016) 'Agricultural labour in the UK' Food Research Collaboration ISBN: 978-1-903-95717-2
Dorling, D. et al.	(2007) 'Poverty, wealth and place in Britain, 1968 to 2005' Joseph Rowntree Foundation ISBN: 978-1-86134-995-8
Eden, Sir F. M. (Bart.)	(1797) 'The State of the Poor, or An History of the Labouring Classes in England (Three volumes)'
Emmerson and Leicester	(2002) 'A survey of the UK benefit system' The Institute for Fiscal Studies Briefing Note No 13
Engels, F.	(1845/1969) 'The Conditions of the Working Class in England - From Personal Observations and Authentic Sources' Panther Books Limited ISBN: 978-0-586-02880-3
English Housing Survey	(2020) 'English Housing Survey: Headline Report, 2019-20' Ministry of Housing, Communities and Local Government
Favara and Imbs	(2012) 'Credit Supply and the Price of Housing' HEC Lausanne
Feinstein, Professor C. H.	(1972) 'National Income Expenditure and Output of the United Kingdom 1855-1965' Cambridge University Press ISBN: 978-0-521-07230-1

Feinstein, Professor C. H.	(1988) 'The Rise and Fall of the Williamson Curve' Cambridge University Press DOI: 10.1017/S0022050700005969
Feinstein, Professor C. H.	(1990) 'New estimates of average earnings in the United Kingdom, 1880-1913' Wiley DOI: 10.1111/j.1468-0289.1990.tb00547.x
Feinstein, Professor C. H.	(1995) 'Changes in nominal wages, the cost of living and real wages in the United Kingdom over two centuries' Edward Elgar Publishing ISBN: 978-1-85278-971-9
Feinstein, Professor C. H.	(1996) 'Conjectures and Contrivances - Economic Growth and the Standard of Living in Britain during the Industrial Revolution' Oxford University Press Pubs. Id. 1167895
Feinstein, Professor C. H.	(1998) 'Pessimism Perpetuated Real Wages & Standard of Living in Britain during & after the Industrial Revolution' Cambridge University Press DOI: 10.1017/S0022050700021100
Ferragina, E. , Tomlinson, M. and Walker, R.	(2013) 'Poverty, Participation And Choice, The Legacy Of Peter Townsend' Joseph Rowntree Foundation ISBN: 978-1-85935-976-1
Fitzpatrick, S. et al.	(2016) 'Destitution in the UK' Joseph Rowntree Foundation ISBN: 978-1-91078-356-6
Fitzpatrick, S. et al.	(2018) 'Destitution in the UK 2018' Joseph Rowntree Foundation ISBN 978-1-911581-35-2
Floud, Professor Sir R., Humphries and Johnson (Ed.)	(2014) 'The Cambridge Economic History of Modern Britain Volume I, 1700-1870' Cambridge University Press ISBN: 978-1-107-63143-4
Floud, Professor Sir R., Humphries and Johnson (Ed.)	(2014) 'The Cambridge Economic History of Modern Britain Volume II, 1870 to the Present' Cambridge University Press ISBN: 978-1-107-68673-1
Floud, Professor Sir R., Wachter and Gregory	(1990) 'Height, health and history - Nutritional status in the United Kingdom, 1750-1980' Cambridge University Press ISBN: 978-0-521-02998-8
Foreman-Peck, Professor J. (Ed.)	(1991) 'New perspectives on the late Victorian economy - Essays in quantitative economic history, 1860-1914' Cambridge University Press ISBN: 978-0-521-89085-3
Freeman, M. D.	(1999) 'Social Investigation in Rural England, 1870-1914' Mark David Freeman PhD Thesis
Freud, Baron D.	(2021) 'Clashing Agendas - Inside the Welfare Trap' Nine Elms Books Limited ISBN: 978-1-910-53352-9
Gazeley, Professor I.	(1989) 'The Cost of Living for Urban Workers in late Victorian and Edwardian Britain' Wiley DOI: 10.1111/j.1468-0289.1989.tb00494.x
Gazeley, Professor I. and Newell, Professor A.	(2007) 'Poverty in Britain in 1904' University of Sussex PRUS Working Paper no. 38
Gazeley, Professor I. and Newell, Professor A.	(2009) 'No Place to Live, Urban Overcrowding in Edwardian Britain' IZA Discussion Paper 4209
Gazeley, Professor I. and Newell, Professor A.	(2009) 'The End of Destitution' IZA Discussion Paper 4295
Gazeley, Professor I. and Newell, Professor A.	(2011) 'The end of destitution: evidence from urban British working households 1904–37' Oxford University Press DOI: 10.1093/oep/gpr032

Gazeley, Professor I. and Verdon, Professor N.	(2014) 'The first poverty line? Davies and Eden's investigation of rural poverty in late 18th century England' Science Direct DOI: 10.1016/j.eeh.2012.09.001
Gazeley, Professor I. et al.	(2017) 'The poor and the poorest, 50 years on: evidence from British Household Expenditure surveys of the 1950s and 1960s' Wiley DOI: 10.1111/rssa.12202
Gazeley, Professor I. et al.	(2017) 'What Really Happened to British Inequality in the Early 20th Century? Evidence from National Household Expenditure Surveys 1890-1961' IZA DP No. 11071
Gazeley, Professor I.	(2003) 'Poverty in Britain, 1900-1965' Palgrave Macmillan ISBN: 979-0-333-71619-1
Giles, C. and Webb, S	(1993) 'Poverty Statistics: a Guide for the Perplexed' Institute for Fiscal Studies ISBN: 978-1-873357-24-9
Gillie, A.	(1996) 'The origin of the poverty line' Wiley DOI: 10.2307/2597970
Gillie, A.	(2008) 'Identifying the Poor in the 1870s and 1880s' Wiley DOI: 10.1111/j.1468-0289.2007.00395.x
Glennerster H. et al.	(2004) 'One hundred years of poverty and policy' Joseph Rowntree Foundation ISBN: 978-1-85935-222-7
Gordon, D. and Pantazis, C	(1997) 'Breadline Britain in the 1990s' Routledge DOI: 10.4324/9780429460173
Grannum, C	(2006) 'Policy briefing: Home ownership' Shelter ISBN: 978-1-903595-63-0
Grant and Williams - Kantar Public	(2017) 'The FCA's Financial Lives Survey 2017 - Technical Report' Kantar Public
Gregory, I. N., Dorling, D. and Southall, H. R.	(2001) 'A century of inequality in England and Wales using standardized geographical units' Royal Geographical society DOI: 10.1111/1475-4762.00033
Gregory, Mclaughlin, Mullender and Sundararajah	(2016) 'New solutions to air pollution challenges in the UK' Imperial College London
Griffin, E.	(2018) 'Diets, Hunger and Living Standards During the British Industrial Revolution' Oxford University Press DOI: 10.1093/pastj/gtx061
Grigoratos and Martini	(2014) 'Non-exhaust traffic related emissions. Brake and tyre wear PM' EU Commission - JRC Report EUR 26648 EN
Harari	(2018) 'Household debt: statistics and impact on economy' House of Commons Library Briefing Paper 7584
Harley, Professor C. K.	(1982) 'British Industrialization Before 1841: Evidence of Slower Growth During the Industrial Revolution' Cambridge University Press DOI: 10.1017/S0022050700027431
Harley, Professor C. K.	(2019) 'The Industrial Revolution in General Equilibrium' University of Oxford Working Paper 170
Harley, Professor C. K. and Crafts, Professor N. F. R.	(2000) 'Simulating the Two Views of the British Industrial Revolution' Cambridge University Press ISSN: 0022-0507
Hatton, Professor T. J., Bailey, R. E.	(2000) 'Seebohm Rowntree and the post-war poverty puzzle' Wiley DOI: 10.1111/1468-0289.00169

Hatton, Professor T. J., Boyer and Bailey	(1994) 'The union wage effect in late nineteenth century Britain' Wiley DOI: 10.2307/2555032
Hatton, Professor T. J., Boyer and Bailey	(2005) 'Unemployment and the UK Labour Market Before, During and After the Golden Age' Cambridge University Press DOI: 10.1017/S1361491604001376
Hick, Dr. R.	(2013) 'On 'Consistent' Poverty' London School of Economics CASE/167
Hicks and Allen	(1999) 'A Century of Change: Trends in UK statistics since 1900' House of Commons Library ISSN: 1368-8456
Hills, Ryland (BofE) and Dimsdale (Oxford)	(2010) 'The UK recession in context — what do three centuries of data tell us?' Bank of England BofE Research and analysis
Hinde, Professor A.	(2003) 'England's Population - A History Since the Domesday Survey' Hodder Education ISBN: 978-0-340-78190-8
HM Treasury	(2019) 'Public Expenditure Statistical Analyses 2019' HM Treasury CP 143
HM Treasury	(2020) 'Public Expenditure Statistical Analyses 2020' HM Treasury CP 276
HM Treasury	(2021) 'Public Expenditure Statistical Analyses 2021' HM Treasury CP 507
Hobsbawm, Professor E. J. E. and George Rudé	(1969) 'Captain Swing' Penguin University Books ISBN: 978-0-140-60013-2
Holgate CBE, Professor S. (Working Party Chair) et al.	(2016) 'Every breath we take: The lifelong impact of air pollution. Report of a working party' Royal College of Physicians ISBN: 978-1-86016-568-9
Holmans, Dr. A.	(2005) 'Historical Statistics of Housing in Britain' University of Cambridge ISBN: 978-1-86190-218-2
Holmans, Dr. A.	(2014) 'Housing need and effective demand in England: A look at "the bigger picture"' University of Cambridge
Holmans, Dr. A.	(2014) 'new estimates of housing demand and need in england, 2011 to 2031' Town & Country Planning Tomorrow Series Paper 16
Holmes, G. S.	(1977) 'King and the Social Structure of Pre-Industrial England' Cambridge University Press DOI: 10.2307/3679187
Hood and Keiller	(2016) 'A survey of the UK benefit system' The Institute for Fiscal Studies Briefing Note No 13
Hopkins et al.	(2018) 'Financial Lives Survey 2017 - Weighted Data Tables User Guide' Financial Conduct Authority
Horrell, Professor S.	(1996) 'Home Demand and British Industrialisation' Cambridge University Press DOI: 10.1017/S0022050700016946
Horrell, S., Humphries, J. and Weisdorf, J.	(2019) 'Family standards of living over the long run, England 1280-1850' University of Warwick Working Paper 419
Howard, Beevers and Dajnak	(2015) 'UP IN THE AIR How to Solve London's Air Quality Crisis: Part 2' Capital City Foundation
Howard, R.	(2015) 'UP IN THE AIR How to Solve London's Air Quality Crisis: Part 1' Capital City Foundation

Hume, Professor R. D.	(2015) 'The Value of Money in Eighteenth-Century England: Incomes, Prices, Buying Power— and Some Problems in Cultural Economics' Henry E. Huntington Library and Art Gallery DOI: 10.1525/hlq.2014.77.4.373
Humphries, Professor J.	(2012) 'Childhood and child labour in the British industrial revolution' Wiley DOI: 10.1111/j.1468-0289.2012.00651.x
Inglis, B.	(1971) 'Poverty and the Industrial Revolution' Panther Books Limited ISBN: 978-0-586-03792-8
Jefferys, J. B. and Walters D.	(1952) 'National Income and Expenditure of the United Kingdom, 1870-1952' Wiley DOI: 10.1111/j.1475-4991.1955.tb01075.x
Jenkins, Professor S. P.	(1999) 'Trends in the UK Income Distribution' Institute for Social and Economic Research
Jenkins, Professor S. P. and Micklewright, Professor J.	(2007) 'New Directions in the Analysis of Inequality and Poverty' Institute for Social and Economic Research ISER Working Paper 2007-11
Jin, W. et al.	(2011) 'Poverty and Inequality in the UK: 2011' Institute for Fiscal Studies ISBN: 978-1-903274-84-2
Johnson, S.	(1755/1758/1818) 'A Dictionary of the English Language'
Jones, F. et al.	(2008) 'The distribution of household income 1977 to 2006/07' Office for National Statistics Economic & Labour Market Review, Vol 2, No 12, pp. 18-31
Jones, F. et al.	(2009) 'The redistribution of household income 1977 to 2006/07' Office for National Statistics Economic & Labour Market Review, Vol. 3, No 1, pp. 31-43
Joyce and Xu	(2019) 'Inequalities in the twenty-first century, Introducing the IFS Deaton Review' The Institute for Fiscal Studies ISBN: 978-1-912-80521-1
Joyce, Mitchell and Norris Keiller	(2017) 'The cost of housing for low-income renters' Institute for Fiscal Studies ISBN: 978-1-911102-66-3
Justiniano, Primiceri, and Tambalotti	(2017) 'Credit Supply and the Housing Boom' Federal Reserve Bank etc. css6-7
Keep	(2020) 'The budget deficit: a short guide' House of Commons Library Briefing Paper 06167
Kelly, M. and O'Grada, C.	(2016) 'Adam Smith, Watch Prices, and the Industrial Revolution' Oxford University Press DOI: 10.1093/qje/qjw026
Kelly, M., O'Grada, C. and Mokyr, J.	(2013) 'Precocious Albion: a New Interpretation of the British Industrial Revolution' University College Dublin WP13/11
Kennedy	(2004) 'Poverty: Measures and Targets' House of Commons Library RP04-23
Kennedy, L. and Solar, P. M.	(2012) 'Markets and Price Fluctuations in England and Ireland, 1785-1913' Taylor Francis ISBN: 978-1-315-85237-9
Keohane and Broughton	(2013) 'The Politics of Housing' National Housing Federation
Kitson, Professor M. and Michie OBE, Professor J.	(2014) 'The De-industrial Revolution - The Rise and Fall of UK Manufacturing, 1870-2010' University of Cambridge Working Paper No. 459
Knowles, J. (Ed.)	(1888) 'The Nineteenth Century. A Monthly Review. Volume XXIII' Keegan Paul

Kyd, James G. (Ed.)	(1952) 'Scottish Population Statistics - Including Webster's Analysis of Population 1755' University of Edinburgh
Laybourn-Langton, Quilter-Pinner and Ho	(2016) 'LETHAL & ILLEGAL Solving London's Air Pollution Crisis' IPPR
Lindert, Professor P. H.	(1986) 'Unequal English Wealth since 1670' The University of Chicago Press DOI: 10.1086/261427
Lindert, Professor P. H.	(1998) 'Three Centuries Of Inequality In Britain And America' University of California Davis Working Paper Series 97-09
Lindert, Professor P. H.	(2000) 'When did inequality rise in Britain and America?' Elsevier Science Inc. DOI: 10.1016/S0926-6437(99)00012-8
Lindert, Professor P. H. and Williamson, Professor J. G.	(1982) 'Revising England's Social Tables 1688-1812' Academic Press, Inc. DOI: 10.1016/0014-4983(82)90009-2
Lindert, Professor P. H. and Williamson, Professor J. G.	(1983) 'English Workers' Living Standards During the Industrial Revolution' Wiley DOI: 10.2307/2598895
Lindert, Professor P. H. and Williamson, Professor J. G.	(1983) 'Reinterpreting Britain's Social Tables' Academic Press, Inc. DOI: 10.1016/0014-4983(83)90044-X
Long et al. (Shelter commissioners)	(2018) 'A vision for social housing' Shelter
Lupton et al.	(2009) 'Growing up in social housing in Britain' Joseph Rowntree Foundation
Lyle, M. A.	(2007) 'Regional agricultural wage variations in early nineteenth-century England' British Agricultural History Society The Agricultural History Review, Vol. 55, No. 1 (2007), pp. 95-106
Lyons, Murphy, Snelling and Green	(2017) 'What More Can Be Done To Build The Homes We Need?' IPPR
Malthus, Rev. T. R.	(1798) 'An Essay on the Principle of Population' Oxford University Press ISBN: 978-0-192-84747-8
Marner, Dr. B.	(2016) 'Deriving Background Concentrations of NOx and NO2' Air Quality Consultants
Marner, Dr. B.	(2016) 'Emissions of Nitrogen Oxides from Modern Diesel Vehicles' Air Quality Consultants
Massie, J.	(1756) 'Calculations of Taxes for a Family of Each Rank, Degree or Class: for One Year'
Massie, J.	(1758) 'A Plan for the Establishment of Charity Houses'
Mathias, P.	(1957) 'The Social Structure in the Eighteenth Century: A Calculation by Joseph Massie' Wiley DOI: 10.2307/2600060
Mayhew, H.	(1851/1987) 'London Labour and the London Poor' Wordsworth Classics ISBN: 978-1-840-22619-5
Mayor of London (GLA)	(2019) 'PM2.5 in London: Roadmap to meeting World Health Organization guidelines by 2030' Greater London Authority
McCloskey, Professor D. N.	(2014) 'Measured, unmeasured, mismeasured, and unjustified pessimism: a review essay of Thomas Piketty's Capital in the twenty-first century' EJPE Erasmus Journal for Philosophy and Economics, Volume 7, Issue 2, Autumn 2014, pp. 73-115

McDonald and Whitehead	(2015) 'new estimates of housing demand and need in England, 2012 to 2037' Town & Country Planning Tomorrow Series Paper 17
McGuinness and Harari	(2019) 'Income inequality in the UK' House of Commons Library Briefing Paper 7484
McLeay, Radia and Thomas	(2014) 'Money creation in the modern economy' Bank of England BofE Quarterly Bulletin
McLeay, Radia and Thomas	(2014) 'Money in the modern economy: an introduction' Bank of England BofE Quarterly Bulletin
Mearns, Rev. A.	(1883) 'The Bitter Cry of Outcast London'
Meen, Professor G.	(2018) 'How should housing affordability be measured?' UK Collaborative Centre for Housing Evidence R2018_02_01
Miles and Monro	(2019) 'UK house prices and three decades of decline in the risk free real interest rate' Bank of England Staff Working Paper No. 837
Ministry of Labour	(1940) 'The Ministry of Labour Gazette' Her Majesty's Stationery Office Vol. 48, No. 12
Ministry of Labour	(1941) 'The Ministry of Labour Gazette' Her Majesty's Stationery Office Vol. 49, No. 1
Ministry of Labour	(1941) 'The Ministry of Labour Gazette' Her Majesty's Stationery Office Vol. 49, No. 2
Mitchell, B. R.	(1988) 'British Historical Statistics' Cambridge University Press ISBN: 978-1-107-40244-7
Mitchell, B. R. and Deane, Professor P. M.	(1962) 'Abstract of Historical Statistics' Cambridge University Press ISBN: 978-0-521-05738-8
Mokyr, Professor J. (Ed.)	(1999) 'The British Industrial Revolution - An Economic Perspective' Westview Press ISBN: 978-8-813-33389-2
Monks, Professor P. et al.	(2019) 'Non-Exhaust Emissions from Road Traffic' Air Quality Expert Group PB14581
Mulheirn, I.	(2019) 'Tackling the UK housing crisis: is supply the answer?' UK Collaborative Centre for Housing Evidence
Neild, W.	(1842) 'Comparative Statement of the Income and Expenditure of Certain Families of the Working Class in Manchester and Dukinfield, in the Years 1836 and 1841' Wiley DOI: 10.2307/2337693
Nesteling, H. P. H.	(1993) 'English population statistics for the first half of the Nineteenth Century : a new answer to old questions' Societe de Demographie Historique DOI: 10.3406/adh.1993.1840
Niemietz, Dr. K.	(2011) 'A New Understanding of Poverty - Poverty Measurement and Policy Implications' The Institute of Economic Affairs ISBN: 978-0-255-36638-0
Niemietz, Dr. K.	(2012) 'Redefining the Poverty Debate - Why a War on Markets is No Substitute for a War on Poverty' The Institute of Economic Affairs ISBN: 978-0-255-36652-6
O'Donoghue (ONS), Goulding (ONS) & Allen (HofC Lib.)	(2004) 'Consumer Price Inflation since 1750' Office for National Statistics Economic Trend 604

Officer, Professor L. H.	(2007) 'What Were the U.K. Earnings Rate and Consumer Price Index Then? A Data Study' University of Illinois at Chicago
Officer, Professor L. H.	(2007) 'What Were the UK Earnings and Prices Then? A Question-and-Answer Guide' MeasuringWorth
Onions, C. T. (Ed.), Little, Fowler and Coulson	(1932/1983) 'The Shorter Oxford English Dictionary on Historical Principles (2 volumes)' Guild Publishing CN 5647
ONS	(2014) 'UK Wages Over the Past Four Decades' Office for National Statistics
ONS	(2021) 'A guide to sources of data on income and earnings' Office for National Statistics
ONS	(2021) 'Average household income, UK: financial year 2020' Office for National Statistics
Orr, J. et al.	(2021) 'Regional differences in short stature in England between 2006 and 2019: A cross-sectional analysis from the National Child Measurement Programme' PLOS Medicine DOI: 10.1371/journal.pmed.1003760
Ortiz-Ospina, Esteban and Hannah Ritchie	(2018) 'What's happening to life expectancy in Britain?' Our World in Data
Palma, N.	(2016) 'Book review of Broadberry, Campbell, Klein, Overton, and van Leeuwen, British Economic Growth, 1270-1870' Maddison-Project Working Paper WP-5
Patriquin, Professor L.	(2007) 'Agrarian Capitalism and Poor Relief in England, 1500–1860' Palgrave Macmillan ISBN: 978-0-230-59138-7
Perkin, Professor H.	(1969/2002) 'The Origins of Modern English Society' Routledge ISBN: 978-0-415-29880-2
Perkin, Professor H.	(1989/2002) 'The Rise of the Professional Society - England Since 1880' Routledge ISBN: 978-0-415-30178-5
Perkin, Professor H.	(1996) 'The Third Revolution - Professional Elites in the Modern World' Routledge ISBN: 978-0-415-14338-1
Phaup, H.	(2015) 'Historical sources of mortgage interest rate statistics' Bank of England
Piddington, Nicol, Garrett and Custard	(2020) 'The Housing Stock of The United Kingdom' BRE Trust PEN02 20
Pinker, Professor S. A.	(2018) 'Enlightenment Now' Allen Lane ISBN: 978-0-241-00431-9
Platt, L.	(2003) 'Putting Childhood Poverty on the Agenda: The Relationship Between Research and Policy in Britain 1800-1950' Young Lives
Polanyi, K.	(1944/2001) 'The Great Transformation: The Political and Economic Origins of Our Time' Beacon Press ISBN: 978-0-8070-5643-x
Pope and Waters	(2016) 'A survey of the UK tax system' The Institute for Fiscal Studies Briefing Note No 09
Raleigh, Veena (Senior Fellow, King's Fund)	(2021) 'What is happening to life expectancy in England' The Kings Fund
Rashid, T. et al.	(2021) 'Life expectancy and risk of death in 6791 communities in England from 2002 to 2019' The Lancet DOI: 10.1016/S2468-2667(21)00205-X

Ravallion, Professor M.	(2013) 'The Idea of Anti-Poverty Policy' National Bureau of Economic Research Working Paper 19210
Ravallion, Professor M.	(2016) 'The Economics of Poverty - History, Measurement and Policy' Oxford University Press ISBN: 978-0-190-21276-6
Ravallion, Professor M.	(2020) 'On the Origins of the Idea of Ending Poverty' National Bureau of Economic Research Working Paper 27808
Razzell, P. E.	(2016) 'Mortality, Marriage and Population Growth in England, 1550-1850' Caliban Books ISBN: 978-0-904573-19-0
Razzell, P. E.	(2018) 'Population Growth and the Increase of Socio-Economic Inequality in England, 1550-1850' Razzell, P.
Registrar General	(1904) 'Census of England and Wales, 1901, General Report with Appendices' Her Majesty's Stationery Office
Ridley, Dr. Viscount M. W.	(2011) 'The Rational Optimist' 4th Estate (Harper Collins) ISBN: 978-0-007-26712-5
Roantree and Shaw	(2017) 'What a difference a day makes: inequality and the tax and benefit system from a long-run perspective' Springer DOI: 10.1007/s10888-017-9362-x
Roser, Max	(2020) 'The Spanish flu (1918-20): The global impact of the largest influenza pandemic in history' Our World in Data
Rosling, Dr., H., Rosling and Ronnlund	(2018) 'Factfulness' Sceptre (Hodder & Stoughton) ISBN: 978-1-473-63746-7
Rowntree, B. Seebohm	(1901) 'Poverty: A Study of Town Life' MacMillan and Co. ISBN 978-1-86134-202-0
Samaras, Professor Z. et al.	(2013) 'Transport related Air Pollution and Health impacts – Integrated Methodologies for Assessing Particulate Matter' TRANSPHORM
Scott, Professor P. M. and Walker, Professor J. T.	(2014) 'Demonstrating Distinction at 'the Lowest Edge of the Black-coated Class': The Family Expenditures of Edwardian Railway Clerks' Henley Business School Discussion Paper Number: IBH-2014-04
Scott, Professor P. M. and Walker, Professor J. T.	(2020) 'The Comfortable, the Rich, and the Super-Rich. What Really Happened to Top British Incomes during the First Half of the Twentieth Century?' Cambridge University Press DOI: 10.1017/S0022050719000767
Scott, Professor P. M., Walker, J. T. and Miskell, P. M.	(2014) 'British Working-class Household Composition, Labour Supply and Commercial Leisure Participation during the 1930s' Henley Business School Discussion Paper Number: IBH-2014-03
Sen, Professor A. K.	(1982) 'Poor, Relatively Speaking' The Economic and Social Research Institute ISBN: 978-0-7070-0055-6
Shaw-Taylor, Dr. L.	(2009) 'The Occupational Structure of England 1750-1871 Some Preliminary Results' University of Cambridge
Shaw-Taylor, Dr. L. and Wrigley, E. A.	(2006) 'The Occupational Structure of England c.1750-1871: A Preliminary Report' University of Cambridge
Shaw-Taylor, Dr. L. et al.	(2010) 'The Occupational structure of England and Wales c.1817-1881' University of Cambridge
Shaw-Taylor, Dr. L. et al.	(2010) 'The Occupational structure of England c.1710 to c.1871 Work in progress' University of Cambridge

180

Smee, W. R.	(1846) 'THE INCOME TAX: Its Extension at the Present Rate Proposed to all Classes'
Snell, Professor K. D. M.	(1985) 'Annals of the Labouring Poor - Social Change in Agrarian England, 1660-1900' Cambridge University Press ISBN: 978-0-521-33558-4
Solomou, Professor S. and Ryland Thomas	(2019) 'Feinstein Fulfilled: Updated Estimates of UK GDP 1841-1920' ESCOE (NIESR) and ONS ISSN: 2631-3588
Spiegelhalter OBE, Professor Sir D. J.	(2017) 'Does air pollution kill 40,000 people each year in the UK?' Winton Centre
Spiegelhalter OBE, Professor Sir D. J.	(2019) 'The Art of Statistics - Learning from Data' Pelican (Penguin Books) ISBN: 978-0-241-25876-7
Starling, B. and Bradbury, D.	(2020) 'The Official History of Britain - Our story in numbers as told by the Office for National Statistics' Harper Collins ISBN: 978-0-008-41219-7
Stroud, P. (Chair)	(2019) 'Equivalisation In Poverty Measures: Can We Do Better?' Social Metrics Commission ISBN: 978-1-911125-52-5
The Intergenerational Commission	(2018) 'A New Generational Contract' Resolution Foundation ISBN: 978-1-999-72011-7
The Trussell Trust	(2019) 'The State of Hunger' The Trussell Trust
Thomas	(2015) 'Analysis of Long-run Historical Data at the Bank of England' Bank of England BofE Archival Worksop
Thompson et al.	(2012) 'Olympic Britain: Social and economic change since the 1908 and 1948 London Games' House of Commons Library
Thompson, E. P.	(1963) 'The Making of the English Working Class' Vintage Books ISBN: 978-0-394-70322-0
Timmers and Achten	(2016) 'Non-exhaust PM emissions from electric vehicles - 134 (2016) 10e17' Atmospheric Environment DOI: 10.1016/j.atmosenv.2016.03.017
Townsend, Professor P.	(1954) 'Measuring Poverty' Wiley DOI: 10.2307/587651
Townsend, Professor P.	(1966) 'Poverty, socialism and Labour in power' Fabian Society Fabian Tract 371
Townsend, Professor P.	(1979) 'Poverty in the United Kingdom' Penguin Books ISBN: 978-0-140-22139-8
Townsend, Professor P.	(2010) 'The meaning of poverty' Wiley DOI: 10.1111/j.1468-4446.2009.01241.x
Turner, C. and NHBC	(2015) 'Homes through the decades' NHBC Foundation ISBN: 978-0-9930691-3-0
Twigger, R.	(1999) 'Inflation: the Value of the Pound 1750-1998' House of Commons Library Research Paper 99/20
UK Statistics Authority	(2019) 'Statistics on air quality and emissions of air pollutants' UK Statistics Authority Assessment Report 344
Vamplew, W.	(1980) 'A Grain of Truth The Nineteenth-Century Corn Averages' British Agricultural History Society The Agricultural History Review, Vol. 28, No. 1 (1980), pp. 1-17 (17 pages)

van de Ven, Dr. J.	(2011) 'Expenditure and Disposable Income Trends of UK Households: Evidence from Micro-Data' National Institute of Economic and Social Research DOI: 10.1177/002795011121800105
Vanderlint, J.	(1734) 'Money Answers all Things'
Voth, H-J.	(2003) 'Living Standards During the Industrial Revolution: An Economist's Guide' American Economic Association DOI: 10.1257/000282803321947083
Watts, Fitzpatrick, Bramley and Watkins	(2014) 'Welfare Sanctions and Conditionality in the UK' Joseph Rowntree Foundation ISBN: 978-1-909-58646-8
Welshman, J.	(2006/2013) 'Underclass: A History of the Excluded Since 1880' Bloomsbury ISBN: 978-1-4725-0498-2
WHO	(2006) 'WHO Air quality guidelines for particulate matter, Ozone, Nitrogen Dioxide and Sulphur Dioxide' World Health Organisation
Williamson, Professor J. G.	(1984) 'Why Was British Growth So Slow During the Industrial Revolution' Cambridge University Press DOI: 10.1017/S0022050700032320
Williamson, Professor J. G.	(1985) 'Did British Capitalism Breed Inequality?' Routledge ISBN: 978-1-138-86489-4
Wilson	(2019) 'Under-occupying social housing: Housing Benefit entitlement' House of Commons Library Briefing Paper 06272
Wilson and Barton	(2018) 'Tackling the under-supply of housing in England' House of Commons Library Briefing Paper 07671
Wilson and Barton	(2020) 'Overcrowded housing (England)' House of Commons Library Briefing Paper 1013
Wilson Fox, A.	(1903) 'Agricultural Wages in England and Wales during the Last Fifty Years' Wiley DOI: 10.2307/2339234
Wilson, W	(2019) 'Stimulating housing supply - Government initiatives (England)' House of Commons Library Briefing Paper 06416
Wolff, J. et al.	(2015) 'A Philosophical Review of Poverty' Joseph Rowntree Foundation ISBN: 978-1-90958-659-8
Wrigley, Professor Sir E. A. and Dr. R. S. Schofield	(1982/1989) 'The Population History of England, 1541-1871, A reconstruction' Cambridge University Press ISBN: 978-0-521-35688-6
Wrigley, Professor Sir E. A. and Dr. R. S. Schofield	(1997) 'English Population History from Family Reconstitution, 1580-1837' Cambridge University Press ISBN: 978-0-521-59015-0
Zmolek, M. A.	(2019) 'The Dark World of Reverend Malthus' University of Nebraska Omaha ISSN: 2476-0269

Internet Data

Bank of England - "Millennium Database"	https://www.bankofengland.co.uk/statistics/research-datasets
BRE Trust - UK Housing Stock Report	https://files.bregroup.com/bretrust/The-Housing-Stock-of-the-United-Kingdom_Report_BRE-Trust.pdf
Building Societies Association - Mortgage interest rates	https://www.bsa.org.uk/BSA/files/f8/f86888ee-716c-4f95-9c63-1dfa26d86742.xlsx
Building Societies Association - Mortgages and housing	https://www.bsa.org.uk/statistics/mortgages-housing
Chartered Institute of Housing	https://www.ukhousingreview.org.uk/ukhr21/compendium.html
Christopher Chantrill - UK Public Revenue	https://ukpublicrevenue.co.uk/
Christopher Chantrill - UK Public Spending	https://ukpublicspending.co.uk/
Clark, Professor G. - Downloads	http://faculty.econ.ucdavis.edu/faculty/gclark/data.html
DEFRA - Air Pollution in the UK	https://uk-air.defra.gov.uk/library/annualreport/
DEFRA - Air Quality and Emissions Statistics	https://www.gov.uk/government/collections/air-quality-and-emissions-statistics
DEFRA - UK Air Information Resource - Data	https://uk-air.defra.gov.uk/data/
Department for Transport - Coronavirus transport use	https://www.gov.uk/government/statistics/transport-use-during-the-coronavirus-covid-19-pandemic
Department for Transport - Vehicle statistics	https://www.gov.uk/government/collections/vehicles-statistics
Department for Work and Pensions - Statistics	https://www.gov.uk/government/collections/dwp-statistical-summaries
Drax Electric Insights	https://electricinsights.co.uk/#/homepage?&_k=o6odgj
Economic Statistics Centre of Excellence	https://www.escoe.ac.uk
Economic Statistics Centre of Excellence - Documents	https://www.escoe.ac.uk/research/historical-data/etarticles/
Economic Statistics Centre of Excellence - Historical data	https://www.escoe.ac.uk/research/historical-data/
Halifax - House price data	https://www.halifax.co.uk/media-centre/house-price-index.html
HM Treasury - Country and regional analysis	https://www.gov.uk/government/collections/country-and-regional-analysis

HM Treasury - Public expenditure statistical analysis	https://www.gov.uk/government/collections/public-expenditure-statistical-analyses-pesa
HMRC - Survey of personal incomes	https://www.gov.uk/government/collections/personal-incomes-statistics
Human Mortality Database	https://www.mortality.org/
Institute for Fiscal Studies - Living standards, poverty and inequality in the UK	https://ifs.org.uk/tools_and_resources/incomes_in_uk
Lindert, Professor P. H. - Downloads	https://gpih.ucdavis.edu/files/
London Air Quality (Imperial College London) - Data	https://www.londonair.org.uk/london/asp/datadownload.asp
London Average Air Quality Levels (Kings College London)	https://data.london.gov.uk/dataset/london-average-air-quality-levels
London Congestion Zone - Camera captures	https://data.london.gov.uk/dataset/vehicles-entering-c-charge-zone-month
Measuring Worth	https://www.measuringworth.com/
Ministry of Housing, Communities and Local Government - English housing survey	https://www.gov.uk/government/collections/english-housing-survey
Ministry of Housing, Communities and Local Government - House building	https://www.gov.uk/government/statistical-data-sets/live-tables-on-house-building
Ministry of Housing, Communities and Local Government - Housing	https://www.gov.uk/government/statistical-data-sets/live-tables-on-dwelling-stock-including-vacants
National Atmospheric Emissions Inventory - Data	https://naei.beis.gov.uk/data/
National Infrastructure Commission - Historic Energy Dataset	https://nic.org.uk/data/all-data/historic-energy/
Nationwide - Housing historic data	https://www.nationwidehousepriceindex.co.uk/resources/
NHS - National child measurement programme	https://digital.nhs.uk/data-and-information/publications/statistical/national-child-measurement-programme
NHS - Workforce statistics	https://digital.nhs.uk/data-and-information/publications/statistical/nhs-workforce-statistics
NOMIS - Official census and labour market statistics	https://www.nomisweb.co.uk/
OECD - Housing prices	https://data.oecd.org/price/housing-prices.htm

Office for Budget Responsibility	https://obr.uk/
Office for Budget Responsibility - Data banks	https://obr.uk/data/
Office for Budget Responsibility - Welfare spending by age (Chart 3.2)	https://obr.uk/docs/dlm_uploads/Welfare-Trends-Report.pdf
Office for Budget Responsibility - Welfare spending by age (Removed)	https://obr.uk/forecasts-in-depth/brief-guides-and-explainers/an-obr-guide-to-welfare-spending/
Ofgem - Electricity prices	https://www.ofgem.gov.uk/data-portal/breakdown-electricity-bill
Ofgem - Energy bills explained	https://www.ofgem.gov.uk/publications-and-updates/infographic-bills-prices-and-profits
Ofgem - Gas prices	https://www.ofgem.gov.uk/data-portal/breakdown-gas-bill
ONS - Average equivalised household disposable income	https://www.ons.gov.uk/peoplepopulationandcommunity/personalandhouseholdfinances/expenditure/datasets/detailedhouseholdexpenditurebyequivaliseddisposableincomedecilegroupoecdmodifiedscaleuktable31e
ONS - Deaths by single year of age	https://www.ons.gov.uk/peoplepopulationandcommunity/birthsdeathsandmarriages/deaths/datasets/deathregistrationssummarytablesenglandandwalesdeathsbysingleyearofagetables
ONS - Deaths registered weekly in England and Wales, provisional	https://www.ons.gov.uk/peoplepopulationandcommunity/birthsdeathsandmarriages/deaths/datasets/weeklyprovisionalfiguresondeathsregisteredinenglandandwales
ONS - Environmental accounts	https://www.ons.gov.uk/economy/environmentalaccounts
ONS - GDP	https://www.ons.gov.uk/economy/grossdomesticproductgdp
ONS - Gross disposable household income	https://www.ons.gov.uk/economy/regionalaccounts/grossdisposablehouseholdincome
ONS - Health inequalities	https://www.ons.gov.uk/peoplepopulationandcommunity/healthandsocialcare/healthinequalities
ONS - House building	https://www.ons.gov.uk/peoplepopulationandcommunity/housing/datasets/ukhousebuildingpermanentdwellingsstartedandcompleted
ONS - Housing	https://www.ons.gov.uk/peoplepopulationandcommunity/housing/datasets/dwellingstockbytenureuk
ONS - Income and wealth	https://www.ons.gov.uk/peoplepopulationandcommunity/personalandhouseholdfinances/incomeandwealth
ONS - Inflation and price indices	https://www.ons.gov.uk/economy/inflationandpriceindices
ONS - Labour force survey, earnings and working hours	https://www.ons.gov.uk/employmentandlabourmarket/peopleinwork/earningsandworkinghours

ONS - Life expectancy	https://www.ons.gov.uk/peoplepopulationandcommunity/health andsocialcare/healthandlifeexpectancies/datasets/lifeexpectancy estimatesallagesuk
ONS - National balance sheet	https://www.ons.gov.uk/economy/nationalaccounts/uksectoracc ounts/datasets/thenationalbalancesheetestimates/current
ONS - National life tables	https://www.ons.gov.uk/peoplepopulationandcommunity/births deathsandmarriages/lifeexpectancies/datasets/nationallifetables unitedkingdomreferencetables
ONS - Percentage of households with durable goods	https://www.ons.gov.uk/file?uri=/peoplepopulationandcommuni ty/personalandhouseholdfinances/expenditure/datasets/percent ageofhouseholdswithdurablegoodsuktablea45/1970tofinancialye arending2018/a45201718rerun.xls
ONS - Population and migration	https://www.ons.gov.uk/peoplepopulationandcommunity/popul ationandmigration
ONS - Population estimates	https://www.ons.gov.uk/peoplepopulationandcommunity/popul ationandmigration/populationestimates
ONS - Population, Our population - Where are we?	https://www.ons.gov.uk/peoplepopulationandcommunity/popul ationandmigration/populationestimates/articles/ourpopulationw herearewehowdidwegetherewherearewegoing/2020-03-27
ONS - Retail Prices Index: average price of selected food items: 1914 to 2004	https://www.ons.gov.uk/file?uri=/economy/inflationandpriceind ices/methodologies/consumerpricesindexcpiandretailpricesindex rpibasketofgoodsandservices/rpiaverageprices19142004tcm771 68515tcm77420253.xls
ONS - UK Families and households	https://www.ons.gov.uk/peoplepopulationandcommunity/births deathsandmarriages/families/datasets/familiesandhouseholdsfa miliesandhouseholds
ONS - Vital statistics, births, deaths and marriages	https://www.ons.gov.uk/peoplepopulationandcommunity/popul ationandmigration/populationestimates/datasets/vitalstatisticsp opulationandhealthreferencetables
ONS - Workbook 4 - Expenditure by Household Characteristics	https://www.ons.gov.uk/file?uri=/peoplepopulationandcommuni ty/personalandhouseholdfinances/expenditure/datasets/familys pendingworkbook4expenditurebyhouseholdcharacteristic/2020/ familyspendingworkbook4expenditurebyhouseholdcharacteristic s.xlsx
Our World in Data	https://ourworldindata.org/
Our World in Data - CO2 and GHG emissions	https://github.com/owid/co2-data
Our World in Data - Coronavirus pandemic (Covid-19)	https://ourworldindata.org/coronavirus
Our World in Data - Excess mortality during the Coronavirus pandemic (COVID-19)	https://ourworldindata.org/excess-mortality-covid
Our World in Data - Excess mortality P-scores	https://ourworldindata.org/grapher/excess-mortality-p-scores-average-baseline
Our World in Data - Life expectancy	https://ourworldindata.org/life-expectancy

Oxford Dictionary - Lexico	https://www.lexico.com/en
Peter Lindert - Data-garden	https://psychology.ucdavis.edu/people/fzlinder/peter-linderts-webpage/data-garden
Rashid et al (Imperial College) - Life expectancy and risk of death in 6791 communities in England	https://globalenvhealth.org/download/24423/
Renewable Energy Foundation	https://www.ref.org.uk
UK Data Service	https://beta.ukdataservice.ac.uk/
UK Government – Air Quality Standards Regulation 2010	https://www.legislation.gov.uk/uksi/2010/1001/made
UK Government - Coronavirus dashboard	https://coronavirus.data.gov.uk/
UK Government - Stat-Xplore	https://stat-xplore.dwp.gov.uk/webapi/jsf/login.xhtml
UK Government BEIS - Annual January prices of road fuels and petroleum products	https://www.gov.uk/government/statistical-data-sets/oil-and-petroleum-products-annual-statistics
UK Government BEIS - Crude oil and petroleum: production, imports and exports	https://www.gov.uk/government/statistical-data-sets/crude-oil-and-petroleum-production-imports-and-exports
UK Government BEIS - Digest of UK Energy Statistics (DUKES)	https://www.gov.uk/government/collections/digest-of-uk-energy-statistics-dukes
UK Government BEIS - Energy Consumption in the UK	https://www.gov.uk/government/statistics/energy-consumption-in-the-uk
UK Government BEIS - Historical coal data: coal production, availability and consumption	https://www.gov.uk/government/statistical-data-sets/historical-coal-data-coal-production-availability-and-consumption
UK Government BEIS - Historical electricity data	https://www.gov.uk/government/statistical-data-sets/historical-electricity-data
UK Government BEIS - Historical gas data: gas production and consumption and fuel input	https://www.gov.uk/government/statistical-data-sets/historical-gas-data-gas-production-and-consumption-and-fuel-input
Vision of Britain - Census	https://www.visionofbritain.org.uk/census/
Wages through history - A. Wilson Fox agricultural wages	https://historyofwages.blogspot.com/2011/02/agricultural-labourers-wages-1850-1914.html
World Bank - Life expectancy	https://data.worldbank.org/indicator/SP.DYN.LE00.IN

Worldometers - Covid-19   https://www.worldometers.info/coronavirus/
Coronavirus Pandemic

Milton Keynes UK
Ingram Content Group UK Ltd.
UKHW021005050923
428034UK00005B/223/J